SOCIAL WORK DIALOGUES

SOCIAL WORK DIALOGUES

Transforming the Canon in Inquiry, Practice, and Education

Stanley L Witkin   Dennis Saleebey

Council on Social Work Education
Alexandria, Virginia

Library of Congress Cataloguing-in-Publication Data

Social work dialogues : transforming the canon in inquiry, practice, and education / [edited by] Stanley L Witkin and Dennis Saleebey.

p. cm.

Includes bibliographical references and index.

Based on discussions at the Transforming Social Work (TSW) gatherings held annually in Vermont since 2000.

ISBN 978–0-87293–123–7 (alk. paper)

1. Social service. 2. Social service—Philosophy. 3. Social work education. 4. Postmodernism. I. Witkin, Stanley L, 1947– II. Saleebey, Dennis. III. Title.

HV40.S6613 2006

361.3—dc22

2006020928

Printed in the United States of America on acid-free paper that meets the American National Standards Institute Z39-48 Standard.

Council on Social Work Education, Inc.

1725 Duke Street, Suite 500

Alexandria, VA 22314-3457

www.cswe.org

Contents

Foreword

A lot is being written these days about uncertainty, change, and the need for transformation in the way we think and act in social work. And so there should be. However, it is becoming extraordinarily more difficult to write about new ways of being and doing that can strike a chord in innovative ways. I therefore sit down to read books like this with a mixture of hope and apprehension. I am apprehensive that I will read yet another tome that is good at stating the problems, but will only make me feel more powerless to tackle them. And yet I am also hopeful that I will read something that will inspire my imagination and make me want to take a leap into relatively unknown territory.

This book is definitely of the latter type. I found it especially intriguing, as the chapters emerge from experiences all contributors shared in the Transforming Social Work Practice, Education, and Inquiry annual meetings of the Global Partnership for Transformative Social Work in Burlington, Vermont. Having attended one of these meetings, I found it fascinating to trace how contributors have drawn their thoughts from these experiences. The chapters really do evoke a sense of "transforming conversations," certainly "good talk," as Ruth Dean terms it in her chapter. They provide a perfect illustration of how an "unconference" can provide an environment that nurtures creative and innovative thinking.

In this sense, I found the book to be a powerful model of one of the things it talks about as important—the capacity to match form and method to philosophy. The need for multiple perspectives, for new and different forms of communication, for a diverse collection of forms of representation and ways of knowing are all regularly mentioned in these pages. Happily, the book neatly demonstrates this diversity and it practices what it preaches—it presents a delicious array of topics, styles, and approaches that do tantalise the intellectual tastebuds and challenge the reader toward more daring innovations.

The whole book attempts to present a smorgasbord of different perspectives on some of the most taken for granted features of social work, and invites us to feast our imaginations on what a radical remaking of some of these very basic foundations might entail. After beginning with an explanation of how the Vermont gatherings emerged in a climate of relative intolerance to new formulations, the beginning chapters attempt to theorize some aspects of these gatherings. Other chapters tackle the "big" questions: the nature of theory and theorizing, emancipatory social work, the use of artistic forms in social work, the implications of uncertainty and ambiguity, the environment, research, and, of course, the contexts in which we educate.

Yet the chapters, while stimulating, are also intellectually satisfying. While often reflective, in being able to link personal experience with more abstract theorizing, they come from this basis to provoke further thinking. The often open-ended approach models uncertainty, at the same time making it exciting enough to take on the anxiety that following such a path often entails. The chapters are written by highly experienced and well-respected authors, all trailblazers in the broad area of postmodern and social constructionist approaches in social work. They come from across the globe—the United States, the United Kingdom, Australia, and Canada. We are privileged to get a feel for each contributor's own personal, individual, and highly original perspective in making meaning of these perspectives within often more mainstream and traditional professional settings.

It is difficult to predict who might not be interested in this book. It can be appreciated at many different levels. Those new to social work will find the book appealing in its illustration of how long-standing social workers and academics find inspiration in personal experiences. Social work academics and practitioners will find that the engagement with and remaking of traditional ideas may give a new lease on life to practice and thinking. Other professionals will find that the themes tackled are common across the professions and that these chapters can offer a concrete way forward for many of us struggling with the challenges new epistemologies and changing social and economic conditions entail.

The book, on another level, also functions as a tribute to the vision and leadership of the editors who are also organizers of the annual Transforming Social Work conferences in Vermont, Stanley Witkin and Dennis Saleebey. These conferences themselves stand out as a highly innovative way of engaging with uncertainty. It is perhaps fitting that this book is published at a time when the Global Partnership is moving to become more international, to include yet more perspectives, and to become yet more culturally inclusive in the ways in which dialogue is fostered.

I hope, on this note, that the book leaves you with the lasting sensation I have—of a long walk in a Vermont forest at fall, surrounded by sunlit, dappled trees and leaves of multicolors, in the company of diverse colleagues, engaged in good talk, on a path that leads—where?—but knowing that the experience will enrich me in ways I can't even imagine.

Jan Fook
Professor in social work studies
School of Social Sciences
University of Southampton
Southampton, United Kingdom

Preface

The idea for this book emerged from the reactions of participants, including ourselves, of the Transforming Social Work Practice, Education, and Inquiry (TSW) gatherings held annually in Burlington, Vermont, since 2000 by the Global Partnership for Transformative Social Work (GPTSW). Motivated in part by frustration from trying to fit the square peg of postmodern thought into the round hole of conventional social work, the TSW meetings were intended to provide a venue for academics, students, and practitioners to discuss with interested colleagues the implications of the "postmodern moment" for social work and for themselves. To accomplish this we believed it was necessary to untether ourselves from the strictures of academic tradition and to explore dialogue and connection as avenues of intellectual development (see chapter 1 for a more detailed explanation).

Following each annual TSW gathering and the excitement it generated, participants expressed an interest in producing a tangible product that could bring a broad range of social workers and others into our conversations. This collection of essays is our response to this interest. Although it is difficult to capture the full sense of what it is like to participate in these gatherings, we hope that these essays give readers some sense of the kinds of discussions and ideas that occur. We hope, too, that students in particular will be inspired by these essays—inspired not only by the ideas generated, but also by the intellectual courage shown by some of the authors to explore new forms and pathways to knowledge. Having the opportunity to read, react to, and discuss with peers and teachers the kinds of ideas presented in this collection may generate the sense of excitement that comes from open dialogue about issues of importance.

As noted in some of the essays, our educational institutions tend to be structured around "modernist" ideas about knowledge and learning (e.g., experts imparting knowledge to the uninformed). Despite organizational rhetoric embracing progressive ideals, it is not always easy in these settings to express new and different ideas (particularly if one is not tenured). We believe that it is vital for social work not only to allow such ideas, but to actively encourage them. Contemporary social issues are highly complex, globally interrelated, and dynamic. Social workers must be able to draw upon multifarious sources of information and different knowledge traditions in a context of permeability and change. To accomplish this requires, in our view, the ability to break out of procrustean beds of thinking—whether called capitalism, science, or some other "metanarrative." We cannot afford to limit ourselves to mainstream approaches to practice, inquiry, and education. Needed too are people who not only "think outside the box" (to use a somewhat tired phrase), but who question the construction and function of "the box" itself and explore the implications of new metaphors. The freedom, even encouragement, to think in this way should be part of all students' education.

Like any work of this type, we owe a great debt to many people who made it possible to have these kinds of dialogues and who enriched them when we did. In chapter 1, we note the forerunners of the TSW gatherings and some of the people involved in these pioneering efforts. In addition, we have been the fortunate beneficiaries of the writings, conversations, and encouragement of others who walk, and in some cases have forged, a similar intellectual path. In many ways the ideas expressed in this book are simply an extension of our ongoing dialogue with these colleagues and friends. Although identifying such individuals risks inadvertently omitting a significant contributor (and we hope we'll be forgiven if we do), we want to mention some who were particularly important to our current thinking. First, we want to thank the authors of the chapters for their willingness to participate in this project, their willingness to stay with it despite its long gestation, and for their diverse and enriching intellectual contributions. For both of us, the late Howard Goldstein was a rich source of compelling and provocative ideas and a supportive colleague and friend; he is missed. In addition, I (Stanley) would like to acknowledge Zvi Eisikovits, Ken Gergen, David Harrison, Shimon Gottschalk, Ray Rist, Michael Mahoney, Roberta Iversen, Mirja Satka, Stephen M. Rose, Kyösti Urponen, Sheldon Rose, Ann Weick, Mary Katherine O'Connor, Joan Laird, and Ann Hartman for their contributions along the way.

In different ways Justin, Shana, and Joshua Witkin have contributed significantly to my current understandings. I want to thank Dennis Saleebey, my coeditor, for his collaboration on this project, his creativity, friendship, and a zillion laughs. This was truly a joint effort that would have been much poorer without Dennis's insight and wisdom. Finally, I want to thank my wife, Fran Joseph, for her support, interest, ideas, and, most significant, for participating in my most transformative conversation.

I (Dennis), too, want to thank many of the same people. Howard Goldstein was a revelation and delight, a real mentor. Ann Hartman and Joan Laird led the way for me early on in transformative thinking in social work. John Romanyshyn, Ernest Becker, Kenneth Gergen, and my dear and intellectually daring wife, Ann Weick, have all given me inspiration and enthusiasm for the postmodern project. And many members of our Global Partnership for Transformative Social Work group have been instrumental in shaping my ideas and beliefs. Finally, Stan Witkin has been a friend, a compatriot, and mentor over the years. And, believe me, we have had a lot of laughs along the uncertain path to transformative thinking. Finally, Stan and I would both like to thank the Council on Social Work Education Council on Publications and our editor, Noemi C. Arthur, for their interest, support, and guidance.

CHAPTER 1

Toward a Transformative Social Work

STANLEY L WITKIN

I have always believed that social work is a noble and important profession. Its nobility comes from its vision of a more tolerant, humane, and just world; its importance from its commitment to serve marginalized and disadvantaged people. Depending on how they are expressed, visions and commitments can be cohesive or divisive, inspiring or dissuading, expansive or constrictive. Therefore, it is not surprising that the meaning of this vision and the dedication to this commitment have been the subjects of frequent disagreements. In part, these disagreements reflect social work's contradictory roles as an instrument of dominant social institutions (such as government) and as an advocate of people oppressed by those institutions—its well-known social control and social change mandates. Straddling these positions is not easy and, in my view, underlies many of the perennial tensions within and between social work practice and research. Attempts to resolve this tension often push the profession toward one or the other position generating both adherents and detractors. For example, the relatively individualistic orientation of social work in the United States in which problems are located within persons is considered by some as an abdication of its primary role as an agent of social change (see, e.g., Courtney & Specht, 1994). Although holding a "both-and" or transcendent position in relation to this contradiction may be possible, so far it has proved to be elusive.

As someone whose career has spanned different sides of these debates, I have experienced the pushes and pulls of working within and outside of the mainstream. While the strategy of "changing the system from within" appealed to me (and brought tangible rewards), Audre Lorde's (1984) caution about not being able to dismantle the master's house using the master's tools seemed more critical to maintaining social work's unique vision. As "standpoint epistemologists" argue, the way we understand the world depends on where we are positioned within it. The significance of these positions, whether based on gender, ethnicity, sexual orientation, or other designation, stems from historical traditions, culturally based beliefs and practices, and contemporary social arrangements. Those in socially marginalized positions tend to have different perspectives on their situations than those more centrally located; however, their voices are often silenced or ignored. Social work—at its best—tries to change this situation by amplifying these voices, demanding that we pay attention, and altering the conditions that produce their marginalization.

These are weighty matters, and social work's emphasis, understandably, has been on substantive issues, for example, how to reduce poverty or homelessness. Less often have the contexts and processes of knowledge production itself assumed center stage. However, questioning why certain practices of knowledge generation and representation are privileged and examining their relationship to dominant assumptions and beliefs can broaden understanding of how such social problems arise and are sustained. And it is here, within these somewhat abstract queries, that the intellectual movement known as postmodernism has been particularly germane. By raising questions about the warrant for dominant beliefs, exposing their underlying assumptions, and critically examining processes of knowledge generation, legitimation, and representation and their influence on what we know or can know, postmodern scholars have diminished the hegemony of official knowledge and opened new avenues for understanding.

Given social work's identity as a socially and politically progressive profession, it may seem strange that it remains somewhat intellectually conservative in its approach to knowledge generation and representation. However, as implied above, it is difficult for a profession struggling for mainstream recognition and resources to adopt an openly critical stance toward the very institutions (in this case, science) in which it wishes to gain acceptance. Even critics, however, find the entrenched authority of Western science, or at least a particular version of science, difficult to dislodge sufficiently so that space is created for alternative systems of understanding. Thus, the social work research community has been relatively silent about attempts by the U.S. government to legislate methodology and undermine fields such as indigenous, ethnic, and queer studies that do not assume a traditional scientific worldview, an issue that is of great concern among educational and cultural studies researchers (see, e.g., Lincoln & Cannella, 2004). Yet, it seems reasonable to ask how the privileging of certain narrowly defined approaches to inquiry influences social work's ability to carry out its core functions and fulfill its aims.

These kinds of issues, I believe, are central for many social workers who have been attracted to the diverse forms of knowing associated with the term *postmodern*. There is unease about the privileging of scientific knowing and its claim to superior truth. There is a questioning of enlightenment themes of rationality, universality, and inevitable progress, viewing them not as inalienable truths, but as a narrative, one way among many ways of making sense of the world. There is a belief that dominant interests and dominant ways of knowing are not independent, but reciprocally supportive. Such musings lead to a sense of disquietude, a desire to explore new ways of learning and knowing, and perhaps most of all, to connect with others who feel similarly. In a significant way these musing have also led to the creation of this book. More concretely, the essays herein were inspired by the authors' participation in one or more meetings that began in 2000 and have been held annually since in Burlington, Vermont. The Transforming Social Work Practice, Inquiry, and Education (TSW) meetings (or gatherings, as we call them) provide an opportunity to explore the transformative potential for social work of what might be broadly considered postmodern thought In a manner reminiscent of the aphorism, "If you build it, they will come," uttered by James Earl Jones in the movie *Field of Dreams* in 1999, Dennis Saleebey and I announced the time and place of our first gathering. Fortunately, enough people were willing to risk participating in this "unconference" (as Sally St. George and Dan Wulff call it in chapter 2) to enable the TSW gatherings to became a reality.

But to appreciate this story it is necessary to go back to 1984 when a small group of social work educators and scholars calling themselves "the group for the study of philosophical issues in social work," which later became the Global Partnership for Transformative Social Work (GPTSW) (www.gptsw.net), began meeting semiregularly.[1] Generally, participants in the study group were looking for a forum where they could share ideas that were considered outside the mainstream of social work scholarship. Such ideas tended to be postmodern in the sense of questioning the dominant canons of empiricism, quantification, and experimentalism and their associated beliefs and assumptions. Interests such as qualitative research, spirituality, the arts, and social construction were fringe topics in social work 15 to 20 years ago (and some would argue still are), and participants were hungry to find kindred spirits with whom they could explore their ideas. Despite a small but dedicated following, the group had only marginal success in establishing itself within the more established venues of the profession. Illustrative of these difficulties were the repeated attempts by the group to establish an annual symposium at the Council on Social Work Education's (CSWE) Annual Program Meeting. To achieve symposium status, a group had to a have a certain number of abstracts submitted and accepted. This proved difficult, and a perennial dirge heard at our informal meetings was the futility of submitting unconventional proposals to the conference abstract reviewers. Finally, at a 1999 meeting, we suggested that rather than continue this exercise in self-flagellation, we consider developing our own venue for these ideas. Despite some uncertainty about the viability of our proposal, the response from those present was positive enough for us to move forward and hope "they would come."

Transforming Conversations

Given the postmodern theme of our proposed gathering and the pivotal role of dialogue, the traditional academic conference did not provide a useful organizing template. Academic conferences, including social work conferences, for the most part, mirror modernist assumptions about knowledge, for example, that language transmits rather than generates knowledge or that researcher/scientists are mere reporters of their "findings." These kinds of assumptions are congruent with brief presentations by experts to largely passive audiences. In many ways, these conferences are the oral counterpart to research writing, which we present in American Psychological Association (APA) style. Knowledge in both venues is viewed as a process of transference via language from one mind, the presenter or author, to another, the audience member or reader. The presenter/author as person largely is absent. Ideas are seen as existing relatively independently of one's personal life or social circumstances. Information beyond professional affiliations and accomplishments is rare. Interaction with conference presenters, if it occurs at all, is generally brief and structured along the lines of questions and answers. This tends to make the relationship between the presenter and audience member hierarchical, impersonal, and distant.

For these reasons, we tried not to be constrained by traditional academic conventions and, in postmodern fashion, to broadly define scholarship. Dialogue seemed central to these aspirations. As conference veterans ourselves, we often heard—and experienced—that the most meaningful conference experiences took place in the unstructured spaces between formal sessions where actual dialogue occurred. Therefore, in our planning, we sought a kind of figure-ground reversal, making the between-session conversations the focus of our time together.

We also believed that trying to separate people from their ideas was misleading and led to impoverished understanding. Our own work was strongly related to our biographies and this seemed true of others we knew. Understanding how ideas connected to personal experience and values enriched their meaning. Additionally, communication is a relational activity. The nature of our relationships—how they are structured, constrained, contextualized, and so on—will influence how and what we communicate. Conversations between people who share some sense of personal connection, that is, who know one another as multidimensioned selves, tend to be different from those within the structured impersonality of professional forums. Less encumbered by rules of proper discourse, the former conversations tend to be more interactive, rich, and stimulating.

To facilitate this type of dialogue, we emphasized small-group, conversational formats rather than presentations; a loose, flexible structure that participants could modify; and activities that fostered personal relationships. In order to create an environment that felt safe, supportive, and conducive to exploration and reflection, we decided to keep the gathering relatively small (30 to 40 participants). Small numbers also gave us the possibility of involving all participants in common activities.

For the most part, participants are academics or aspiring academics (i.e., doctoral students), although some practitioners have attended. Inviting participants from outside the United States also has been important. Their participation has added a richness to our dialogues that would not be possible with an all-U.S. group.

We were fortunate to locate a setting that perfectly met our needs—a small conference center located on 300 wooded acres along the shores of Lake Champlain in Burlington, Vermont. Available only to nonprofit groups, the center also offered lodging and meals at modest prices. We decided to hold the gatherings in late September or October to take advantage of the incomparable fall foliage of Vermont. This bucolic setting has been an important aspect of our gatherings. It is an environment that inspires reflection, creative thinking, and connection.

What Does a Typical Program Look Like?

In our initial invitation letter to prospective participants we wrote,

> We would like to invite you to participate in an exciting, challenging, and unique meeting on "Transforming Social Work Practice and Inquiry" to be held from September 28 to October 1, 2000, in Burlington, Vermont. Approximately 40 participants will meet in one of four groups organized

> around the themes of social constructionism, the arts, strengths and resilience, and spirituality. Groups will explore possibilities, developments, prospects, and strategies for transforming social work practice and inquiry within and across these four areas.
>
> In contrast to the usual paper presentation, question-and-answer conference format, we envision a meeting that invites conferring, discussing, sharing, debating, demonstrating, laughing, even engaging in—gasp—the illusive dialogue. (All the things we do in between and after the formal sessions at conferences!) We want to encourage spirited discussion and the expression of passionate ideas within a context of safety, mutuality, and respect.
>
> To further enrich this experience, and encourage a playful and energetic frame of mind, we have included opportunities for fun, outdoor excursions, and even commerce with nature.

Although the substantive themes and group activities have changed over the years, the focus on creating a safe, respectful environment for dialogue has remained constant. Recent gatherings have been based on topics selected by participants from a menu of ideas related to the postmodern and social work themes of the gathering. Based on their topic choices, participants are assigned to discussion groups of five to eight people. To illustrate the nature of our recent discussions, the following are two topics chosen for the 2004 gathering.

1. ETHICS

A central feature of postmodern thought has been its opposition to "metanarratives," particularly as expressed in universal doctrines. In the area of ethics this position has generated tensions within groups that feel drawn to some aspects of postmodernism but see themselves as having a socially activist agenda. For example, the idea of universal human rights has been an important part of some groups' attempts to provide protections to vulnerable groups. A related tension has been between those who promote universalist codes of ethics and those proposing more relational or situational perspectives such as an ethic of care or discourse ethics. This discussion group will explore ethics from these (and possibly other) perspectives, considering official positions (e.g., *Code of Ethics of the National Association of Social Workers*) and how they influence the profession. What might an alternative look like? How might it influence our teaching, practice, or inquiry? Are there ways to reconcile the tensions noted above?

2. CRITIQUE AND VISION

The various strands of critique that have emerged from the postmodern moment have been highly effective in identifying the shortcomings of modernist-oriented perspectives and their associated practices. In fact, some would say they have been *too effective*, creating a situation in which all but one's own perspective is dismantled under a barrage of critique. But what is left when the dust clears? What is the affirmative vision that a postmodern perspective offers to social work? Answering this question in a cogent and accessible way seems critical to the eventual acceptance of these perspectives. This group will grapple with this issue of balancing critique and vision: How do we maintain a critical consciousness while generating excitement about possible futures?

Despite the consistent focus on exploring postmodern expressions for social work, each year generates new and often unpredictable group dynamics and ideas. Different discussion questions, new participants, and changes in the larger social context ensure that no two meetings are alike. At the same time, we have found that transcending presuppositions and traditional ways of doing things is not easy, even within a group ostensibly committed to exploring the nonconventional. For example, it is common practice at the beginning of meetings to engage in some type of introduction. Usually this is done in a way that reinscribes an individualistic concept of persons (e.g., "I am . . ."). When this was pointed out and participants were requested to come up with introductions that did not assume encapsulated, separate selves, there was a sense of discomfort and disorientation, with some participants wanting to introduce themselves "in the old-fashioned way." However, once reluctances were overcome, developing introductions based on different assumptions was informative and set a tone of playful exploration at the gathering.

Within each discussion group one participant acts as a facilitator. This person keeps track of time, encourages balanced participation, and helps the group address the agreed upon topics. Following several hours of discussion, each group is asked to share its experience with the rest of the gathering. Rather that the typical "reporting out" summarizing of the conversation, we encourage activities that give the larger group the opportunity to participate in and contribute to the smaller group's dialogue. This has led to some creative exercises and activities that, at least in a small way, enable everyone to participate in all the discussions (for example, see chapter 14).

Another important part of the gathering is the "nonacademic" group activities: various group outings that take advantage of Vermont's natural beauty and cultural attractions. As with the discussion topics, participants choose from a menu of activities designed to accommodate different interests and physical demands. Although on the surface these activities seem merely pleasant diversions from the "real work" of the gathering, they contribute importantly to relationship development and dialogue among participants. Conversations tend to take on a different quality when hiking along a mountain path or driving through the fall foliage of the Green Mountains. Ideas generated during these activities often are brought back to the small groups or continued in other venues after people return home.

After almost three days together, the gathering ends with all participants meeting and sharing reflections and comments on their experiences. New conversational directions emerge as individuals react to commonalities and differences among participants. This discussion among all participants also provides a sense of closure to the gathering and generates new possibilities for the future.

Transformation—A Key Concept

Transformation is a central, organizing concept of the TSW gatherings. It functions as a point of convergence among participants, foregrounding the belief in the desirability of and need for change at many levels (see Dennis Saleebey's discussion of personal and institutional transformation in chapter 14). Within this context, transformation represents a "deep" kind of change that is qualitatively significant. Such change can be contrasted with incremental or additive changes. These tend to be grounded in and retain the rules, presuppositions, and beliefs that undergird the object(s) of change. Consider, for example, a teaching skills program that focuses on techniques to increase speaking clarity, write comprehensive syllabi, construct fair tests, and assign interesting homework. Changes in these areas may lead to better teaching as evidenced on student evaluations. However, to the extent that the program leaves assumptions and beliefs about teaching and learning untouched, it is unlikely to be transformative. Instructors will continue to teach largely in the same way as they did before, albeit perhaps with more skill; however, what it means to be a "good teacher" remains unchanged. There is no shift in the basic metaphors, language, underlying conceptual models, or way that teaching quality is understood.

In contrast, transformative change would likely involve a reformulated understanding of teaching and learning and the relationship between them. For example, the metaphor of students as "empty vessels" to be filled with facts might be replaced with one of students as active cocreators of knowledge. In this example transformation may take on a metamorphic quality. There is a change in the appearance, form, or even the character of the former practice. Rather than enhancing current practices, there is a relational redefinition that may render old practices (such as developing more comprehensive syllabi) obsolete or lead to new practices. This might require change in how teaching and learning are "languaged" (even including the words *teaching* and *learning*) in order to dislodge the definitional baggage that accumulates with use over time.

Transformation is relational (one might even argue that the social acknowledgment of change is a precondition for its occurrence). Whether at a personal or more macro level, a qualitative shift in the web of connectedness among people invites change among all involved (which may also generate resistance to change). The teacher who no longer prestructures a course with a syllabus but asks students to cocreate the course with her or him is changing the relationship between teacher and students and, possibly, what it means to function as a teacher and a student. For some students this may seem like an exciting opportunity, while for others such a relationship may be threatening. Attempts at transformative change that challenge foundational assumptions and beliefs upon which relationships have developed can generate a sense of uncertainty or feeling of upheaval, which may be resisted. This is more likely to occur if the change is unilateral; for example, if a teacher simply announces the change rather than negotiates it with the students. The former is an exercise of the teacher's authority and unlikely to generate transformative change. In contrast, engaging students in authentic dialogue can create the relational conditions conducive to transformation.

Dialogue and Discourse

With the realization that language constitutes rather than reflects what we take to be reality (itself a transformative change), there has been increased interest in how the use of language generates and maintains beliefs and practices. For academics and practitioners, dialogue—in the classroom, therapy room, meeting room, or legislative hearing—is the means we use to generate the conceptual shifts that characterize transformation. Thus, dialogue is central to the TSW gatherings, both as a vehicle for exploring transformation and as a way of practicing it.

But the constructive use of dialogue ("good talk," as Ruth Dean calls it in chapter 3), particularly in the service of transformative change, is not easy. Our individualist traditions, while serving us well in some ways, also create challenges to adopting an open orientation to different views. Believing one exists in a state of individual separateness invites actions that ultimately are self-serving. Such a stance engenders cautiousness (or even suspiciousness) toward others since their actions are likely to be self-aggrandizing (Gergen, 1994).

Individualism can be understood as an ideology that is manifested in various discourses. I use *discourse* in the Foucauldian sense of language, rules, and practices that regulate how we conceptualize and express knowledge. Understanding discourses and how they operate helps us to consider how they shape and limit our conversations. Without these considerations, we risk supporting the very discourses that give rise to the objects, relations, or conditions that we wish to change. One way this occurs is by controlling the rules of argument, the forms of its expression, and the criteria for its resolution. For instance, limiting arguments to methodological flaws in research or claims of objectivity may ignore challenges to the presuppositions that frame the substance of the debate and influence the formulation of intelligible questions.

A challenge at an interpersonal level is how to engage in dialogue that increases awareness of multiple discourses, not in order to identify the superior one, but to expand relational resources and possibilities. One way to consider this is to show how the workings of discourse (that is, its methods of making sense) keep alternative knowledges from becoming visible or legitimate. This was what Foucault attempted in his "genealogies," for example, by showing how the synchronicity of history was imposed on events (Prado, 2000).

Exploring discourses through dialogue involves critique. Keeping critique part of the conversation can be difficult because of its negative connotation. In part, this comes from viewing critique as synonymous with criticism. However, whereas criticism suggests finding fault or judging harshly, critique implies analysis and evaluation. From this perspective, critique is ongoing and constructive. Foucault expressed the spirit of this view in his suggestion that critique is needed to keep accepted ideas and practices from ossifying and becoming rigid over time, and also to explore the limits of discourse in order to free us to think in new ways (Cooper & Blair, 2002). That is, critique is a necessary dimension of constructive dialogue.

The practice of "problematization" creates a context for this type of critique. To problematize is not to take for granted what is taken for granted, but to treat such beliefs and assumptions as ways of understanding that have gained a status that renders them relatively impervious or invisible to critique. When we problematize we view this status, not as a reflection of the ways things "really are," but of some social process such as a relation of power (Smith, 1987). Foucault argued that to problematize (which he contrasted with polemics) was to engage in ethical dialogue. He wrote, "Problematization is a search for understanding, based on a reciprocal, interrogative model, that privileges inquiry over advocacy"(as cited in Cooper & Blair, 2002, p. 520). That is, instead of defending ideas, interlocutors explore their limits with the aim of enhancing understanding. By working to keep our conversations truly dialogical, we can increase awareness of multiple ways of understanding and how authority operates to favor certain conceptualizations over others. We begin to notice, as R. D. Laing reminds us, of what (or even that) we fail to notice. We come to understand that through the fluid, interactional, embodied, inchoate, and interdependent process of dialogue we can enlarge the range of possibilities available to us. This spirit pervades the conversations that take place at the TSW gatherings.

An Entrée to the Gathering

The chapters that constitute this book represent some of the varied topics that have been explored at our gatherings. The various writing styles are indicative of how the authors approach their topic and are representative of the different ways participants communicate. Some chapters are written as standard academic papers (for example, Richard Pozutto's chapter 4 on theory), while others read more like personal essays (for example, Allan Irving's chapter 10 on the "off-frame"). Other than requesting that each chapter begin with some description of how the authors' participation in the gatherings connected to their paper, we made no attempt to impose a uniform format on the chapters.

Chapters 2 and 3 give readers a sense what it is like to participate in these gatherings and how dialogue plays a central role. Sally St. George and Dan Wulff describe how what they call the "un-conference" provides opportunities for meaningful dialogue in chapter 2. The importance of personal connection is evident throughout their chapter: from their description of the initial contact informing them of the gathering to their participation in the event itself. They also discuss their efforts to sustain and implement positive aspects of the gatherings by sharing ideas and trying out new practices with colleagues and students.

Ruth Grossman Dean (chapter 3) also explores the connection between the gatherings and other settings. Her concern is the elusive qualities of "good talk," "conversations that exude energy and send our thoughts in new directions." Ruth contemplates why, even at our TSW gatherings, discussion sometimes gets bogged down. In an attempt to identify some qualities of good talk, she explores practice and educational situations. Again, the idea of personal relationship is salient. Finally, she wonders (and asks us to consider) whether good talk is what happens during a conversation, or is it something that continues to develop and change as ideas become part of other conversations?

Good talk also is important to Richard Pozutto (chapter 4), but his focus is on how we talk about the world through the use of theory. He contrasts two views of theory (favoring a modern or postmodern interpretation) based on an analysis of two foundational social work texts. He explores the implications of these different conceptions of theory for practice, including how practice itself is understood. Moving away from Truth as the ultimate criterion of theory, Richard considers other criteria such as the ability to accommodate (versus eliminate) multiple perspectives.

The process of theorizing (and inquiry) as an everyday aspect of social work rather than the formal properties of theory is the focus of Brenda Solomon's chapter 5. Drawing on the institutional ethnography approach of sociologist Dorothy E. Smith, and Ann Weick's recent work on social work knowledge, Brenda explores the meaning-making activities of social workers. In particular, her analysis of social caretaking as a form of theorizing opens new space for understanding how knowledges are legitimated.

Social work theory and theorizing must also be understood within the historical context of the profession. Mel Gray and Richard Pozutto (chapter 6) examine some of the historical trends that have shaped contemporary social work to be, in their view, a conservative profession. Written in the form of a dialogue, they explore whether and how an emancipatory practice can operate within this conservative legacy.

Similar issues, albeit from a different perspective, concern Nigel Parton (chapter 7). He wonders how social work is responding to the ever increasing complexity and uncertainty of contemporary life. Consistent perhaps with its conservative heritage, he argues that the profession's response to this "postmodern turn" has been to turn "back" to modernist approaches emphasizing control and rationality. Indicative of the latter is the evidence-based practice movement. The problem, Nigel argues, is not the desire for evidence per se, but the narrowness and rigidity by which it is defined and the centrality it has assumed. To remedy this situation he proposes an expanded conception of evidence that can address more postmodern and social constructionist approaches. He concludes with a discussion of "constructive social work" and its potential contributions to practice in a world of ambiguity and uncertainty.

A social constructionist vision is not without its tensions. As a "a devoted naturalist," Fred H. Besthorn (chapter 8) struggles with how to reconcile his essentialist view of nature with some ideas associated with social construction. For Fred the notion of dialogue should not be limited to persons, but extended to nature itself. This is not a simple either/or dilemma as some aspects of social construction are highly congruent with Fred's thinking. For instance, he acknowledges the importance of constructionist thinking to countering privileged narratives. On the other hand, he worries that the belief that nature is socially constructed will diminish social workers' ability to take action on behalf of the environment. Fred invites us into his internal dialogue around these issues as he seeks to find "a balance that expands the boundaries of reciprocal discourse to include the voices of nature in the way we understand ourselves and our place in *relationship* to the rest of the sentient world." Expanding the dialogue is also of concern to Adrienne Chambon (chapter 9). Rather than nature, she looks to the world of art as a means of telling about and representing social life. Based on her work at the Canadian Centre for Victims of Torture, Adrienne explores how selected poetry, prose, photographs, paintings, and films communicate the experience of refugees. As she writes, "They deal with questions of memory and traces of things passed. Of being in between worlds, metaphorically, also physically. They address displacement, lack of home, seeking home. They include institutional decisions that shape the course of persons' lives: Crossing a border or not; obtaining a passport or being sent back; knowing and not knowing what will be one's fate. They convey personal and group experiences." For social workers, inured to the cries of "clients," these forms of representation can create powerful connections to their struggles and triumphs.

This desire to reconnect to life is apparent in Allan Irving's remarkably personal and passionate chapter 10. His sense of being on the "off-frame," of being in a world no longer intelligible via modernist concepts, led him to revisit the works of Friedrich Nietzsche and Samuel Beckett and to examine some ideas of Michel Foucault and Ludwig Wittgenstein. Allan discusses how each of their ideas takes him farther down the path of the postmodern. Finally, in a moment of epiphanic anguish, he realizes "that I wasn't mad just truly postmodern." He concludes with a fantasy lecture to a social work class, titled "Ceremonies of Patching, Rituals of Chaos," in which he passionately pleads for the abandonment of the modernist project of universality, certainty, and domination, and the development of a social work that entertains a "multitruthed world" and new sites and forms of knowledge.

Creating space for such knowledges requires new analyses of the concepts that organize much of our thinking about the world. Katherine Tyson McCrea (chapter 11) takes on this task in her investigation of the concept of causality. She attempts to show the limitations of the current, dominant conception of causality, demonstrating that there are other ways to think about cause. Her discussion looks at various heuristics or metaphors that guide and limit inquiry. She takes us on a historical journey discussing the causal models of Aristotle, St. Thomas Aquinas, Descartes, David Hume, and Immanuel Kant. This is followed by summaries of the present-day work of William Winsatt, Roy Bhaskar, and R. C. Lewontin and a discussion of the recent concept of emergence and its relationship to consciousness. She concludes with a revisioning of causal validity in a way that can be used in research while retaining the complexities of the concept.

Another central concept in social work is ethics. Indeed, some would argue that social work itself can be considered as an expression of applied ethics. Teaching students to appreciate and apply the complexities of ethical thinking to practice has always been challenging. It is even more challenging when ethics is reconsidered from a postmodern perspective. Margaret Rhodes (chapter 12) bravely takes on this task. In particular, she explores how the teaching of ethics can more squarely address the issue of social justice. Using a case-plus-theory method, Margaret describes the typical approach to ethical decision making, which she believes overemphasizes professional and legal obligations, and contrasts it with an approach that places social justice in a central position. Embracing rather than reducing the complexity of the case, she proposes ways to have students consider the multiple meanings and entrée points that any case offers. She asks them to experiment with using different concepts to begin their analyses and to consider who is included and excluded by each. Based on her analysis she proposes four steps of ethical decision making that invite examination of multiple perspectives.

Teaching from a postmodern perspective is challenging. Universities, as Susan E. Roche points out (in chapter 13), are decidedly modernist in their organization and practices. Students who have had successful academic careers within the realms of right and wrong answers and teachers as authorities may balk at this different and uncertain approach to education. Susan takes us to two sites to consider this issue. First we visit a small discussion group of social work educators and doctoral students at the TSW gathering. These participants struggle with a variety of instructional and organizational issues related to adopting a postmodern educational stance. Next we go to a practice class of master of social work students. Here the focus is more on the challenges of learning the unfamiliar language and perspective of postmodern practice, particularly when it is not endorsed in their field settings. Constructively using her in-between location, Susan shows how these groups can be brought together to form a colearning relationship that opens up new possibilities for practice.

Finally, Dennis Saleebey (chapter 14) closes out this volume with his own thoughts on transformation: how it is manifest in the authors' essays, and how, through relationship building and a kind of Habermasian ideal speech situation, the gatherings themselves become a context for, and an example of, transformation. He concludes with some suggestions about how to return some of the transformative ardor generated at the gathering back to our colleagues and workplaces.

So there you have it, a small entrée into a large, ongoing conversation about social work and postmodern thought taking place in various sites such as classrooms, journals, books, and social agencies. As readers of this collection you not only have an opportunity to share in the fruits of the TSW dialogues, but also to be participants. Just as this book is an extension of these dialogues, we hope that you, too, will take up these words and enrich the conversation with new ideas, commentaries, and interpretations.

Notes

1. The original name of this group was the "Gooseneck Group," after the location where the group first met. The founders were Roberta Imre, Glenn Haworth, Dennis Saleebey, Ann Weick, Ann Hartman, Joan Laird, Howard Goldstein, Ed Sherman, and Jerry Wakefield.

References

Cooper, M., & Blair, C. (2002). Foucault's ethics. *Qualitative Inquiry, 8*(4) 511–531.

Courtney, M., & Specht, H. (1994). *Unfaithful angels: How social work has abandoned its mission*. New York: Free Press.

Gergen, K. (1994). *Realities and relationships: Soundings in social construction*. Cambridge, MA: Harvard University Press.

Lincoln, Y. S., & Cannella, G. S. (2004). Dangerous discourses, methodological conservatism and governmental regimes of truth. *Qualitative Inquiry, 10*(1), 5–14.

Lorde, A. (1984). *Sister outsider: Essays and speeches*. Trumansburg, NY: Crossing Press.

Prado, C. G. (2000). *Starting with Foucault: An introduction to genealogy* (2nd ed.). Boulder, CO: Westview Press.

Smith, D. E. (1987). *The everyday world is problematic: A feminist sociology*. Boston: Northeastern University Press.

CHAPTER 2

The Un-Conference

SALLY ST. GEORGE and DAN WULFF

All professions hold conferences. Conducting a computer search by Googling the key terms *professional* and *conference* yields over 20,000,000 hits! It would seem that there is a conference in every major city in the United States on any given day of the year on a rich variety of topics. Searching through social science databases shows that professional conference going is the focus of considerable study and commentary (e.g., Bell, 1998; Chesterfield, 2000; Shaffer, McNinch, & Erwin, 1997; VanZandt, 1992).

The importance that professional conference going holds for attendees covers a wide range. Some professionals attend conferences regularly and find the workshops and networking opportunities useful and stimulating. Many attend conferences in order to garner continuing education requirements and/or enjoy an authorized hiatus from work duties. Others do not attend at all.

Conferences can provide valuable networking opportunities and a broad spectrum of workshops and experiences that provides many levels of professional development. Opportunities to hear and see the writers and originators of programs; meet with new professional acquaintances, prospective supervisors, and students; learn new practice skills; and to have a "professional vacation" all seem to be important. Yet, we wonder, are these opportunities good enough? Do they push participants and the field to innovation and change, or do they just maintain the status quo? Do they provide new ideas for old dilemmas, or do they package ideas for easy consumption, popularity, and potential profits? Do they help us to relate to our worlds in new, more effective ways? For those of us in helping professions, do conferences challenge us to tackle the persistent social problems that plague our world?

We have participated in many professional conferences that have been organized in the basic and customary format. With this format everything is set up months (or years) in advance, ideally with all sessions and workshops built around a major theme determined by an organizing committee. The organizers of these conferences make the decisions regarding how the conference is conducted and what workshops are offered and when (which may or may not correspond with what the participants want). It is up to each participant's discretion primarily to actually attend the chosen workshops or paper presentations or substitute with networking, tourist activities, sitting in the bar, or retreating to one's room. Oftentimes these conferences include several hundred or even more than a thousand participants and convene in major cities at major hotels. Most of us who have attended the state or national conferences of our professional organizations are familiar with this format.

We have come across an alternative type of conference in the past few years that better meets our needs than the traditional conference model. It is flexibly organized around (a) the issues as presented by the participants when they arrive, (b) developing and deepening relationships, and (c) having fun. This conference, Transforming Social Work Practice, Education, and Inquiry, is held in Vermont and is limited to around 40 invited people. We experience this conference as very validating, stimulating, and regenerating, both professionally and personally.

In this chapter we will discuss this conference; we refer to it as the un-conference because of its unconventional form and process. This un-conference was created by and for social work educators who generally subscribe to a philosophy and work ethic grounded in social constructionism. The impetus for the development of this conference was the marginalization of this point of view at large, well-established social work conferences. After struggling for years to be accepted to present their ideas at these conferences, the people in this group decided that it would be more productive and generative to meet separately and conduct their own conference in accordance with their principles and preferences.

This conference has a decidedly improvisational flavor, built more around placing people together in conversations of their own design and development rather than structuring informational sessions whereby *presenters* provide information to an *audience*. This structure is built upon the belief that the process of conversing will itself produce desirable and useful results (e.g., information, support, creative ideas). The annual un-conference is organized with the suggestion of a plan or theme that is broad enough to include all the participants and specific enough to stimulate some excitement. The specific agenda is fleshed out by the group when it convenes at the conference site. Typically, five or six topical areas are identified and participants select one. Conversations usually continue in a free-flowing and evolving manner, including much improvised time with various members of the conference during breaks, evening hours, or on the varying social adventures available.

Both of us attended the Vermont un-conference in the fall of 2001 organized by Stanley Witkin and Dennis Saleebey. The unique appeal of this un-conference began when we received a letter of invitation. We felt that we were receiving a *personal* invitation from a person or persons who knew us and our work (to *some* degree through professional meetings). This was very different from a form letter or general advertisement directed to a mass audience.

We were also very interested in the other invitees. When we received follow-up correspondence, we examined the other E-mail addresses listed in the notices sent by Stan and Dennis. We recognized a few names, but most were people we had not yet met. We felt like we were deliberately being invited to join a group that shared some interests we also held—nontraditional or alternative approaches to social work and social work education. We had come to think of ourselves as somewhat out of sync with traditional approaches to social work and social work education, so for us to find what we considered a support group for these ideas made up of others from around the country and around the world was very appealing.

As a professional couple, we have the good fortune of working at the same school and have been actively integrating the fields of social work and family therapy at their professional intersections or boundaries in our program. The tensions that exist between the professional domains of social work and family therapy make true or fundamental integration within our curriculum quite problematic. The un-conference is a haven for us. Since 2001 we have both attended this meeting yearly—it is our first priority in our academic conference plans.

Going to Vermont

We have found the conference to be inexpensive—organized with little overhead costs and without a need to turn a profit. This no-frills approach seems to keep the focus on our reason for attending—to converse and interact.

The setting is a lodge in the woods on the shore of Lake Champlain at the height of the fall foliage season. Upon arrival, our initial feeling is that we are joining a group of adults at a summer camp. The un-conference hosts (Stan and Dennis) act as greeters and make a few opening remarks when we first gather. Despite some efforts by the group to look at them as organizers and decision makers, Stan and Dennis consistently maintain that they are group members just as we all are. The group accepts this, but throughout the conference there are moments when Stan and Dennis have to reiterate their position.

Everyone is valued for her or his ideas. The varied life and professional experiences, as well as the various work contexts, guarantee that each person brings unique perspectives. Bringing in what we already know is complemented by each person's willingness to listen and stretch into unknown territory. While most of us are quite opinionated and hold passionate views, there is an appreciation for others' views; that is, we respect others for their views and look for ways these different ideas could enrich our own.

Wearing casual, warm clothes and being on the edge of crisp Lake Champlain seems to provide a context for us not to fear "making waves," offering our thoughts in progress, relaxing our grip on rigid ideas, and truly listening to ideas different from our own. The relaxed atmosphere provides the opportunity to interact in a more open and sincere manner. Rather than posturing and trying to build up one's image or to promote one's agenda or book, the time is spent in a common effort to tackle—through honest discussions—some difficult dilemmas in teaching and practicing social work. Collegiality is promoted by joint interest in and agreement with the enormity of the dilemmas we ponder in our discussions. Freedom to discuss in meaningful ways is encouraged, expected, and enacted—this is a welcome format where we strive to investigate our own ideas more honestly and vigorously.

At this conference, we are in residence with one another so that there is a greater chance of continuing conversations with different configurations of people fluidly throughout our time together. Conversations can be focused and serious or light and funny. One may speak at length or in small bits. One can pursue topics or let them go. Without a specific a priori agenda, the conversations can move as needed to meaningfully engage the participants.

There is a retreat quality; as we are working, we are also being renewed by the stimulation and hope of critically reflecting upon the status quo. There is a feeling that we are holding our basic and most cherished ideas up to the light for examination. These activities broaden our vision and relationships to go beyond narrow "professional" ways of interacting. Meeting and talking with people who share the need for pushing the boundaries of "what is acceptable" in the pursuit of better ways of teaching and practicing social work is validating and enlightening. We are able to genuinely learn from one another in ways that could not have been anticipated or planned. Our conversations are alive and renewing and, best of all, pertinent to bettering our world.

As we said, our conversations are diverse and we can choose from a list of broad categories. We spend a significant amount of our time at the un-conference with a small group (six to seven people) so that we have a chance to pursue topics at length and more in depth. Sally's favorite discussions have been those that have centered on teaching. A focus one year was how our teaching practices need to be parallel to the social work practices that we are teaching so that student learning is reinforced by congruency between the content *and the process* of presenting. We tackled the sacred cow issue of research and grants and how they have been privileged in the academy over the classroom and teaching. We have talked about the problems our students face as they incur student loans and then, after graduating, land poorly paid positions and how this serves as a disincentive to commit to social work as a profession.

Most recently we have discussed the advantages and disadvantages of continuing to conduct practica in traditionally familiar ways—those practices that serve to create carbon copies of supervisors rather than encourage innovative practices. Why not channel the students' energy and enthusiasm into providing services that sponsoring practicum agencies cannot provide, rather than having them just learn someone's job? The students can learn about the agency by doing some valuable extra work rather than shadowing a worker to emulate what that worker does. Couldn't practica provide creative and unique services to those clients who might be left out of the agency's customary service delivery? These discussions about practica have continued back in our home school. The ideas tossed around in this group at the un-conference and the support of the other conference participants has given us the courage to pursue them back in our home school context. Furthermore, we talk about *living* social constructionist principles in our classrooms, in academic departments, and within our home communities and our private lives.

A topic of interest for Dan has been the possibilities of using the arts in social work and social work education. Art, music, theater, and improvisation are large, untapped sources of wisdom and learning within social work. Creative brainstorming of ideas that are not logical, rational, or traditional is both challenging and fun. How does the arts-based social work educator nurture these practices within an established school that clearly privileges only the scientific? How do we evaluate these practices? Do education and training in nontraditional ways (the arts) adequately prepare students to assume social work jobs? Should we prepare students to fit into jobs as they exist, or should we stretch students to reenvision their jobs of the future? Can art be socially activist? The application of performance in our academic department and university was initiated in these Vermont discussions. We will discuss later in the chapter some specific performances that we produced for our faculty that were a direct result of these un-conference conversations.

Going Home

Each year we leave with a sense of commitment and responsibility to develop and activate "the Vermont ideas" with our colleagues at our university. Dan recalled having felt the same desire to keep the spirit of the ideas going after the first Vermont conference, but those good intentions faded upon returning to the "real world" and its pressing daily demands. What seemed to be so invigorating and promising was lost for a year, reappearing at the second Vermont conference. After the second conference, we were determined not to let this happen again. Upon our return this time we were intent on finding a way to share our experiences with our colleagues.

We started by simply reporting our experiences at the un-conference in a general faculty meeting and followed that up by continuing to discuss our Vermont learnings/thoughts in conversations of other committee meetings with faculty, staff, students, and alumni. The invigorating feeling of taking time to discuss issues at length, the excitement of playing with innovative ideas, the hopefulness of challenging the status quo, and our hope to bring these ideas into practice at our school were the topics that we highlighted. The process of importing ideas from other programs, universities, and professionals fuels our development and creativity. The value of external conferences and meetings for our school's growth could be enormous if each faculty member brought in the new and different that he or she found. It is a rather slow process, but we are seeing our colleagues bringing back what they have experienced in their conferences and continuing their efforts to expand those ideas in our school.

The retreat nature of the conference brought home some other ideas as well. The setting, company, and focused attention to discussion served as a respite from our busy, fragmented lives. We started thinking about how we might transfer that same sense of relief and balance to our professional lives once we return home. The fast pace of our everyday academic life began to seem to us to be the culprit in stimulating our stress and distress. We wondered if we could invite this energizing and generative way of being and interacting in our professional roles to transform the hectic pace that we (and our colleagues) feel. Toward that end we have begun to infuse small segments of creative and generative talk about social work issues into our regular faculty meetings. We raise questions that are designed to invite more people to talk about the issues in ways that feel genuinely constructive. Our purpose is to expand how we converse regarding issues that go into making departmental decisions. For example, when a committee offered its proposed solution to an ongoing internal dilemma, we asked about the alternatives the committee had considered but discarded in favor of the solution presented to us. By this, we encourage transparency in our departmental decision making. We try to invite openness in generating and evaluating various alternatives involved in any decision.

We ask how our curriculum changes support the overall mission of the school, how they will affect our larger community and the community's view of us, and how curriculum changes affect student field experiences. These critical and complex questions can be considered ponderous and heavy for some who would prefer simpler and quicker decisions. So advocating for this sort of generative and inclusive process often requires a healthy dose of boldness and resolve. We credit our Vermont time with encouraging us to have the vision and the courage to ask these questions of ourselves, our colleagues, and our students.

In addition to our ordinary administrative discourse, we have begun to add discussions of other issues. From our faculty discussions, a teaching group of full-time and part-time faculty now come together monthly to talk specifically about our teaching experiences and practices. The group decided to read *What the Best College Teachers Do* by Ken Bain (2004) and discuss it, shared various ideas regarding grading and teacher expectations, and took a long look at the dominant teaching narratives that tell teachers to conform to traditional practices that do not seem to stimulate students to really learn. Our latest discussion concerned the messages that our students are receiving to be compliant and how we, as teachers, may unwittingly participate in these messages. We are beginning to systematically study and deconstruct our teaching practices to see the degree to which we encourage (or fail to encourage) our students to be leaders of change in the field. Do we engage in teaching practices that enliven our students and encourage them to excel in the communities in which they are working or encourage them to "follow the rules" or "stay in line"? Much of what students experience throughout their school years from an early age is to do what the teacher says—not to stray outside of what they are explicitly told to do. To engage in that form of teaching of graduate students may inadvertently encourage our students to silence their criticisms or ideas on how to be more effective and helpful to their clients.

Even our regular committee work has been highly influenced by our Vermont dialogues. The respectful and honoring type of conversations we experienced in Vermont seemed worth continuing back in the real world where so often the committee-room discourses are disempowering, discounting, and disillusioning—in a word, quite unmannerly. We are now working on ways to use "good manners" with one another in *all* our collegial interactions. Common courtesies in relationships are often neglected or altogether discarded when we meet to discuss administrative and business-related issues.

The deliberate staging of performances as instructional and compelling was another idea discussed in Vermont that we wanted to "take root" in our home school. We created performances as catalysts to stimulate dialogue regarding diversity issues in our faculty meetings. For example, we wrote a script in which Dan played the role/character of "Mr. Racism" who was interviewed as if he were a guest on a television talk show. Sally and another colleague served as the talk-show hosts. The script led into an improvised section where others in the audience (not part of the script) were so engaged in this performance that they offered their impromptu questions to Mr. Racism. Many in attendance at this performance reported a sense of strong engagement with this issue by virtue of the nontraditional method and performance. This event was followed by further discussions and other attempts to raise our awareness of how racism works in our lives.

To continue with another diversity theme, we orchestrated our own version of the play *The Vagina Monologues* in which actual letters, E-mail exchanges, and statements written by members of our department (including students) were read by actors under the glow of a single lamp in an otherwise darkened auditorium. The intention of this performance was to make public what had been spoken in whispers, through gossip, and in other limited forms of communication so that we might reflect upon these semiprivate (or semipublic) conversations in terms of what they "said about us" as a department. This *Monologues* format was another attempt to consider everyday interpersonal issues in a new, more generative and intriguing light.

We are working to bring the Vermont ideas into our Master of Science in Social Work/Marriage and Family Therapy Specialization Program. In our program, we are looking for ways to encourage more voice and participation of our students. With our program's collaborative orientation, we are examining our role as administrators to see if we are too "in control." Do our students sense the kind of participation in the program and in their own learning that we purport to be the case? We are looking for *ways to investigate* this question that also embody the principles of generative collaboration. In terms of our annual state conference, we are studying ways that conference *themes* (content) and conference *designs* (process) can be more congruent and mutually reinforcing. Perhaps the "medium" can be in concert with the "message."

We have also hosted two small invitation-only conferences so that we could create a very intimate and participatory conference experience. We hold an annual retreat for our students so that they may experience this kind of intimate professional/personal connection as we all strive to live the principles we stand for and espouse professionally. The retreat is informal and fun and is designed to promote connectedness among students and alumni by sharing food, symbolic activities, and letters of support and encouragement written for our students by family members and other professionals. The students do not know many of the professionals who are writing to them, and that makes it even more powerful for all of us when we realize that people who do not know the students personally are invested in their progress and success.

All Is Not "Peaches and Cream"

It would be fair to say that many of our attempts to bring the Vermont-stimulated ideas home are met with mixed reactions. Some colleagues share our excitement and willingness to develop and try new ideas in our professional sphere. But some appear to be less appreciative and more hesitant about the ideas and suggestions we bring.

For example, some of the feedback we received from our questions about decision making in committee and faculty meetings indicated that we were slowing down the process of reaching solutions/conclusions too much. Our goal is/was not to slow things down (or be "obstructionist" to decision making). Rather, it is/was our intention to encourage reflective consideration of all relevant alternatives before deciding what to do, and we have stated this in response to the feedback. Despite declaring our intent to promote effective and transparent decision making, we still experience criticism and disagreement.

Another example of experiencing controversy came from the performances. Raising the issues of inequities in our school sparked many reactions, some supportive and some very negative. Such a topic rather naturally engenders strong feelings, and we prepared for these reactions by relying on the support of our planning group and the merit of the principles for which we were standing. In light of these reactions to the performances, we had to think of ways to modify our approach to alternatively address the topic of inequities without sacrificing the principles. This reflexive process exemplifies our Vermont thinking. Rather than seeing the performances as failures or problematic, they were instrumental in shaping our subsequent efforts.

Regarding the invitation-only meetings/conferences that we have planned, the charge of exclusivity is another illustration of the difficulty of putting our Vermont ideas into practice. The desirability of smallness in meetings invariably leaves some people out, creating hard feelings. Elitism is not our goal, and like the Vermont un-conference planners, we welcome those who would like to join us in future endeavors. The small, open-structured meetings are highly prized by some but not everyone. Additional invitations do not threaten the overall size and shape of these events. The interest in these small events has not, to date, overwhelmed their character or design.

Sustaining the Unconventional

We see the purpose of professional meetings to spark ideas that will be folded into the ongoing practices of the conference goers. Yearly respites are nice but not enough. The generative nature of conferences should yield questions and attention to issues. They could likely be unsettling experiences, driving us back to the drawing board to rethink our ideas and our practices. Most conferences are not planned so that ideas are presented in ways conducive to maintenance year-round. Continuous avenues of communication and opportunities to maintain interaction among the conference participants throughout the year is an important, but largely unexplored and undeveloped, area. We wonder how the energy generated among participants might be nurtured between the annual un-conference dates.

The greatest value of this un-conference may be its isomorphism with the participants' practices and teaching approaches already in motion. The un-conference nurtures many ideas and projects we have already envisioned or begun back home. This conference gives the message that unconventional ideas are okay—and perhaps even vital. We are buoyed when we return from the un-conference. One example of such a boost has been the development of our online journal, *The Qualitative Report*. Knowledge dissemination and conversations among professionals can be accomplished on the Internet as well as in person. Envisioning online journals as *learning communities* or sites of dialogue and innovation can expand the potential of social work and provide genuine opportunities to be inclusive of many voices and viewpoints. We have participated in an all-online journal since 1996 (see *The Qualitative Report* at www.nova.edu/ssss/QR), first as reviewers and now as coeditors. *The Qualitative Report* is dedicated to helping all authors of qualitative research from any field (regardless of their experience level in publishing) disseminate their ideas via the Internet. We actively assist authors in getting their papers in the best possible form so that others may read and know their work/ideas. It is our belief that helping others publish their work for a worldwide audience to read at no cost is a profoundly democratic activity.

This alternative vision for a conference matches the free-flowing and wide-ranging talk about social problems, what needs to be done about them, and the most effective ways to educate future social workers. The unconventional conference format frees us and allows us to think unconventionally about how social work has approached (and is approaching or has failed to approach) difficult societal issues and, perhaps most important, how effective our field has been in addressing these issues.

With social work's mission in mind, we take a clear-eyed look at our performance as a field and our track record in producing practitioners who critically examine what effect(s) we have had on the persistent social problems of our world. This critical review reflects rather harshly on the field of social work, but for our group, this review serves to enervate us and stimulate generative dialogues. We are not despairing of our world's condition—we are excited to believe that we have important work yet to do. The recalcitrant nature of our social problems spurs us on to challenge beliefs of the status quo and practices that are likely implicated in the persistence of these problems.

The un-conference provides an experience for us that motivates us to innovate in our work as social workers and social work educators. It validates our ideas and provides the framework for us to delve into new and different ideas as well. Many of the attributes of this type of conference might well be applied to the larger, more traditional variety of conference. This way of un-conferencing privileges the individual conference goer as the site of learning, using those persons explicitly in the design and running of the conference experience. The potential of un-conferencing is yet to be fully explored, but our experiences to date have clearly convinced us to expand our exploration of this territory.

References

Bain, K. (2004). *What the best college teachers do*. Cambridge, MA: Harvard University Press.

Bell, J. M. (1998). The professional meeting: Revenue generation versus meaningful dialogue. *Journal of Family Nursing, 4*(4), 347–349.

Chesterfield, R. (2000). Using multi-dimensional scaling to promote dialogue among development professionals in conference settings. *Development in Practice, 10*(2), 244–249.

Shaffer, G. L., McNinch, G. H., & Erwin, R., Jr. (1997). Professional conferences: Who attends them; who does not; and why? *College Student Journal, 31*(3), 382–386.

VanZandt, C. E. (1992). Making the most of professional conferences: Beyond sweaty palms and boring meetings. *School Counselor, 39*(4), 263–267.

CHAPTER 3

"Good Talk"

The Art of Transforming Conversations

RUTH GROSSMAN DEAN

"Good talk" is what educators long for in classrooms, at conferences, and, in written form, in journals. We hope to experience, encourage, or be part of conversations that stimulate, challenge, or even change our thinking. But if our conversations are to be transformative, then we may need to transform the kinds of conversations we have with one another. How do we create possibilities for good talk at meetings, in professional journals, and in the classes that we teach? And how do we create venues for conversations in which participants' creative, passionate, and personal voices are released and not stifled? What kinds of in-between, or open, "liminal" spaces allow this to happen?

Good talk has been a primary goal at the Transforming Social Work Practice, Inquiry, and Education meetings held for the last five years by the Global Partnership for Transformative Social Work—the group whose members have authored the chapters in this book. Choosing a bucolic setting on the edge of a lake in Vermont, the planners have done away with the formalities usually associated with professional meetings. There is no call for papers or competition over who will be selected to present; in fact, there are no presentations. Instead, a series of topics of mutual interest is proposed by the conference organizers, and members choose the study group topic with which they will engage for the duration of the meeting. Groups are small (a limit of 10 people or so) and discussions proceed according to the participants' mutual interests. Toward the end of the conference, the salient points of each discussion are shared with the entire group of conference attendees. We are encouraged to present our material in creative ways that involve the whole group. The process is informal and spontaneity is key.

Conversations extend beyond the group meetings as members walk around the lake, hike, sightsee, eat, drink, and socialize. These conditions often lend themselves to good talk, but this is by no means a certainty—even in these idyllic surroundings. At times, discussions get bogged down, or never get going. In the small discussion groups, one person may dominate or another may go off on a tangent just when a good exchange seems to be starting. Or the talk may become competitive as members "show and tell" what they know or do.

Hence, the reason for this inquiry. I have participated in and led group discussions at this and other conferences. Sometimes the talk is stimulating and group members participate with excitement; at other times it becomes tedious and boredom sets in. As a teacher, I have had similar experiences in the classroom. And so, I have become curious about the specific conditions that contribute to good talk. While accepting that serendipity plays a part, I wonder if there are ways to increase the likelihood that good talk will occur. Are certain skills involved, are there strategies to be employed that would make this outcome more likely? For the purposes of this chapter, I am assuming that conditions contributing to good talk in conferences and in classrooms are similar.

In using the expression *good talk* I do *not* mean talk that is respectful and sensitive. Let's take that as a given. What I am referring to are the kinds of conversations that exude energy and send our thoughts in new directions. In these exchanges one person's ideas build on another's in a synergistic process. It's hard to say exactly what happens when the conversation takes off, but we *know* these moments when we encounter them.

Let me give an example. At one Vermont meeting (2004), I was one of six people who had signed up for the group on relationships. Our task was to discuss the ways that "Social construction and related approaches have extended and reinvigorated ideas about relationship(s)," such as the relationships of "student-teacher, client-practitioner, faculty-faculty, researcher-subject." We were to consider the ways these relationships have changed, the implications of these changes, the challenges they offer, and the possibilities for new models. We had three hours in the morning, a break for lunch, and a two-hour period in the afternoon at the end of which we would have to decide how to present our discussion to the larger group.

This was no small task, but we took it on enthusiastically, introduced ourselves, and with the help of our facilitator, began to talk. We covered a lot of territory in the morning. We considered the up- and downside of more collaborative relationships with students. We heard about different teaching methods, such as beginning classes with a minute of silence and experiential exercises that brought feelings into the classroom and more attention to process. We considered action research as a method that challenged the traditional relationship between researcher and subject and wondered why social work didn't make more use of this model. We heard about fieldwork in public housing that stretched the boundaries of time, place, and the relationship between client and practitioner as students ate dinner and attended evening meetings with the residents. By the time of the lunch break we had shared and learned a lot and all of us felt good about the morning's conversation. As we headed to lunch I told one of the group members about the chapter I was writing on good talk, mulling over whether the discussion had fulfilled my very subjective definition. It had certainly been interesting, but I thought that something was missing.

When we resumed our meeting in the afternoon, my colleague asked me to say more about my ideas of good talk. In response, I asked if we could try to go deeper in our ongoing conversation. People were intrigued with this idea (never actually defined). By the end of the day, we were in agreement that something different and exiting had happened. In this afternoon session, we related ideas about teaching, research, writing, and working with colleagues to personal philosophies. We revealed how our interests were shaped by the stage of life that we inhabited. We saw how teaching and research agendas and methods and relationships with colleagues were influenced by aging, or motherhood, or a sense of limited time and shifting priorities.

One of us spoke about the sense of a widening generation gap between herself and her students as she aged. Another aging colleague told us of being less willing to have certain debates and arguments with some of her colleagues. She had a sense of her own mortality and she didn't want to spend her time that way. A third member told us of the ways being a mother had changed her teaching. And a fourth considered how to achieve her goals as a new teacher within a 10-year period, given that her career would be foreshortened because of her older husband's retirement. We were more open and vulnerable in this discussion and more expressive of feelings as we shared stories and information. When we reached the end of our allotted time together, we understood something about the changing quality of relationship(s) through our discussion of the ways our relationships with students and colleagues were changing. We also had the direct experience of the deepening of our relationships with one another. We had enacted a postmodern principle by revealing that "context"—in this case, the personal contexts of our lives—was intricately interwoven in our ways of knowing and being. As we separated, we agreed that this had been good talk.

The possibility that this experience might have even been transformative was suggested during the "reporting back" session. The group whose topic was "Selfhood" presented by inviting us to return to our original groups and discuss what it would mean to exist in a society in which there was no concept of self. When our group reassembled, we shared a perplexity about tackling this difficult assignment. There was a paucity of words. Then, one member suggested that we take each other's hands and so we did. Another suggested a minute of silence, and without any discussion we complied. When the time ended, we said little to each other about the experience except to acknowledge that in those five minutes, the sense of the group was very strong. The ease and unanimity with which this response occurred, and the sense of connection that it provided, made it seem that our relationship to one another had changed as a result of our discussion the previous day. We now experienced the group as a unity and our separate selves as part of that unity.

How did this come about? What were the characteristics of the small-group discussion that contributed to good talk? It seems that

1. Paying attention to the process and naming the desire to "go deeper" *was* helpful.
2. Knowing something about the personal context in which a person's ideas and beliefs are formed makes the information more meaningful and easier to build on.
3. Participants' openness and their willingness to be somewhat vulnerable and include emotions as well as ideas is important.

These tentative ideas about good talk can serve as an introduction to this chapter. But how else to study this subject? What literature might provide a beginning understanding? Communication theory suggests ways of improving the outcomes of small-group discussions through making talk more precise. Within this field of study, there are models for framing conversations, examples of lines of questioning, and considerations of ways to deal with conflict and achieve consensus. These discussions define good talk according to its effectiveness in reaching goals.

In addition to communication theory, there have been some recent developments in social work writing and in discussions of pedagogy that inform this exploration. First, editors of several journals have begun to experiment with new forms of writing in an effort to enliven the discourse, make it more accessible and consistent with contemporary sensibilities (Altman & Messler Davies, 2001; Goldstein, 1998; Witkin, 2000). A close look at the characteristics associated with "good writing" might contribute to understanding what accounts for good talk.

Additionally, there is a growing body of literature on pedagogy and diversity (see for example Tusmith & Reddy, 2002; Basham, 2004). In this discourse, the focus is on finding ways to enable classroom discussions in which students and teachers talk in meaningful ways across and about differences. The differences most prominently noted are race, culture, ethnicity, and sexual orientation. Invariably, when these subjects come up in class discussions and at meetings, differences in beliefs and values emerge and add to the strain. The "talk" can be difficult—awkward at best, and often painful, stilted, and unrewarding. While we would all agree that it is "good" to talk about these matters, it is rare when the talk is actually "good."

In the material that follows, I will explore these developments in writing and pedagogy in an effort to answer the questions I initially posed—what makes talk "good" and what makes "good talk" happen? I will conclude with a story from my teaching experience from which further insights can be drawn. Ultimately, my interest is in discovering strategies that liberate the voices of all participants and support and sustain good talk.

New Formats for Writing

In his first "Notes" as editor of *Families in Society* in 1998, Howard Goldstein welcomed the contributions of human service professionals on the front lines and of those who write from the orientation of the humanities, as he sought "diversity of opinion, energizing ideas, and provocative discourse" (p. 229). He added alternative formats to the journal, such as a series on "Writers at Work," as a way of trying to make this possible.

To extrapolate from Goldstein's ideas, one could say that good talk requires the contributions of multiple voices—especially those who speak from direct experience. As editor, he took responsibility for creating a journal that was more inclusive. He tried to elicit contributions from practitioners whose writing might invoke the creative and artistic aspects of social work. He sought autobiographies, experiential and narrative writings, and invited "essays that capture the personal, 'what it's like' particularities of becoming and being a student or a professional—and, not the least, a client" (Goldstein, 1998, p. 229).

As teachers and leaders of group discussions, could we set the stage for good talk by encouraging the contributions of all participants and creating an atmosphere that does more than give lip service to this idea? What conditions enable those who are not always heard to speak up?

In the October 2000 issue of *Social Work*, Stanley Witkin, then editor, experimented with writing styles not usually associated with professional journals by soliciting articles in the forms of essays, a memoir, and an autoethnography (see Donahue, 2000; Kanua, 2000; Rose, 2000; Sternbach, 2000; Weick, 2000). In this experimental set of writings, the authors are visible and vulnerable; the writing includes self-disclosures and personal narratives. It is honest, wry, reflective, and at times, recursive, with the writer commenting on the writing. Vivid details bring the writing alive and capture attention. Personal accounts are used to strengthen generalizations. There is a back-and-forth between experience and reflection—with neither taking over the writing. It is this balance between personal anecdote and general theory that is important.

How many of us have witnessed a failure of communication when someone begins to tell a personal story in a meeting or class and goes on and on, seeming to get lost in the details. "What is the point?" we listeners wonder. We long for a general conclusion that will help us understand what the anecdote was intended to convey. The other extreme can be equally problematic. Some writers and speakers present their ideas as if they had a direct line on the truth. There is no sense of the context for the speaker's remarks and no way of understanding how the persona of the speaker is related to the idea being presented. The speech is distant and detached and the speaker exudes authority without our knowing whence this authority derives. When authors and speakers provide personal and historical contexts for their remarks, the reader can critically evaluate their ideas within these contexts. Much is lost when such details are not included.

When ideas are situated in a lived experience, the listener or reader can build a relational connection with the speaker or writer. This relational connection reinforces further interest and provokes associations and responses in the listener. Good talk and good writing "recruit the . . . imagination" and allow the reader or listener to participate in the creation of meaning through associations and new awareness (Bruner, 1986, p. 25). New formats for conversations written and spoken invoke new ways of relating to one another, and new ways of relating can break up our usual ways of thinking and take us outside our habitual frames.

Conversation (or writing) becomes exciting—when it takes us to new places. This is also one of the goals of teaching about diversity. Educators who teach courses on racism, social justice, and cross-cultural work are interested in improving dialogue among members of different groups toward the goals of social justice and understanding. Writings concerning pedagogy and diversity are also about good talk.

Talking About Diversity

The discourse on pedagogy and diversity has several features. One focus is on strategies for creating the kind of environment in which discussions among members of different groups can best occur. Another focus concerns the defining features of effective conversations. What are teachers trying to achieve? Finally, a few writers focus on the philosophical or psychological "spaces" in which these discussions can more easily take place (Basham, 2004; Irving & Young, 2004). In the material that follows I would like to relate each of these aspects of conversations about diversity to the matter of good talk.

STRATEGIES

In the strategic writing, educators recommend preparing in advance for the kinds of tensions that can erupt during sensitive conversations. They suggest establishing a framework for class discussions with ground rules. These rules could include requiring confidentiality, speaking only for oneself (and not one's group), sharing time, maintaining respect, and challenging ideas without attacking the person holding them (Miller, Hyde, & Ruth, 2004). There are suggestions of "striving to create egalitarian space," listening carefully, and maintaining open-mindedness (Miller, Donner, & Fraser, 2004, p. 388). The importance of understanding current and past historical, political, and social contexts in which the conversations take place is stressed (Miller, Donner, & Fraser). There is also a suggestion that mechanisms be considered for dealing with stuck conversations, such as dividing into caucus groups or going around the circle with all members of the class being expected (but not required) to speak in turn (Miller, Donner, & Fraser). With all of these different ways of structuring the conversation, it is important that ground rules are established collaboratively with students choosing the rules they want for their class.

This possibility of a collaborative structuring of discussions is worth considering. If members of a class developed a set of guidelines together that they could all endorse, would they then hold each other accountable for maintaining these norms? The teacher's role would be very different if all participants took responsibility for the quality of class discussions. Imagine a classroom in which students were able to give each other feedback in ways that promoted understanding and good talk. What if students were expected to stay engaged and speak as directly and openly to one another as possible?

Might this strategy also be useful if applied to conversations with colleagues at meetings? We presume a certain level of fairness in these collegial discussions, but it doesn't always occur. Are there ways that all of us might be more active in maintaining standards of discourse and determining when and how to apply these standards? This would require more explicit attention to process and desired norms.

Ground rules and structures are important, but they only take us so far. They may help to avoid disasters in discussions and promote respectful discourse, but they don't necessarily lead to good talk. Some might argue that too much structure would dampen conversations, stifle the possibility of "good" fights and healthy disagreement, and make all participants so self-conscious that good talk would be impossible. While setting the rules in advance might seem protective, it could constrain talk. For language to be creative, expectations would need to develop, as part of the talk, through experience and experiment and not be set rigidly as law about what is consensually acceptable in social work (Adrienne Chambon, personal communication,

September 10, 2004). Attention to process and structure in our group and class discussions might help us determine what is actually helpful to or destructive of good talk.

CONDITIONS ASSOCIATED WITH GOOD TALK

Some educators speak of *dialogue* as a necessary condition to conversations that can become transformative, and they reference the work of Mikhail Bakhtin, who thought that the self can only exist in dialogue with others (as cited in Rozas, 2004). Two characteristics of conversation associated with the concept of dialogue are openness and reciprocity. In dialogue, individuals *strive to* address one another as equal subjects with equal power and opportunity in the conversation.

We strive for equality in classrooms and groups while knowing that participants enter discussions with preexisting expectations and assumptions regarding power and equality. Some of us are uneasy intellectually, others carry a social sense of disempowerment. In educational contexts, the teacher has considerable power that does not disappear despite efforts to create a democratic classroom. But even with these constraints, it may be possible through dialogue, transparency, and openness for teachers to level the playing field to some extent.

How does dialogue lead to transformation? If people are truly open in conversation they can gain deeper understandings of one another over time. Empathic connections are achieved through reflecting on what is said. Self-understanding is enhanced as participants come to see themselves through the eyes of another. Sharing one's personal identity is a crucial condition to dialogue. As participants become connected to each other's experiences, they begin to define and redefine themselves within the interaction (Rozas, 2004). It is in this sense that the self exists and is transformed through dialogue with others. The concept of dialogue is more about the stance one takes in conversation and less about the content. It is about listening and reflecting as well as speaking.

We tend to take listening for granted, and yet it is an art that involves skill and practice. According to communication theorists, the ability to listen is related to the willingness to be a "message receiver" (Bormann & Bormann, 1976). To receive a message you must be willing to give up your perspective for a moment in order to concentrate. Giving feedback and restating the message helps to ensure that the message has been understood. It is important to focus on and remember details. However, these details can be forgotten if they are not embedded in an understanding of the structure or main outline of a comment (Bormann & Bormann). Finally, the interpersonal context in which the conversation takes place affects the ability of the participants to listen. If there is mistrust or other negative feeling about the speaker, it is less likely that the message will be received (Bormann & Bormann).

In a standard exercise often used in class (sometimes referred to as a "fish bowl"), two members of the group engage in dialogue while the rest listen. Each might be instructed to restate the other's message and check to see if it has been accurately remembered and understood. This is similar to techniques used in couples therapy where each partner is asked to restate the other's point and focus on getting it right—not on responding to it (White, 1986/1987) Promoting good listening might require that the discussion leader or teacher encourage dialogue when it occurs through structuring opportunities to give feedback and ascertain if understanding is being reached. Would this lead to good talk and would it stimulate further dialogue between other participants?

Asking questions is related to listening well and achieving understanding. Questions can move us forward to new insights. Forms of questioning can become interventions to raise consciousness or increase awareness. When we ask questions and put our assumptions aside for the moment, we admit to "not knowing" (Finlayson, 2001). Questioning that contributes to conversation derives from a perspective of exploration of differences, collaboration, and empathy (Finlayson). By creating an atmosphere in which people feel free to ask questions from their personal perspectives and engage their differences, we increase the probability of talk that is interesting and exciting.

In the literature concerning pedagogy and diversity, another concept mentioned is complexity. In courses on diversity there is an attempt to help students move from stereotypes and reductionistic, simplistic ways of thinking about others and themselves, to richer, more complex understandings (Miller, Donner, & Fraser, 2004). Why is "complexity" so important?

Neurobiologists have identified complexity as an essential quality of healthy biological systems; families and communities can also be thought of as complex systems (Siegel, 2003). Complexity in systems evolves through the processes of differentiation and integration.

When applied to the art of conversation, the notion of complexity as a desired outcome promotes the importance of differentiating ideas, refining concepts, and developing detailed descriptions. It also suggests the need to integrate and find common threads and connections between ideas. Balance is important. To achieve complexity, conversations must veer off into exciting, new, unpredictable paths while not dissolving into chaos.

Thus far, I have highlighted features of the pedagogy and diversity discourse that I consider relevant to this discussion of good talk. These include the use of agreed upon rules, the development of dialogue, and the search for more complex understandings. Earlier, in looking at experimental journal writing, such characteristics as referencing lived experience and balancing the interplay between experience and theory were noted as important hallmarks of good talk or writing. Another consideration to be explored relates to the kinds of "spaces" that lend themselves to experimentation and exciting conversations.

SPACES ASSOCIATED WITH GOOD TALK

Conversations occur in spaces that can be defined in physical, philosophical, and psychological terms. In social work, as a postmodern perspective has entered the curriculum, students have been expected to embrace multiple perspectives simultaneously. In psychological terms, they must tolerate the uncertainty that comes when objective knowledge and universal truths are seen as contextual and as maintaining the dominant hierarchies and power structures in society. For many students, grasping these ideas requires moving to a new cognitive "space."

Irving and Young (2004) speak of classrooms "as processes, transitional in-between, borderland places where there are no hasty resolutions of complexities" (p. 215). The concept of borderlands refers to places where two or more groups or cultures meet, come up against each other's edges, and overlap. These spaces literally exist in geography, for example, in towns at the Texas border with Mexico where the cultures of Mexico and the United States mingle and become new, hybrid formations. They also pertain to "metaphorical regions of the mind where possibilities and potentialities are all around for new subject and cultural formations, new kinds of selves and new kinds of community" (as cited in Irving & Young, 2004, p. 219). In the metaphorical and mental spaces of the borderlands, there is openness to shifting meanings, discontinuities and places of joining, of dreams, ruptures, and contradictions (Irving & Young, 2004).

Other ways of describing these spaces include liminality—a continuous process of change and openness—and Third Space, a location of "in between-ness" that resists the usual rigid categories of culture (Irving & Young, 2004, p. 221). If we could inhabit these kinds of spaces, how would they affect the conversations we would have with one another? Would we "walk out of one culture and into another" as Anzaldua (1990, p. 377) describes, and could we inhabit all cultures—and experience a new form of consciousness? Here is another set of conditions for good talk. It involves more permeable boundaries and a willingness to tolerate ambiguity and lack of resolution while new possibilities are tried on and lived with.

This is a daunting assignment. Neurobiological theory, cited earlier, suggests that there is a need to balance chaos with order. The openness associated with borderlands, liminality, and Third Spaces resists order and organization. In order to move out of familiar and comfortable spaces in conversation and inhabit borderlands we need enough of a sense of trust to take risks. Psychological concepts associated with Winnicott (1965) provide some guidance here (pp. 37–45). The idea of a "holding environment" was used initially by Winnicott to mean both a mother's literal, physical "holding" of her baby and her provision of psychologically sensitive care based on an empathic sense of what her infant needs. It is a concept associated with ideas of containment.

When this concept is applied to group or classroom discussions it refers to a climate in which strong feelings and powerful ideas can be "held" and contained by group norms or by a group leader. Ground rules that promote respect for all participants may be helpful if participants are going to take risks and step into new spaces. "Holding" each other's feelings includes trying them on, inhabiting them, and then working toward greater understanding from this insider position. In this way boundaries are destabilized and borderlands come into existence where experimentation and creativity are possible.

Discussion

In the preceding material, I have looked for ideas that might aid in answering the questions I raised originally—What makes talk "good," and what makes "good talk" happen? I started with a look at the experiments in professional literature that include multiple voices and alternative formats. In these experiments the voice of the writer was present, and personal experience was balanced with more general concepts and theories. What made this writing particularly powerful was the ability of the writer to find and convey to the reader the connections between personal experience and general theories. This material demonstrates how essential it is to good talk or good writing that speakers or writers situate themselves in their communications, making it more possible for the reader or listener to develop a relational connection with what is said or written.

These ideas are supported and expanded by those educators who champion experiential approaches to teaching and learning. As participants bring more of themselves into the conversation, the learning space evolves and expands (Kolb, 2002).

The discourse on diversity and pedagogy provided additional guidelines in the search for conditions of good talk. The educators involved in cross-cultural communication and education recommend collaboratively creating structures that help groups stay involved in discussions that are difficult (Miller, Donner, & Fraser, 2004). These structures will need to evolve with the conversation.

In highlighting the importance of dialogue, the diversity writings remind us of the kind of relationship that comes into being when two people deeply engage with one another. This includes listening well, checking out meanings, responding directly and honestly, and asking for feedback. This also includes ideas about complexity. In order to fully represent the complex nature of the phenomenon we discuss, it is important to make distinctions between ideas and develop more detailed descriptions through questioning. Often when beginning students discuss their clients in class, they include every possible detail known. Part of the task of the educators is to help them sort through the deluge of information collected and determine those details most useful to their purposes. But differentiation is only part of the meaning of complexity. It is also important to draw connections and integrate materials. How do students learn the art of pulling together seemingly disparate pieces of information into a coherent whole? These processes of differentiation and integration are important aspects of the educational process and they could help to improve discussions.

What if we approached discussions in classes or meetings by encouraging people to speak back and forth to one another in a dialogic fashion and develop more complex understandings? This talk might be interesting for those who observed it as well as for those who participated in it directly.

These same principles might also apply in discussions with our colleagues. Engaging in dialogue, asking questions that differentiate and make distinctions, and finding ways to integrate ideas and connect them to other thoughts and theories would enhance the possibilities for good talk. It is important that a balance is achieved between the familiar and the unfamiliar, between creativity and order.

The writings about space remind us that we need to step into new relationships and new territory with colleagues and students. If we were to create some of the structures and conditions already cited, they would produce a sense of inhabiting new places like the borderlands of which Irving and Young (2004) speak. In these places the talk would be different, challenging, and provocative.

In summary, good talk

1. Includes a diversity of voices and encourages the participation of those who speak from direct experience.
2. Is personal, yet it balances personal expression with an awareness of group need. It is both personal and relational.
3. Contains a back-and-forth between experience and reflec-

tion, a balance between personal anecdote and general theory with neither taking over.

4. Occurs with structures that promote trust, yet these structures best evolve within the experience of conversation—otherwise they stifle and constrain.
5. Involves dialogue in which people engage as equals, listen well, and develop understanding through feedback and reflection.
6. Moves toward complexity as efforts to differentiate are balanced with efforts to integrate.
7. Takes us into new spaces that are open and in flux and promote creativity.

As teachers and group leaders, we can encourage good talk by

1. Modeling ways of including those personal details that provide more fullness to our contributions while maintaining privacy.
2. Helping the group develop structures that promote a sense of trust as these evolve from conversations.
3. Demonstrating the art of dialogue, of listening respectfully, and of engaging as equals.
4. Questioning in ways that differentiate while finding integrative themes and threads.

We cannot know what talk will be like once we enter unfamiliar territory. This new territory might even transform our ideas of what counts as good talk. A recent experience with a former student required me to recast my evaluations of classroom discussions and ideas of what constitutes good talk.

A Teaching Borderland

I had just finished giving a speech at a school event, attended by many alumnae, when a young woman approached me at the podium. "Do you remember me?" she asked. "My name is Karen and I was in your class when we had that difficult discussion about your case. I recognized her and began to recall the discussion she referred to. I remembered that a few years earlier, in an effort to help the students in my advanced practice class talk about the challenges of cross-racial and cross-cultural work, I told them about a difficult experience I had while working with a 10-year-old African American boy and his family. (Aspects of this work have been described in more detail in "The Myth of Cross-Cultural Competence" [Dean, 2001]). After providing a little background information, here is the story I told my students:

After some time of weekly appointments between myself and the child, Malik, Mrs. W., who was his great-aunt and guardian, began questioning the usefulness of our interviews, since Malik continued to get in trouble at school. In an effort to persuade her that the meetings were important, I explained that Malik was changing in some ways. He was becoming more open with me, asking many questions, and we were engaged in important discussions. I considered this a good sign in a boy whose ability to trust had been badly damaged by multiple losses. He had lived with five different relatives before moving in with Mrs. W. when he was six. "What have you two been talking about?" she asked. In an uncharacteristic move, I decided to share some of the content of our interviews hoping it would persuade her to let the work continue.

I told her that Malik had been asking me questions about race—"Are white people and black people really alike or different?" and prejudice—"How did prejudice begin?" and privilege—"How does the man who owns the store get to own it?" I told her that I had encouraged him to talk with her and his Afro-Caribbean teacher about these questions, and I had also tried to answer his questions the best I could. As I explained all of this to Mrs. W., it was obvious that she was not pleased that I, a white woman, was having these discussions with her nephew. "Why isn't he asking me these questions?" she asked with considerable annoyance. I thought (but did not say) that he was afraid to ask her questions because she scolded him so often. I did suggest that this was an important question for us to think about, but she wasn't really interested in discussing it with me.

At the time of my next scheduled appointment with Malik, he was not at his after-school program when I went to pick him up. The director of the program, Mrs. S., asked to speak with me. She informed me, on Mrs. W.'s behalf, that I was not to see him any longer. Mrs. S. was Mrs. W.'s messenger, but she also had her own agenda that now entered the conversation. She told me that she thought it was destructive for black boys to work with white female counselors because it leads to an idealization of white women while putting down black women. She did not welcome any discussion of these ideas but instead referred me to reading material about white privilege and guilt and concluded our discussion. My efforts to meet with Malik and say good-bye were stonewalled, and I was not successful in my attempts to have any further conversation with Mrs. W. about her concerns.

As I told this story, the students were extremely attentive. They were a diverse group, fairly evenly divided between white students and students of color who were Asian, African American, and Hispanic. At the end of my presentation, in order to involve the entire class in the discussion, I suggested that we go around the room with students offering any thoughts or comments they wanted to share about the case and about the issue of cross-cultural work. (The option of "passing" and not speaking was also available.) The first student to speak was a young black woman who was visibly upset.

She said, "A few years ago, I would have responded differently, but now I am the mother of a three-year-old black boy. He thinks white women are better than black women. I don't know where he gets this except from TV—he certainly doesn't hear it from me and my husband. It hurts me deeply that he is getting this message and it concerns me very much."

The class took in this powerful remark and I expressed my appreciation for her willingness to be so direct and open with us. Without taking a position, she was raising questions about the ways that working with a white, female therapist could affect her son. As we continued around the table, most of the students of color were critical of my work. They spoke of my lack of appreciation for the ways my relationship with Malik would have been perceived by his guardian and his after-school teacher. They admonished me for not working harder to involve these women and honor their roles in Malik's life. They spoke of the limited understanding white people can have of what it is like to be black and poor. Although a few of the comments were harsh, I knew they were well intended and I also thought they were fair. Despite meeting regularly with Mrs. W. and trying to involve her, I had missed some important clues about her reactions. And I had settled for a very superficial relationship with the after-school teacher. I had to admit to myself and my students that I should have tried harder to engage these important women in Malik's life and that there were limits to my ability to understand their lives as black women.

When it was time for Karen, the former student now standing in front of me at the conference, to speak, she burst into tears. "I went into this profession so that I could work with all people—black and white. I want to work with black kids and now you are telling me I can't do this because I'm white," she sobbed to her classmates. After she spoke other students raised similar issues. An Asian student spoke of her expectation that she would mostly work with people she was different from and she wanted to believe this was possible. The comments continued—there was much debate but little resolution when the class ended. A couple of students came to me before the next class and expressed their concern about the way we left things and so we tried to process what had happened in the next class. But there continued to be no sense of resolution and I was unsure of what I might have done to make the discussion more successful. I deemed it a failure—hardly an example of good talk.

Standing before me at the conference, Karen explained, "Now I live in New York and work in the South Bronx. Everyday I travel to work on a bus where I am the only white person, and my experience at work is similar. I am one of very few white persons working in a high school with mostly black and Hispanic kids. I think of that class discussion every day as I travel to work. I once thought I could do cross-cultural work and I still like it, but I am so much more aware of my limitations. I think of your experience with Malik and I have so many questions about what is and is not possible."

I told her that I had resumed work with Malik in the past year after Mrs. W. placed him in a foster home and turned over custody to the Department of Social Services. While he was still having difficulties, I felt hopeful that our work and his foster family, whose members were very supportive and loving, might help him do better in school and in life. She was pleased by that news and again mentioned that she thought about our practice class often. Others were waiting to speak with me, so there was no opportunity to find out more about her work and the ways her thinking had changed. But her comments led me to question my definition of good talk.

I would never have said that the discussion in those two practice classes had been good. There were some of the hallmarks of good discussions: students were open and honest, all participated, most spoke from their personal experiences, there was considerable give-and-take, and the complexity of cross-cultural matters was very evident. Strong feelings were expressed, but I was not sure that as the teacher I had contained them. I feared that students were left with raw feelings and a lack of closure.

Educators have written about the potential damage that can be done when students have poor experiences in courses discussing race and racism. It has been suggested that "open, raw and unprocessed emotions, unexplored questions, misinterpreted content result in a message that race is a 'dangerous' topic, best avoided" (Miller, Hyde, & Ruth, 2004, p. 417). I feared that I had unleashed difficult content and had failed to help students deal with it effectively.

But Karen's comments revealed another possibility. Can we know what will count as good talk at the time it is spoken? In a postmodern sense, the meaning of the class discussions had continued to evolve for Karen as her life and experience changed. The discussion had stayed with her and been reworked in her mind in the light of new and continuously evolving experiences. While the talk in class may not have seemed "good" to her when she was a student, she made it clear that it was one of the most important learning experiences that had occurred during her time at school.

In the true sense of borderlands—there could be no resolution of the class discussion at the time it occurred. Its meaning changed for Karen and became more complex as it mingled with the new spaces of her professional life. By bringing the news of her ongoing considerations back to my awareness, she allowed me to be part of this continuous process of meaningful development and transition. My learning evolved as well. Karen's story reinforced the idea that there needs to be room for important intellectual differences and strong or upsetting feelings in classrooms and meetings. Perhaps the teacher or group leader's role is to provoke lively and difficult discussions and encourage students or group members to respond honestly and personally. If strong feelings and differences emerge, instead of feeling the necessity to resolve issues, it is important to learn to live with ambiguity and let meaning evolve over time.

This suggests an additional way of defining good talk as a concept in motion—not fixed and always recognizable. All we can do is begin conversations and make them as "good" as possible. We cannot know how their meaning and value will evolve and be transformed.

References

Altman, N., & Davies, J. M. (2001). Introduction. *Psychoanalytic Dialogues, 11*(6), 823.

Anzaldua, G. (1990). La conscience de la mestiza: Towards a new consciousness. In G. Anzaldua (Ed.), *Making face, making soul—Haciendo Caras: Creative and critical perspectives by feminists of color* (pp. 377–389). San Francisco: Aunt Lute Foundation Books.

Basham, K. (2004). Weaving a tapestry: Anti-racism and the pedagogy of clinical social work practice. *Smith College Studies in Social Work, 74*(2), 289–314.

Bormann, E. G., & Bormann, N. C. (1976). *Effective small group communication*. Minneapolis, MN: Burgess Publishing Company.

Bruner, J. (1986). *Actual minds, possible worlds*. Cambridge, MA: Harvard University Press.

Dean, R. G. (2001). The myth of cross-cultural competence. *Families in Society, 82*(6), 623–630.

Donahue, A. B. (2000). Riding the mental health pendulum: Mixed messages in the era of neurobiology and self-help movements. *Social Work, 45*(5), 427–439.

Finlayson, A. (2001). *Questions that work: How to ask questions that will help you succeed in any business situation*. New York: AMACOM.

Goldstein, H. (1998). Looking ahead. *Families in Society, 79*(3), 227–230.

Irving, A., & Young, T. (2004). "Perpetual liminality": Re-readings of subjectivity and diversity in clinical social work classrooms. *Smith College Studies in Social Work, 74*(2), 213–227.

Kanua, U. K. (2000). "Being" native vs. "going native"; Conducting social work research as an insider. *Social Work, 45*(5), 439–448.

Kolb, A. Y. (2002). The evolution of a conversational learning space: An experiential approach to knowledge creation. In A. C. Baker, P. J. Jensen, & D. A. Kolb, (Eds.), *Conversational learning: An experiential approach to knowledge creation.* Westport, CT: Quorum Books.

Miller, J., Donner, S., & Fraser, E. (2004). Talking when talking is tough: Taking on conversations about race, sexual orientation, gender, class and other aspects of social identity. *Smith College Studies in Social Work, 74*(2), 377–392.

Miller, J., Hyde, C. A., & Ruth, B. J. (2004). Teaching about race and racism in social work: Challenges for white educators. *Smith College Studies in Social Work, 74*(2), 409–426.

Rose, S. M. (2000). Reflections on empowerment practice. *Social Work, 45*(5), 403–412.

Rozas, L. W. (2004). On translating ourselves: Understanding dialogue and its role in social work education. *Smith College Studies in Social Work, 74*(2), 229–242.

Siegel, D. J. (2003). An interpersonal neurobiology of psychotherapy: The developing mind and the resolution of trauma. In M. F. Solomon & D. J. Siegel (Eds.), *Healing trauma* (pp. 1–56). New York: W.W. Norton.

Sternbach, J. (2000). Lessons learned about working with men: A prison memoir. *Social Work, 45*(5), 413–424.

Tusmith, B., & Reddy, M. T. (2002). *Race in the college classroom: Pedagogy and politics.* New Brunswick, NJ: Rutgers University Press.

Weick, A. (2000). Hidden voices. *Social Work, 45*(5), 395–402.
White, M. (1986/1987). Couples therapy: Urgency for sameness and appreciation of difference. *Dulwich Centre Newsletter*, 11–13.
Winnicott, D. W. (1965). *The maturational process and the facilitating environment*. London: Hogarth Press.
Witkin, S. (2000). Editorial: Writing social work. *Social Work, 45*(5), 389–394.

CHAPTER 4

Understanding Theory, Practicing Social Work

RICHARD POZZUTO

I am a "returning academic." I came back after a 25-year period when I was a practitioner with strong intellectual interests. Then, unbound by an academic position and the related time demands, I had the opportunity to read as broadly as I wished.

When I returned to academia, I felt less comfortable intellectually compared with my earlier experiences. The reasons were not immediately clear to me. Certainly things had changed in higher education, but the structural changes were not the cause of my discomfort. Something was askew in the communications with my colleagues and in my discussions with other members of the campus community. It was as if we were speaking the same language but not sharing common meanings when we spoke.

The Transforming Social Work conference in Vermont in 2002 was a different experience. Communications, while still requiring some noticeable negotiations even on basic issues, were comfortable. It was much easier to understand and be understood. The language had not changed very much, but the ease of communication had increased greatly. While the conference participants, from my perspective, were quite knowledgeable, they were not narrowly focused specialists. It was easy to find common intellectual interests. For example, my independent reading tends to focus on that border between social theory and philosophy. The participants both recognized and valued that area. The camplike atmosphere, rural setting, common meals, and group activities promoted relaxed dialogue. There was time and willingness to find the common, and there was an interest in what could be.

The experience stayed with me long after the conference. I began to look a little more closely at the discussions within my academic unit. I realized over the years that I began to think more in terms of "processes" than "objects," and more in terms of "meanings" than "fact." My interests were more in what people "did" to produce change than in what "caused" change. Both positions were grounded in theory but in quite different ways. This chapter revolves around the understanding of the idea of theory, its function in the conceptualization of social work, and the consequences for social work practice of different approaches to theory. It attempts to identify differences in order to promote dialogue. It assumes dialogue requires enough similarity to make communication possible and enough difference to make it interesting.

What Is Social Work Theory and Why Is It Important?

The role of theory in social work practice is unclear. In fact, whether theory is important has long been contested (Penna, 2004). For some, the usefulness of theory for social work practice remains an issue (Thyer, 2001; Ungar, 2004). There are even questions about the nature of theory itself.

One may immediately apprehend that the theory one adopts to guide social work practice will influence what is done in the course practice. Within clinical social work the difference between cognitive-behavioral practice and existential practice illustrates the difference. Cognitive-behavior practice is focused upon correcting errors in thinking, such as polarized thinking or overgeneralization, which then contribute to incorrect interpretation and subsequent problematic behavior. Existential practice focuses upon the meaning life holds for the client, the expansion of awareness, and authenticity. Of perhaps greater importance is the more subtle distinction: the way one defines theory will have an even greater impact on the way one practices social work.

There are currently two alternate definitions of social work theory in the literature. These definitions are informed by different ways of looking at the world. By examining the two major perspectives on social work theory, one finds that each assumes a different view of the world—the technical-rational and the generative. In turn, each model of theory presents distinctly different views on the nature of social work practice. By understanding these very different approaches to theory, the social worker can make more informed decisions about how to apply theory: what to do in relation to helping a client.

These differences are not new to social work though they are often presented around different issues, and often the proponents of the varying perspectives speak past each other, a point not lost on Peile (1988). Martha Heineman [Pieper] (1981) challenged what she considered to be the dominant perspective in social work research: logical positivism. Schuerman (1982), Hudson (1982), and Brekke (1986) countered. Each of these defenses was an attempt to ward off relativism. Kondrat (1992), to be discussed later, suggested different forms of knowledge. Rosen (1994) claimed this was unscientific, and in a later work (Rosen, 2003) went on to classify the works of Davis (1985); Gergen (1985); Karger (1983); Peile (1988); Rodwell (1998); and Witkin (1998) as inappropriate for scientific research.

Similar issues have been raised in terms of postmodernism. Gray (1995) suggested there are ethical implications to social work theory and that a critical, reflective perspective was an improvement. Pease (2002) saw a postmodern perspective enhancing empowerment practice. Hugman (2003) found postmodernism enhancing our vision of values and ethics. At the same time, Howe (1994) suggested postmodern theory is fragmenting social work's intellectual outlook. Ungar (2004) considered postmodernism too theoretical so far, and Piele and McCouat (1997) were concerned about the relativism inherent in the perspective. Finally, assuming a modernist definition, Barber (1996) found social work resistant to science. In part, all of these discussions rest on varying definitions and functions of theory.

As Arnd-Caddigan and Pozzuto (in press) have discussed, many of the varying perspectives on research, theory, and practice ultimately rest upon beliefs that are not subject to empirical verification. Recognizing the differing foundations, often missing from the debate, allows for the possibility of cross-perspective dialogue.

Two Kinds of Theory

Social work as profession and practice is molded by and contributes to the intellectual currents of the time. As Foucault (1978) has made clear, these intellectual currents are neither value neutral nor necessarily progressing toward a more just social world. Foucault suggested that under the thoughts, themes, and images of a professional practice such as social work, under its "manifest discourse" (p. 48), there are rules for the discourses themselves. These rules, which are themselves covert, define and limit what can be considered legitimate perspectives and theories in social work.

Social work theories comprise a discourse within social work. Under the surface of the theories are the rules for the discourse. These concealed rules place limitations on practice. By making those rules explicit, the social work practitioner can identify the limitations imposed by any particular theory or range of theories. The practitioner thus informed can then make better judgments concerning the degree to which a given theoretical orientation can promote or inhibit the maintenance of individual or collective well-being, or, for that matter, a just society.

Schön (1983) has articulated one of the ways of looking at the underlying assumptions about theory. Drawing upon the work of Habermas (1972), he approached the relationship between theory and practice by distinguishing between technical-rational and reflective practice. From a technical-rational perspective, professional activity "consists in instrumental problem solving made rigorous by the application of scientific theory and technique" (Schön, p. 21). Floersch (2004), citing the work of Fook (2002), described the technical-rational approach as a "top down" (p. 163) approach. In other words, theory in this view is the starting point, and practice is the application of that theory. The desire for such a grounding in social work is not new. Porter Lee's 1929 address, "Social Work as Cause and Function," suggested a movement away from social causes toward a technical problem-solving approach (Lee, 1939). In Floersch's words, the social worker would apply the "necessary skills to fix or transform objects" (p. 163). While this may be consistent with the assumptions of some forms of theory, it may not be consistent with the mission of social work.

The National Association of Social Workers (NASW) *Code of Ethics* (1999) states, "The primary mission of the social work profession is to enhance human well-being and help meet the basic human needs of all people, with particular attention to the needs and empowerment of people who are vulnerable, oppressed, and living in poverty" (p. 1). Enhancing human well-being is a value-driven principle as is meeting basic human needs. These principles assume a set of values, these being about collective responsibility for human well-being and equitable satisfaction of basic human needs, and use them as the foundation for the primary mission of the profession. It is possible to conceptualize the primary mission if a technical-rational approach is adopted. Given this perspective, values are reduced to rational choices between technical alternatives (Habermas, 1972). Such a conceptualization is consistent with both a narrow definition of science and the promotion of social work as an application of science.

An alternate interpretation of social work is that it is generative. If it is a profession that seeks to assist people in creating satisfying lives, not choosing between fixed alternatives, and assists in establishing a social context that promotes human well-being and the satisfaction of basic human needs, then at its best social work is an attempt to consciously create a just social order. This kind of activity is based on a very different type of theory from that which narrowly defines the nature of problems, then dictates skills that are aimed at the solution of those circumscribed problems. This issue has been addressed by Kondrat (1992, 1995). She distinguished between technical-rational theory, which she identified as intended for explanation, and a theory intended for understanding. In this sense explanation refers to a statement or series of statements that points to causes and consequences of some object or process. The explanation is consistent with rules or laws applicable to the object or process. Understanding, on the other hand, refers to grasping how people in life give meaning to their actions and the social world around them. Kondrat, following the lead of Habermas (1972), considered theory intended for understanding to have a broader practical interest. It provides a basis for intentional social acts, including those that maintain, reproduce, or transform a social order. Kondrat favored the latter form of theory for social work.

Perhaps she was correct, but, more important, she helped identify the complexity of the term *theory*. Kondrat's work met with strong opposition (Rosen, 1994) and, in many ways, has remained of interest primarily within the academic community.

Two Perspectives of Theory in Social Work

Some words take on a naturalness. They seem to have an accepted, unproblematic meaning. Within social work, though the issue is broader, theory is one of those terms. Social work students, practitioners, and academics all use the term theory with ease. While each knows there are a variety of practice theories, at a different level, there are different scholarly understandings of theory itself. The differences are often obscured by the apparent unaffected nature of the term. Within the social work context, taken together, Francis Turner's (1996) *Social Work Treatment: Interlocking Theoretical Approaches* and Malcolm Payne's (1997) *Modern Social Work Theory* address various theories and diverse notions of theory itself. Turner presented a single definition as a foundation for various practice approaches. Payne, in contrast, identified two forms of theory, in his terms *positivist* and *postmodern*. In the following sections both Turner's and Payne's definitions of theory will be examined, along with the function of language in each perspective.

TURNER'S SOCIAL WORK TREATMENT

Turner's work, now in a fourth edition, first appeared in 1974, while Payne's work appeared in 1991 and is in its third edition. Both texts are influential in social work education and together they illustrate the range of understanding within social work of the term theory. An examination of the two works allows for an exploration of the differences in understanding, use, and implications of social work theory.

Turner's (1996) work includes a brief section, titled "What Is Theory?" Here, drawing upon Hearn (1958) and Siporin (1989), Turner defined theory "as a model of reality appropriate to a particular discipline (1996, p. 2)." This perspective on theory is consistent with Schön's (1983) technical-rational perspective previously introduced and a positivist approach to theory discussed later. It tends to depict social work as a technical activity, as the paragraphs below will address.

In discussing theory, Turner (1996) stated that there are four associated terms necessary for understanding theory: concepts, facts, hypotheses, and principles. For Turner, concepts "are abstractions representing logical descriptions of reality that a discipline develops to describe the phenomena with which it is dealing" (pp. 2–3). This may be a description of an object or relationships between objects. Further, Turner noted that these concepts are used to communicate with others both within and across disciplines. He also stated that the concept is not the phenomenon itself and warned against mistaking it for concrete reality (reification).

Facts, for Turner, "are concepts that have been empirically verified . . . they are testable observations related to the concepts with which they deal" (p. 3). Theories "emerge from the process of ordering facts in a meaningful way" (p. 3). From Turner's perspective then, theories are meaningful, ordered sets of statements relative to facts and to stringing facts together in a cogent way.

Turner (1996) used the term *fact* in a dual manner. In one sense, facts are tested and verified, and in the other they have the potential for being tested and verified. This would produce two forms of theory: proven theory and verifiable theory. For our purposes, this is not a significant distinction. The fundamental understanding of theory is the same in either case; theory is a set of statements about the relationships between facts and/or concepts. This is a formal understanding. Turner recognized that the term theory is sometimes used informally to refer to "personal opinion" or even as a pejorative term implying too distant, unreal, or impractical.

In his approach to defining theory, Turner used the term *statement* but did not address it. As a working definition for our purposes statement means referring to stating, declaring, or making known. Statement is an aspect of language. Theory as "ordered sets of statements" is a linguistic presentation of relationships among concepts and/or facts. Also, in considering theory, most of our knowledge about theory comes either in spoken or written form. The link between language and theory cannot be broken. They cannot be independent. In some fashion theory rests upon a foundation of written or spoken language. This is outside the parameters of Turner's considerations, but it is significant to understanding the different forms of theory.

Turner made a number of assumptions about language that suggest he was subscribing to a correspondence theory of language. These assumptions have to do with the relationship of concepts, objects, and facts. Given a correspondence theory perspective, language is assumed to be neutral and corresponds with or reflects the objects of an independently existing, objective world (Rorty, 1979). From this perspective, a word or concept corresponds to an object in the world. It is assumed that empirical experience helps adjust concepts to the objects of reality. Concepts and, hence, language are derivative of objective reality. This is very similar to the "doctrine of physicalism" developed by Otto Neurath and the Vienna Circle (Sarkar, 1996), often referred to as positivism.

The Vienna Circle claimed that all sciences share a common language and that all scientific terms could be restated as, or reduced to, a set of basic statements, or protocol sentences, describing immediate experience or perception (Sarkar, 1996). Members of the circle were aware that nonscientific languages also existed—ones that expressed emotion, sentiment, fantasies, or other nonobjective aspects of daily life. While these statements may convey sentiment, they were essentially meaningless from a scientific perspective. Given this view of language, the doctrine of physicalism, as developed by the Vienna Circle, meant the reduction of all scientific terms to the terms of an objective physics, namely, objectively existing objects. The unity of scientific method, which flows from the unity of science thesis of the Vienna Circle, a thesis resting upon the support of the doctrine of physicalism, implies that the procedures for testing and supporting statements in all sciences are essentially the same. Language, theory, and method are unified into a single perspective. Underlying this perspective is the belief that these elements refer to an objective reality that exists apart from the people who make statements about it. True statements are accurate descriptions of that reality, and untrue statements do not accurately reflect reality.

Turner did not address the philosophy of science, nor did he need to. To the degree that he explored the nature of theory he presented a position within the current idioms of positivism. He is certainly not alone and works from a well-established intellectual tradition.

DE SAUSSURE'S APPROACH TO LANGUAGE

There are other theories of language besides a correspondence theory. De Saussure (1966), often considered the founder of modern linguistics, presented a quite different theory. From this perspective, words (de Saussure used the word *sign* as a more inclusive term) are arbitrary. That is, the word itself bears an arbitrary relationship to an external reality. The English and French languages' concept of *tree* can serve as an example of this principle.

When spoken, the sound used to express the concept tree is different depending upon the language. The French sound and the English sound serve equally as well but they are different. The sound's linkage to the concept is arbitrary; it is not determined by the concept itself. In fact, with any given language—for example, English—the concept tree need not be expressed by the sound usually associated with the word. Any utterance, as long as it is socially agreed upon, can be used to represent the concept. Again, the link between the concept and the expression of the concept is arbitrary.

De Saussure (1966) did not stop there. He additionally stated that the link between the concept and "objective reality" is also arbitrary. This is closer to the heart of the issues regarding the examination of theory. This arbitrariness is not questioning the existence of reality; it is questioning the dividing of reality into particular concepts or categories. If language simply reflected what existed in reality, then the concepts of one language, if accurate, could easily be translated into another language. They would be referring to the same object in the "reality." This, however, is not the case. Languages do not use equivalent concepts. Culler (1986) made the point this way:

> It is obvious that the sound sequences of *fleuve* and *rivière* are signifiers of French but not of English, whereas *river* and *stream* are English but not French. Less obvious, but more significantly, the organization of the conceptual plane is also different in English and French. The signified "river" is opposed to "stream" solely in terms of size, whereas a "fleuve" differs from a "rivière" not because it is necessarily larger but because it flows into the sea, while a "rivière" does not. In short, "fleuve" and "rivière" are not signified or concepts of English. They represent a different articulation of the conceptual plane. (pp. 33–34)

As illustrated by the point above, the English language and the French language take reality and divide it up differently. This differentiation occurs within the context of existing language, which provides a tool in organizing and interpreting reality as we understand it (Bakhtin, 1981). From this perspective language is not "an accurate reflection" of what exists but is a tool in forming distinctions in what exists. Reality without interpretation does not include its division into separate categories, as a correspondence theory of language seems to suggest.

For a correspondence theory of language, meaning is derived from the fit of the language to reality. If, as de Saussure (1966) suggested, language does not fit preexisting divisions of reality, how does it derive meaning? In short, de Saussure's answer is that language is a system. Meaning is derived from the system and the relation of words within the system; that is, a word has meaning in relation to other words.

De Saussure's (1966) observations about the relationship between language and reality imply that reality exists, but a particular organization of reality is dependent upon language. We use language in thinking about reality and we use language in conveying our thoughts to others. If our organization of reality is dependent upon our language, then, in this sense, language defines reality. It does not simply reflect it (Rorty 1979).

Turner's (1996) definition of theory does not fit de Saussure's (1966) perspective on language. Turner defined theory as an articulation from the discovery of reality, while concepts for de Saussure actively construct our reality. As stated earlier, Turner's definition of theory is consistent with a correspondence theory of language. The alternate perspective of language, given the link between theory and language, presents a foundation for an alternate view of theory. Payne's (1997) dual perspective on theory addresses this issue.

PAYNE'S MODERN SOCIAL WORK THEORY

Payne's (1997) work includes a section, titled "What Are Social Work Practice 'Theories'?" He suggested there are two major competing perspectives on theory, one positivist and the other postmodern. Payne's iteration of positivist theory is very similar to Turner's definition of theory and need not be restated here. What Payne adds is an alternate perspective on theory.

Payne (1997) noted that from a positivist perspective knowledge rests upon the fit between concept and the "objective reality," but from a postmodern perspective, knowledge has a different meaning (p. 29). Postmodernists see knowledge as a representation of reality using ideas and words in a language of symbols. Payne is implying that representation does not necessarily mean reflection, as in mirroring, and, for the postmodernist, knowledge is not a reflection of reality.

From Payne's (1997) perspective, postmodern theory is an active component in the creation of reality. This is not to imply that it is an active component in creating the substance of reality itself but an active component in constructing human knowledge or an understanding of reality. We can only know reality via our physical and intellectual capabilities. These capabilities do not comprehend reality on its terms but rather on ours. We see with our eyes, hear with our ears, and think with our mind. Our eyes and ears perceive light and sound within parameters limited by physical ability and expectations (Simmons & Chabris, 1999). Thinking is expressed linguistically, which is limited by the form of the language. Because knowledge is a human product, it necessarily bears the mark of humanity. From this perspective theory is about how humans know the world, not about the world itself. However, this does not lessen the utility of theory in navigating the world.

Several implications flow from these distinctions illustrated by Payne (1997) and Turner (1996) in understanding theory and the practice that might follow from it. One of the more obvious issues has to do with social work research methods. Turner's technical definition of theory is consistent with the most common understanding of theory proposed by social work research texts. This approach emphasizes the "discovery" of an "objectively existing" world. There is emphasis upon the "objectivity" of the study and the "validity" of the concept and measurement. Validity, from Turner's perspective, refers to the fit between the concept and the object in reality.

If, however, one assumes that the division of reality into objects and the categorization of those objects are both human creative actions, then validity in the sense described above is meaningless. There is no independent, external, objective object to which to attach a concept. Assuming a degree of creditability to a postmodern perspective, there is a very basic conflict. Theory, as Turner (1996) understands it, does not fit the assumptions of a postmodern perspective. In a sense, the languages of Turner's theory and a postmodern theory are foreign to each other and not easily translatable because of their conceptual differences. As the forms of theory guide research and practice, their "languages" influence the form that research or practice takes. These languages are passed on to the accounts of the research and practice, again presenting significant translation difficulties.

Language and Practice

Thus far we have been dealing with language as if it were a system of isolated words. Simply looking at this page illustrates that words are placed together to convey meaning. The ordering of the words, either written or spoken, according to Foucault (1978), is not neutral. The positivist notion of theory rests upon the belief that the language of science, in terms of both words and presentation, is neutral and only reflects an underlying reality. De Saussure's (1966) perspective seriously challenged the correspondence of words with a presumed reality, be it for ordinary language or scientific language. More recently, Bhaskar (1978) has suggested it can be both ways depending upon the subject matter. Houston (2001) has advocated this perspective for social work. Is reality the unfolding of universal laws as the positivist would have it, or is reality, to some degree, a conscious human creation as the postmodernist would have it? The implications for practice are significant.

Bakhtin (1981) was an early challenger of the notion that the act of communication via language could be neutral. He referred to what he called *the utterance*, an act of speech that always occurs within a social and historical context, and always in relationship to an "other." One speaks to an other. The other may be the person to whom one is directly speaking, a hypothesized other, or a dialogue within one's own mind. The utterance may be intended to communicate or, it may be, in itself, doing something. For example, the utterance, "You are under arrest," conveys meaning but is also an act of performance. It is performing an arrest in a particular social and relational context.

Utterances are spoken by an individual with a specific history and within a specific social context. Hence, they are always historical and social products. The particular utterance carries the stamp of the individual, a social history, and the intent within the particular situation. One may speak, for example, American English, because that is the culture in which one was raised. This individual's vocabulary reflects his or her lived experiences, and the connotations she or he associates with words are more uniquely his or hers. Even so, those connotations rest within a social context. One's utterances are intentional and purposeful, though not always successful. One chooses what one says and says it to achieve a purpose. Additionally, it would be a mistake to imagine isolated, fixed utterances. They actually occur in dialogues wherein the very process of the dialogue contributes to the shaping of the utterances.

In Bakhtin's (1981) terms each utterance is double-voiced. It carries the voice of the past but occurs within an ongoing dialogue. Each word has multiple possible meanings. Simple words like *right* might mean morally proper, a prerogative, a license, a claim, or even a direction, not to mention to correct, to stand up, to amend, or to proceed straightaway. The listener must find the intent of the word in order for the utterance to be meaningful. The double-voiced nature of the utterance provides the parameters for the interpretation. This is not simple. Several statements may be made back and forth trying to clarify the meaning of utterances. Each actor is speculating about the context in order to find meaning. To the extent that the speculation is part of the dialogue, the speculation then becomes part of the context for grasping the meaning. Perhaps the way to look at this is to see dialogue and communication as an ongoing, self-referential process. Since we are all born into preexisting, ongoing communications, there is no world for us without this process. In that sense there is no beginning point. The process has always been there. The apparent stability of a word or statement is anchored in the ongoing process and not in an external truth.

But what does all this have to do with theory? Turner (1996) defined theory as statements about the relationship between concepts and/or facts. We have already addressed the relationship of concept to reality. Bakhtin (1981) said that the statement itself is also a social product and has meaning only within a social and historical context. From Bakhtin's perspective, the mechanism for conveying theory has meaning only as a social process, rather than as a value-free referent to some objective reality. Thus, theory promotes an agenda through a particular way of seeing and acting in the world. In this sense theory can not be uncoupled from action. It is not passive but active, not an echo of reality but generative.

While theory is a term in the English language, the potential meanings for theory are quite diverse. One form of theory explains human behavior by reference to external factors (Smith 1996). Causal events produce particular effects: human behaviors.

Another form of theory attempts to understand the reasons that motivate particular human acts. Theorizing, that is, humans using theory, depends upon the perspective. It is a different act from one perspective to another.

The Nature of Practice

Given these two perspectives on theory, what is practice? In part, this has been answered by Schön (1983). A positivist—or in Schön's terms, the technical-rational—approach is the application of the known regularities of the social order: instrumental problem solving based upon scientific theory. The positivists discover reality and we fit ourselves, and, perhaps more profoundly, our clients, to that reality. The alternate view sees theory as a human construction that provides a way of viewing reality. The emphasis here is upon *a* way as opposed to *the* way. The alternate view, we may call it postmodern or a social construction perspective, though the two terms are not entirely synonymous, recognizes multiple ways of organizing reality, hence multiple ways of viewing reality.

Each of these views opens and closes possibilities. A positivist perspective tends to project the past into the future since it assumes a consistency of concepts. A postmodern approach leaves a future quite open. The importance of the theory from the latter perspective may rest not in its accuracy in depicting reality but it its utility in constructing a desired social world. The issue, reduced to the simplistic, is to what extent should social work practice fit people to the existing social patterns and to what extent should social work foster the creation of new patterns?

Schön's (1983) alternative to technical rationality is reflection-in-action. The reflective practitioner focuses upon the acts of practice, sometimes retrospectively and sometimes concurrent with the very acts. Schön tried to differentiate this reflection from a technical-rational perspective by introducing the notion of "knowing-in-action." He stated:

> When we go about the spontaneous, intuitive performance of the actions of everyday life, we show ourselves to be knowledgeable in a special way. Often we cannot say what it is that we know. When we try to describe it we find ourselves at a loss, or we produce descriptions that are obviously inappropriate. Our knowing is ordinarily tacit, implicit in our patterns of action and in our feel for the stuff with which we are dealing. It seems right to say that our knowing is *in* our action. (p. 49)

This kind of knowledge does not lend itself to a positivist theory or description; rather it is how we experience our daily lives. It is thinking about what we are doing, but a form of thinking that is outside the bounds of formal, positivist theory. It is not the application of theory to a problem but the application of experience to action. Some of the experience is mediated linguistically in that we are aware of it through language. Other experiences are not mediated this way. Again drawing on Floersch (2004) and Fook (2002), knowledge in action is "bottom up." In other words, ad hoc theories emerge in relation to the specific situation in which the social worker is involved, rather than grand theories providing strictures that the worker apply predetermined techniques that are assumed to be effective across broad contexts.

In addition to different linguistic foundations, different forms of theory hold different assumptions about individuals, societies, and their relationship. For social work, person-in-environment has different meanings depending upon the form brought to bear upon it. This person-in-environment relation is fundamental to social work practice. It is multifaceted, as the next section will begin to articulate.

The Individual and Society

There is a further step that gets one closer to an understanding of social work practice, but two sets of concepts need to be introduced. The first set focuses on the individual and the other focuses on the social.

There are various ways of thinking about the individual. George Herbert Mead (1934) suggested that all human beings experience a self. The self is not an innate structure one is born with, but a capacity that develops through the ongoing social context into which the individual is born. According to Mead, it is the interactions with others that provide the foundation for awareness of self. This self-awareness means that we, as humans, can perceive our self, talk with our self, judge our self, and, perhaps most significant, plan for our self. This self-awareness allows us to be both subject and object; we become, within the social context, self-directing (Mead). Our plans result in acts. They, the acts, are not responses to the world but intentional behaviors to achieve some desired state in relation to the world; they are constructed by the individual. This does not imply that they are constructed well or that they are successful. The consequences may be quite unintended. The act is dependent upon what the individual "takes into account" in its construction.

There are no rigid rules for what is taken into account. The everyday experiences of the individuals and the social context provide parameters for what is likely to be taken into account. Practice theory for social workers is one of the parameters. Two individuals, or for that matter, the same individual at two different points in time, will not necessarily take the same things into account in constructing an act. Their awareness changes with the process of living. This is not an awareness of an objective experience but the awareness of lived experience with all the intermeshing of value, sentiment, interpretation, reflection, narration, and context. This gives rise to the possibility of multiple and changing realities.

The construction of acts changes over time given life experience and reflection upon experiences. One's past experiences are taken into account in constructing future acts. In this process one's consciousness of self changes. In turn, one's perception, talk, and judgment of the self changes as well. Again, from this perspective, the self is not an immutable thing but rather the result of the continual process of coping in the world. The self, then, is better viewed as process than as object. This process occurs within a social context. This thought brings us to our next issue, the social. This conception of self is, of course, not the only one and is not necessarily consistent with both forms of theory under consideration. It is a conceptualization of self consistent with the author's perspective and useful in furthering examining forms of theory.

Berger and Luckmann (1967) developed a paradigm of social reality based upon three interrelated social processes: externalization, objectivation, and internalization. Externalization, the "stuff" out of which all social formations are made, is the "ongoing outpouring of human beings into the world, both in the physical and the mental activities of men [*sic*]" (Berger, 1969, p. 8). From this perspective, the social world exists only as the product of human activity. It is the result of the process of living.

According to Berger and Luckmann (1967), this externalized human activity strikes us as if it were a thing, not an activity, a social fact in Durkheim's (see Giddens, 1972) terms: the "of courseness" of Geertz (1983). The link between the activity and its originator becomes lost, giving the externalized activity its "thing-like" quality. It is through the process of objectivation, according to Berger and Luckmann, that this thing-like quality is achieved. For example, when I was a new driver, traffic lights seemed to have a power of enforcement of some sort. Quite by accident one day I went through a red light. I expected something to happen, perhaps sirens, hidden police officers to appear, immediate arrest, something. In fact, nothing happened. I became aware that I was not compelled by the object to stop. That, in fact, stopping was a voluntary act on my part. For the traffic light to have an effect, in essence, I had to agree to its meaning. It was not a thing over and against me. This structure of the social world was really an interaction that my chosen act could potentially modify.

The third process in Berger and Luckmann's (1967) model is internalization. This process refers to the incorporation of external reality into the structures of one's consciousness. A similar and more common term is socialization. This is essentially how one learns to play the game of life from players who are already participating in it. The more meaningful the players are to one, the more significance they have, that is, the more one internalizes those significant others' versions of reality.

For Berger and Luckmann (1967), this is not a sequential model. All three processes occur simultaneously and continually. They are never completed. In fact, dividing the three moments of the paradigm into separate categories can only be done heuristically. The experience of life does not offer such separation. From this perspective, social reality is maintained and recreated through an ongoing process, both of which, the reality and the process, are subject to modification and transformation. It is the acts of the self that are the stuff of the reality. This is, of course, the reality in which the self develops.

Implications for Practice

Social work is one form of human activity. It has a clearly identified purpose that is found in the *Code of Ethics* (NASW, 1999). The *Code of Ethics* identifies what we are to do and provides some conceptual context for terms such as *empowerment, oppression, individual well-being,* and so on. Drawing upon

Mead's (1934) notion of the self in formulating acts, one might conclude that social workers take into account the factors identified by the guidelines of their profession in formulating their acts. Social workers also take into account their understanding of the world; this brings the conversation back to theory. Part of social workers' knowledge of the world is their grasp of relevant theory. While the *Code of Ethics* provides some guidance about *what* social workers do, theory suggests *how* they do it. The issue for our purposes is not the content of the theory but the nature of the theory itself.

Turner's (1996) notion of theory, as illustrated above, leads to instrumental problem solving by the application of discovered rules. Given Berger and Luckmann's (1967) perspective, this instrumental problem solving becomes externalized and the stuff of social reality. In part, the theory, to the degree that it informs practice, contributes to the construction of the social world that it purports to reflect. In some cases this means that the theory supports the status quo, or keeps members of the society within the existing social relations. The informed social worker may ask herself or himself, "Does this "reality" serve the mission of social work? Do the existing social relations provide opportunities for addressing "empowerment" and "individual and societal well-being"? This is not to imply that social work practice is directly responsible for the organization of society. The construction of the social world is never that direct, determined, or uniformly informed. Many factors are required for social acts to be completed. The act must be reasonably conceived, physically possible, manageable through cooperation or coercion, uninterrupted, and of sufficient priority. Social workers, *or* for that matter, people in general, cannot create the world, intentionally or not, in any fashion they wish. Aspects of the action will always be contested. The contesting is also externalized and hence part of the social world. The point is that, from the author's perspective, the worldview contained within

Turner's (1996) notion of theory seems antithetical to the mission of social work. The mission seems generative, intended to improve the social structure, hence *to* change social structure. Turner's sense of theory does not allow for one to get beyond a given theory in order to accomplish this task.

Turner used the phrase, "interlocking theoretical approaches," in the title of his work. Assuming a unified conception of theory, perhaps this could be accurate. Assuming multiple perspectives on theory itself, it is highly unlikely. The unified approach reduces the recognition of difference and, if accepted, limits possible forms of practice.

On the other hand, the postmodern or constructionist notion of theory recognizes theory as an interpretation of the world, a story, if you like, of how the world works. It is a method of organizing thoughts about the world and establishing what to take into account when constructing acts. One interpretation does not negate another. Multiple interpretations are possible and each may have utility. As the interpretations are employed they offer new stuff to be included in further interpretations. This notion theory is consistent with Schön's (1983) concept of reflective practice.

From this perspective, theory is not imposed upon the world, nor is the expertise of the social worker imposed upon the client. Both the social worker and the client have an interpretation of the world, a commonsense theory of how the world works. Each can gain from the understanding of the other and the other's theory. Together, incorporating the knowledge of both client and social worker, acts can be constructed to form intentional behaviors to achieve some desired state in relation to the world.

This is a complicated and challenging task. Bruner (1986, 1990) suggested that everyone has at least an implicit theory of action. In *Acts of Meaning* (1990) he referred to this as a folk psychology. This is essentially an understanding of how the world works. These understandings, theories if you like, differ depending upon one's reference group. The potential reference groups are varied and may include families, communities, or professions. Usually the social worker and the client have different understandings of the world. Most likely, both of these understandings encompass the role of the other and the relation between self and other; added to the mixture is the element of power.

If one accepts the social work mission as the cocreation of acts to achieve desired states, it is not the function of the social worker to "correct" the client. Rather, social worker and client collaborate on the construction of acts, which, in principle, means drawing upon the knowledge of both. Both the client and social worker "know" something. The task is each recognizing the knowledge of the other and using it in a creative process. For the social worker this means flexibility concerning one's professional status, and for the client this means accepting help and initiating actions. The resulting generative, cooperative relationship with clients provides a dynamic working arrangement of mutual respect. The "fixedness" of the social world may dissipate and possibly become more transparent, allowing for real change. This, of course, is not the only approach to social work practice. It is not an approach consistent with Turner's definition of theory, the social worker as expert, or an instrumental problem-solving perspective.

Conclusion

What is the role of theory in social work practice? The answer to this question depends on the underlying view of theory. If the social worker adopts a positivist view of theory, as Turner (1996) has done, the worker will understand theory to be a reflection of objective reality. This top-down view of theory is based on the correspondence theory of language, and ultimately leads the worker to the technical-rational application of skills to correct or adjust the situation/client. If, on the other hand, the worker determines that theory in part constitutes the social world rather than reflecting the "givenness" of that world, she or he will use theory very differently and will engage in very different types of interventions. The postmodern understanding of theory will lead the worker to question how the theory contributes to rather than only reflects the social world. The social worker may look for the political significance of the theory within the current social context. Such a worker is likely to engage in interventions that emerge in the process of interacting with a specific client in a specific context. This type of social worker is not the technician of Porter Lee's (1939) vision, but a professional who can think critically and apply professional judgment and skillful use of self to help clients achieve an improved quality of life.

While the content of a practice theory may guide the practitioner to think in one set of terms or another, the form of theory also influences practice by implied and often obscured assumptions about the social world. To the degree that these assumptions can be brought to light, the practitioner can reflect upon his or her practice, making a more informed choice in practice approaches. A recognition of difference is required for choice.

Postscript

This discussion started with a series of musings about the difficulties in communication because of different perspectives between my colleagues and me regarding what I considered practical questions and what my colleagues considered abstract, philosophical reflections. Our daily academic practice will continue to be problematic unless we recognize and respect difference. Each of us knows our own perspective and how it contrasts with others. In a similar manner, we should strive to understand the discourse underneath social work theory and how the concealed rules of that discourse shape theory and practice, a discourse that also shapes our social world.

I doubt that I could have written this chapter when I first returned to academia. I did not understand then what I understand now. I could not see clearly enough the differences in perspective. My independent reading during my hiatus had influenced my thinking more than I realized. I was using myself as an anchor point but was not aware of my movement. At the same time the "naturalness" of my position for me obscured the perspectives of many of my colleagues from me. A recognition of difference was required to understand my new position as well as to produce this chapter.

References

Arnd-Caddigan, M., & Pozzuto, R. (in press). Truth in our time. *Qualitative social work*.

Bakhtin, M. (1981). *The dialogic imagination: Four essays*. Austin: University of Texas Press.

Barber, J. G. (1996). Science and social work: Are they compatible? *Research on Social Work Practice, 6*(3), 379–388.

Berger, P. (1969). *The sacred canopy*. Garden City, NY: Doubleday.

Berger, P., & Luckmann, T. (1967). *The social construction of reality*. New York: Doubleday.

Bhaskar, R. (1978). *A realist theory of science*. Atlantic Highlands, NJ: Humanities Press.

Brekke, J. (1986). Scientific imperatives in social work research: Pluralism is not skepticism. *Social Service Review, 61*, 370–373.

Bruner, J. (1986). *Actual minds, possible worlds*. Cambridge, MA: Harvard University Press.

Bruner, J. (1990). *Acts of meaning*. Cambridge, MA: Harvard University Press.

Culler, J. (1986). *Ferdinand de Saussure*. Ithaca, NY: Cornell University Press.

Davis, L. (1985). Female and male voices in social work. *Social Work, 30*, 106–113.

de Saussure, F. (1966). *Course in general linguistics*. New York: McGraw-Hill.

Floersch, J. (2004). A method for investigating practitioner use of theory in practice. *Qualitative Social Work, 3*(2), 161–177.

Fook, J. (2002). Theorizing from practice: Towards an inclusive approach to social work research. *Qualitative Social Work, 1*(1), 79–95.

Foucault, M. (1978). *The history of sexuality*. New York: Pantheon.

Geertz, C. (1983). *Local knowledge: Further essays in interpretive anthropology*. New York: Basic Books.

Gergen, K. J. (1985). The social constructionist movement in modern psychology. *American Psychologist, 40*, 260–275.

Giddens, A. (Ed.). (1972). *Emile Durkheim: Selected writings*. Cambridge, UK: Cambridge University Press.

Gray, M. (1995). The ethical implications of current theoretical developments in social work. *British Journal of Social Work, 25*, 55–70.

Habermas, J. (1972). *Knowledge and human interest*. Boston: Beacon Press.

Hearn, G. (1958). *Theory building in social work*. Toronto, Ontario, Canada: University of Toronto Press.

Heineman, M. H. (1981). The obsolete scientific imperative in social work research. *Social Service Review, 55*, 371–395.

Houston, S. (2001). Beyond social constructionism: Critical realism and social work. *British Journal of Social Work, 31*(6), 845–861.

Howe, D. (1994). Modernity, postmodernity and social work. *British Journal of Social Work, 24*(5), 513–532.

Hudson, W. (1982). Scientific imperatives in social work research and practice. *Social Service Review, 56*, 246–258.

Hugman, R. (2003). Professional values and ethics in social work: Reconsidering postmodernism? *British Journal of Social Work, 33*(8), 1025–1041.

Karger, H. J. (1983). Science, research, and social work: Who controls the profession? *Social Work, 28*, 200–205.

Kondrat, M. E. (1992). Reclaiming the practical: Formal and substantive rationality in social work. *Social Service Review, 66*(2), 237–255.

Kondrat, M. E. (1995). Concept, act, and interest in professional practice: Implications of an empowerment perspective. *Social Service Review, 69*(3), 405–428.

Kondrat, M. E. (1999). Who is the "self" in self-awareness from a critical theory perspective? *Social Service Review, 73*(4), 451–477.

Lee, P. (1939). Social work: Cause and function. In F. Lowry (Ed.), *Readings in social case work, 1920–1938: Selected reprints for the case work practitioner* (pp. 22–30). New York: Columbia University Press.

Mead, G. H. (1934). *Mind, self & society from the standpoint of a social behaviorist*. Chicago: University of Chicago Press.

National Association of Social Workers. (1999). *Code of ethics of the National Association of Social Workers*. Washington, DC: NASW Press.

Payne, M. (1997). *Modern social work theory*. Chicago: Lyceum.

Pease, B. (2002). Rethinking empowerment: A postmodern reappraisal for emancipatory practice. *British Journal of Social Work, 32*(2), 135.

Penna, S. (2004). On the perils of applying theory to practice. *Critical Social Work, 5*(1). Retrieved from http://www.criticalsocialwork.com/units/socialwork/critical.nsf/982f0e5f06b5c9a285256d6e006cff78/504291075acb6a6785256efd0053704c?OpenDocument

Piele, C. (1988). Research paradigms in social work: From stalemate to creative synthesis. *Social Service Review, 62*, 1–19.

Piele, C., & McCouat, M. (1997). The rise of relativism: The future of theory and knowledge development in social work. *British Journal of Social Work, 27*(3), 343–360.

Rodwell, M. K. (1998). *Social work, constructivist research*. New York: Garland Press.

Rorty, R. (1979). *Philosophy and the mirror of nature*. Princeton, NJ: Princeton University Press.

Rosen, A. (1994). Knowledge use in direct practice. *Social Service Review, 68*(4), 561–577.

Rosen, A. (2003). Evidence-based social work practice: Challenges and promises. *Social Work Research, 27*(4), 197–208.

Sarkar, S. (Ed.). (1996). *The legacy of the Vienna Circle*. New York: Garland Press.

Schön, D. A. (1983). *The reflective practitioner*. New York: Basic Books.

Schuerman, J. (1982). The obsolete scientific imperative in social work researach. *Social Services Review, 56,* 144–146.

Simmons, D., & Chabris, C. (1999). Gorillas in our midst: Sustained inattentional blindness for dynamic events. *Perception, 28*, 1059–1074.

Siporin, M. (1989). Metamodels, models and basics: An essay review. *Social Science Review, 63*(3), 474–480.

Smith, D. E. (1996). *The everyday world as problematic*. Boston: Northeastern University Press.

Thyer, B. A. (2001). What is the role of theory in research on social work practice? *Journal of Social Work Education, 37*(1), 9–17.

Turner, F. J. (Ed.). (1996). *Social work treatment*. New York: The Free Press.

Ungar, M. (2004). Surviving as a postmodern social worker: Two Ps and three Rs of direct practice. *Social Work, 49*(3), 488–496.

Witkin, S. L. (1998). Empirical clinical practice: A critical analysis. *Social Work, 36*, 158–165.

CHAPTER 5

Taking "Guilty Knowledge" Seriously

Theorizing, Everyday Inquiry, and Action as "Social Caretaking"

BRENDA SOLOMON

In the following pages, I discuss Ann Weick's (1999, 2000) writings about social caretaking and what she calls "guilty knowledge." I consider the ways that my position as a subject with limited social authority to name my own body and experience intersects with Ann's notion of guilty knowledge and social caretaking in social work. From there, I respond to Ann's call to take up the overlooked knowledge and skills particular to our field and speak of them without guilt but with conviction. Using the same ideas at play in my understanding of guilty knowledge, social caretaking, and the self—ones that aim to disrupt the marginalized position of social workers and social work knowledge—I propose the use of the term *theorizing* to "language," in part, what social workers do. I stress theorizing as a feature of social caretaking as Weick discusses it. Finally, I present one illustration of how theorizing as an *everyday inquiry* and *action* operates in social work practice. My concluding remarks underscore the importance of listening carefully as we endeavor to take ourselves as social workers and the knowledge we generate seriously.

Ann Weick's Guilty Knowledge and Social Caretaking

Ann Weick wrote two related pieces on the marginalization of social work knowledge. In the first piece, "Guilty Knowledge" (1999), Ann lays out an analysis of how we as social workers understand what we know within a hierarchy of knowledges. She dubs this knowledge *guilty knowledge*—guilty in that it is a relatively less valued knowledge, one that is easily discounted and largely operates out of sight. Weick's is a perfectly eloquent consideration of social work and practice knowledge. In it Ann explains how guilty knowledge is formed through an "oppression of knowledge" (p. 329) so that the "inherent value" (p. 329) of what social workers, along with other marginalized groups, know "is denied and those who might wish to claim it are intimidated into silence" (p. 329). To explain further in Weick's words,

> What children know, what women and people of color know, and what social workers know is not knowledge that has place or status in the knowledge hierarchy. It is dismissed as soft, fanciful, and without substance. Because it is so widely disparaged as having no merit, the very act of calling these claims into question is silenced (p. 329).

As prelude to the next piece, she concludes that "the language of social work is a language of care and caring" (Weick, 1999, p. 332). She signals social workers to speak with "confidence and clarity" (p. 332) and "freely acknowledge" (p. 332) what they know has worth.

In the second piece, "Hidden Voices" (2000), Ann grapples more directly with how social work "has been unable to give voice to its work" (p. 396). She laments, "The problem of defining what social workers do continues to plague us" (p. 396). More specifically, she states, "social workers have not been able to give adequate voice to the skills that distinguish them from other helping professions" (p. 398).

In both pieces, Ann lays out the challenges we face in making claims to knowledge. She considers the problem of legitimacy for social workers within the professions and then within social work, particularly, as various factions of the field take up the traditions of medicine and academia to gain recognition. In these works, Ann takes steps to draw attention to knowledges and practices most endemic to the field—those knowledges and practices that make social work distinct, yet, at best, have been overlooked or underappreciated, if not sublimated and marginalized. Finally, she refers to these knowledges and practices together as "social caretaking" (Weick, 2000, p. 395), explaining the association between caretaking and the experience of knowing as follows,

> If the analogy of home-centered caretaking is accurate, then social work can be seen as an extension of family caretaking. Because it shares caretaking functions, it suffers the same fate. The problem with this state of affairs is that the work to which women dedicate their lives becomes a world of private knowledge. The invisibility of the work renders women invisible, not only to others but also to themselves. Although we can enjoy a certain satisfaction in recognizing the truth of the matter within the confines of our own heads, it is difficult to remain confident without some external validation... it takes unusual strength to maintain clarity about the effect of one's own experience, especially when that experience is ignored, dismissed, or actively denigrated. (p. 397)

Ann's ideas and struggles that she articulates in these two pieces feel strangely close to what I think and struggle with but have not been able to adequately express. Like Ann, I have a desire for our field to have ways of talking about (and thinking and doing) social work that notes its distinct value. It has been a source of frustration for me as well that our field is largely recognized by practices brought in line, along with other helping professionals' methods, toward meeting standards for insurance and government funding.

Meeting standards generated from practices outside the profession shifts attention away from practices that honor the foremost traditions in social work so as to confound our thoughts and actions that assume a "preoccupation with human well-being" (Weick, 2000, p. 399), giving "private concerns public weight" (p. 399), and "meeting and being with the people" (p. 399) in order to help them. Especially in "Hidden Voices," Ann draws attention to and names the features of social work that she believes should be (re)incorporated into our discussion of who we are and what we do. She instructs us first to underscore our place alongside the people we work with, and, second, to pay homage to our roots—to practices traditionally constituted as women's work and left to them to do—caretaking, social, or otherwise.

In a very scholarly and personal way, Ann dares us to sort it out among ourselves. Ironically, our proximity to people in despair and at the margins—that is, in how we do our work and how our work is characterized—seems, often enough, reason to discount what we know. As I understand what Ann has to say to us, it is by guilt that we have sufficiently agreed to keep our ways of work to ourselves—to distance ourselves from how we know what we know and to contort ourselves to measure up to standards formed and imposed from outside our field. Our guilt is made in connection with our awareness that a close regard for people's suffering—the starting point of our practice—does not fit with or serve the separating intentions of dominant professional discourses.

Guilty Knowledge, Social Caretaking, and Self

As I mentioned earlier, I am interested in theorizing and everyday inquiry and action as a way to talk about what social workers do. Some of my ideas about this appear in a piece on theorizing in child welfare practice (see Solomon, 2002). I also discussed my thoughts at one of the Transforming Social Work meetings in Burlington, Vermont, where I joined a group of social work scholars charged with the task of talking about theory in social work. While there may be many ways to account for what was said in that group, what struck me most was what I discovered after the meetings had ended and I had reread several of the group's members' related writings. This is how I connected with Ann's ideas, especially how she expressed them in the two pieces I discussed in the previous section.

Before reading Ann's rendition of knowledge and social work, which underscores how social work is a feature of underappreciated caretaking, I was simply concerned with theorizing as a way of talking about what social workers do. I had not thought about the connection between theorizing and caretaking, or, for that matter, guilty knowledge. In a way, I find this odd—especially that I did not consider a relationship between theorizing and caretaking. Actually, I have written a good deal about welfare to work and women's work, particularly caring labor in the nursing home industry (see Solomon, 2001, 2003, in press). While I have made many of the connections Ann makes between women's labor in the home and in the marketplace—and have thought about those connections with regard to social work as well—I have avoided a direct appraisal of social work and caring labor. As with all that goes into forming guilty knowledge as Ann explains it, in my case, to overlook caring is not a simple matter. Without a full account of its complexity, unquestionably, my overlooking complies with a guilty knowledge. While I write about caring labor and feel strongly about exposing the ways it is an underpaid and underappreciated labor, I remain ambivalent about talking about myself as a social caretaker or about social work in some way as caretaking, even as it is social.

Largely, I believe this ambivalence is tied to my desire to be accepted as a scholar. I am too aware of how caretaking may be held in contrast to scholarly work. Especially since the social facts used to make sense of me as a subject insist upon reducing me singularly to the essential and opposing form—woman—there remains an accompanying invitation to hold my work (*her* scholarship) with suspicion. Certainly, this was Ann's point—that caretaking, women's work, subjugated knowledge, and the marginalization of social work and social workers are all linked. It would follow then that the position of both woman and social worker together would amplify subordination. Thus, as I am rendered woman and social worker, I face an easy acceptance of my work as care over scholarship.

While, I confess that I have taken up my place and knowledge with guilt, I am inspired by Ann's courageous claims. Thus, in these remaining pages, I attempt to follow her lead and rearticulate my work (theorizing) as a matter of social caretaking—after all. More so, I believe that this may be useful to the broader project that Ann proposes of making hidden voices of social work audible.

As I see it, I can go about taking up my work as social caretaking, if I do it in a way that is similar to how I go about trying to talk back to the social renderings of myself as a gendered-sexualized subject. That is, if I can try to complicate social caretaking in the way that I try to complicate who I am as subject, then I may be able to use the term *social caretaking* with force and without guilt. For me, the guilt that Ann describes, in part, has to do with not being recognized on my own terms and being noticed instead in terms of dominant scripts. Unfortunately, I am more or less stuck with these dominant scripts—particularly of gender-sexuality and, for that matter, care—and have to work creatively with them. For the most part, I have tried to make sense of myself to others with language and meanings that overlook or exclude what I aim to say. This seems to be the problem Ann describes in "Guilty Knowledge" and "Hidden Voices"—that social workers have difficulty being known and articulating what they know in terms that meet accepted knowledge structures.

For instance, while I'd rather not be made knowable by way of social categories of race, class, gender, and sexuality, among others, I am made subject by these categories just the same. Consequently, I tend to discuss my sense of self in relation to those terms, simply, I tend to use the categories to claim a complexity that the categories cannot adequately recognize and name. Thus, I say things such as, "I have yet to declare a gender and that without some sort of gender position there is no way for me to articulate a sexuality position—sexuality is in part determined by gender signification." That is, I use common social terms to attempt to articulate a social position for myself beyond what is commonly intended and accomplished with those terms. In some way and perhaps only for moments at a time, I turn the intention of the discourse on itself—it does not render me absurd and incomprehensible—but rather, as I use it, I demonstrate the discourse's own shortcomings and absurdities. Now, imagine applying some of this language play toward articulating social work knowledge.

Theorizing as Social Caretaking

I understand that to make social sense of social work, we, as social workers, often end up using terms that do not necessarily fit with what we aim to say. Like caretaking, these terms have been around for a while and have histories.[1] While we must contend with those histories, we can attempt to retool words to our service (see Atmore, 1999; Bingham, 1994; Smith, 1990a, 1990b). Such is my interest with the term theorizing. As I see it, theorizing is a way to language social work using familiar terminology related to scientific knowledge (i.e., theory), but rather than static and finished knowledge, it highlights the complex action of using and making knowledge in the ever renegotiated contexts of social work. In turn, by using the term theorizing, I am interested in paying homage to social work's roots, particularly social caretaking, and in (re)claiming the complexities that have been largely wrought out of social care, which, at least, involve theoretical- and philosophical-related inquiries and actions. That is, part of how I can use social caretaking forcefully and without guilt is to refuse to accept its traditional rendition, one that contrasts caretaking with knowledge.

Like Ann, my purpose here is to underscore the importance of social work in terms of its history of oppression linked to gender-based labor or social caretaking. For me, to do this involves making the complex features of that work—operating beyond essential notions of gender and care—visible in our claim. I am interested in talking/writing about social caretaking in terms that show particularly how the accomplishment of social work—a less valued and underpaid woman-designated work—has always required that the mostly women who are doing it also perform valued and better-paid man-based labor. (This relates to the ideas that men can and do care, and women can and do think, and, further, that caring takes thinking and thinking takes caring.) If you take this view, then a gendered division of labor is less about gender-based practices and sensibilities and more about division-based intentions.

Consider, if you will, my ethnography of a welfare-to-work nursing assistant training program (Solomon, 1999). In it I showed how the so-called caring labor that nursing assistants were trained to do involved much of the same labor they performed at home, which is commonly called mothering or caregiving. At the same time, upon careful examination of this labor, I found that what was accepted as caring, or care/labor required a good deal of what commonly constitutes heavy and hazardous work. That is, the actualities of the work were less so one or the other—a women's work domain of care labor or a man's work domain of heavy and hazardous labor—but more so an amalgam of both.

What seemed important to the characterization of the work was that women's bodies were performing it, that it was likened to the labor performed at home by mothers, and that it was indeed and after all called caring. However, I have argued that because the heavy and hazardous features of nursing assistant work had to be done with care in close proximity to and involving people's bodies—with attention to the aches and pains and desires of the persons being manipulated and lifted—it made it a more difficult labor than what is traditionally thought of as either heavy and hazardous or caring work alone. More so, this difficult and complex labor was left to poor, disenfranchised, and disproportionately black and Latina women to do with inadequate pay and benefits. The point is: we can value or devalue work by how we name it, who performs it, and what history of labor we embed it in. From studying nursing assistants' work, I found such divisions point to an intention to divide, even (or especially) as that intention was wrapped in the language of mothering and romanticized notions of love and family.

Theorizing, Everyday Inquiry, and Action

By studying theorizing, rather than theory, my intention is to shift focus from accepted dominant interpretations of life and practices that intend to privilege one theory over another. Rather, my interest is toward the taken-for-granted processes of everyday meaning making. For me, this way of study-analysis-practice for social work, if you will, has been and remains heavily informed by institutional ethnography, a method of inquiry developed by Canadian sociologist Dorothy E. Smith (1987).

Smith's method begins from the standpoint of marginalized people to make visible the ways that their everyday lives hook into larger organizing social processes and ideologies. Smith's intention is to produce knowledge from, about, and for marginalized people. As with textual and discourse analyses in social work, institutional ethnography has been used largely by scholars to conduct research. However, what I am interested in is its application to social work beyond research to help make sense of what we do more commonly in terms of social work. Simply, you could say (or I am saying) that theorizing by social workers is how social work is commonly accomplished and reaccomplished. It is part of our everyday practice. In this way, it ordinarily operates without remark or attention. Therefore, I am interested in drawing out the processes of theorizing—making them visible, speakable, and (re)negotiable. I want to show how they are, after all, self-conscious processes that allow for an ongoing critique of what is used to inquire and make sense of what is going on in social workers' professional lives and the lives of the people they serve.

Because theorizing is part of how social work is accomplished, it involves both deconstructive and reconstructive processes. First, it involves seeing how things are put together. Then, it involves reforming those arrangements toward better service. For instance, as social workers consider how ideas and actions used in social work hook into a history of control and contest, theorizing is deconstructive. At the same time, as social workers consciously consider less accepted or alternative ideas and actions, complicating standard analyses used over time to arrive at more encompassing responses closer to the lives of the people they work with, theorizing is reconstructive. Consistent with the goals and values of the profession, such critical analyses allow for conceptualizing and processing people in ways that are more helpful to them, at less expense to them, or at closer approximations toward their emancipation. In our theorizing, we consider the extent to which we are doing the bidding of institutions on the one hand, and trying to surface ideas, practices, and beliefs to further the causes and better the lives of the people we serve on the other hand.

Before I go any further, I want to say a few words about using theorizing along with everyday inquiry and action, I want to talk about stringing these terms together in the way that I do here. As I explained earlier, theorizing is simply a way to draw attention to and name meaning making in social work. It retools accepted language used to signify knowledge products or theories and focuses instead on the processes involved in producing knowledge in ongoing, everyday social work activities.

I place theorizing alongside inquiry because I associate theorizing less with dominant ways of making meaning (grand theory-related ways) and more with social constructionist/postmodern ways of making meaning (in this case, inquiry). Thus, theorizing is tentative, open, and unsettled. It is often carried out in the form of a dialogue and engages in possibility, performance, and play. It responds to changes and ways that do not fit standards. How it operates as well as what it makes possible is social caretaking. That is, theorizing contributes to and is part of how social caretaking is produced. The ever-shifting terrain on which social caretaking is performed requires ongoing, thoughtful deliberations about actions that make social care possible at any point or in a series of moments.

Following that, I say inquiry and action together (as in theorizing, everyday inquiry, and action) because I mean to suggest that theorizing in social work is an intellectual-active process; our inquiries and actions are closely linked, and there is equal emphasis on looking into and doing or thinking and acting. I add "ing" to theorize because I want to suggest in-the-moment inquiry and meaning making and response. This social caretaking that we do is tender and warm and smart and fierce all at once. In this way, it is more difficult than either a supposed theory work or care work.

Finally, between theorizing and inquiry and action I add, *everyday*. I do this to draw attention to the common ongoing complexities of social living that social workers respond to and analyze. Everyday is how Dorothy E. Smith explains her approach of institutional ethnography as in "the everyday as problematic" (1987). It is an absolutely wonderful word to put alongside problematic for the purposes of inquiry as Dorothy uses it. It is as purposeful when Ann uses it in "Hidden Voices" (Weick, 2000) to explain social caretaking. In her words, "It [social caretaking] concerns itself with the everyday tribulations of human life met with consciousness and intent" (p. 401). For me, the everyday challenges that social workers face with people who are directed to them or seek their help is what makes it a work, as Gerald A. J. de Montigny (1995) has described, one "contaminated by daily life" (p. 221) in which our hands get dirty. We do not theorize at a distance; we are in the lines of the story and our actions are judged along with our clients' actions. We are implicated in these ways: by what is available to us and what we use to help others. This is not a fault of social work, it is what contributes to our distinct position; we are in the field—in the places people occupy and in the bellies of institutions as we try to figure out what will work or how to find ways to help. Therefore, to do work that actually does help requires thoughtful, active caring every day—if not also every night,[2] and at times, minute by minute. Taken together, theorizing, everyday inquiry, and action may tell part of the story of how social work is performed and social caretaking is accomplished.

Noticing and Naming Theorizing, Everyday Inquiry, and Action

I now turn to the ways I see theorizing and everyday inquiry and action operating in social work. That is, I propose that the practices involved in what I am calling theorizing and everyday inquiry and action are happening regularly as features of social work. I am simply drawing attention to them and casting them in some way that I think may be useful to the field. With that in mind, in the following paragraphs, I illustrate theorizing and everyday inquiry and action, drawing on earlier experiences I had while working at a small counseling center. Please keep in mind that my example shows only a few ways that theorizing operates in social work.

At the center where I once worked, therapists and counselors used a variety of practice approaches, though few at the time utilized approaches that were associated with constructionist and postmodern positions such as narrative, strength-based, and dialogic. While I did not accept all of what was entailed in the methods others used, I welcomed their possible utility in my work. At one point I became particularly interested in Freudian analysis and the questions Freud raised during his time that were considered outrageous if not worse than the postmodern ideas of what was then my doctoral education. I took to Judith Butler's account of Freud in her 1997 book, *The Psychic Life of Power*, appreciating that postmodern thinkers could see the value in retracing some of Freud's analyses. By reading Freud and then Butler's interpretation of Freud, I began to more fully appreciate knowledge formation—how it occurred in my work and in the lives of the people I saw at the center. I felt closer to the processes by which knowledge was formed, accepted, ignored, and reinterpreted and retooled to fit another purpose at another time. By reading Freud and then Butler, I was reminded that ideas are not static; they are passed around, reinvigorated, and manipulated. I was also reminded that the acceptance or dismissal of ideas is not static. I remember feeling very hopeful. Even while it might not have been widely accepted knowledge, knowledge was something that the people I worked with and I could form and honor together. That is, we could treat our opinions and ideas with the sort of worth granted to the esteemed knowledge of our time.

As I became especially interested in Freud's notion of melancholy and Butler's (1997) reinterpretation of it, I began to think about the absence of knowledge or about the relationship between absent knowledge and present (-day) knowledge. In a way, I was interested in knowledge that might be in the imagination but yet to be formed and articulated (see Butler, 1997). This allowed me to think more fully about how the despair of people is linked to the absence of certain possible ways of making themselves sociably knowable to themselves and others. (Of course, this absence of knowledge may at least partially account for my frustration with accepted language forms of gender-sexuality to construct a self and Ann's frustration with standard forms of help to construct a knowable social work.) Further, I used these ideas to work with people at the center, holding a broader range of knowledges up for analysis as the people I met with tried to make sense of their lives and form a direction. In this way, they could make sense of the sense that was made of them and consider possible directions for their lives beyond former limits that intruded on their imaginations.

At the time, I found a great way to access possibilities was through music. I was working with several young people who carried their music with them. It didn't take much to include their music in our work together. We would listen to songs that seemed to most express their position or feelings of the day. I remember our exchange as it went on sounded less and less like conversation and more like poetry, as we spoke at times using lyrics. At once, we seemed to have moved outside of traditional methods of talk and ways of forming and recognizing knowledge, and accessed something between us that, from my position anyway, made us feel more directly knowable to one another and implicitly connected. Even if we couldn't figure out how to change the world in our hour-long weekly sessions (a goal I shared with the young people with whom I met, although they pursued it more vigorously), it seemed at least that we changed what was possible between us. By doing so, we created new possibilities for relating to yet others outside of our sessions. Although these sessions were intended for the benefit of the person I was seeing at the center, I believe that we both felt the sway of the chances we took together.

In my work at the center, I aimed not to override or discount various dominant or standard knowledges. By theorizing, I drew an array of knowledges into the analysis. As a social worker enlisting theories, I considered the social power of various ideas and ways, "insistently challenging the assumptions about the value of what we know" (Weick 1999, p. 329). By theorizing, the dimensions of help made possible by enlisting one or another theory or practice approach was made visible and negotiable. Thus theorizing, in this way, required a complex knowledge of theories and their application in various fields used to make sense of people's everyday lives. It also required knowledge of counterclaims to grand theories and alternatives to dominant ways of processing people.

As part of this everyday theorizing, I considered how those credited with making knowledge and the knowledges that they form largely serve those with greatest social power, maintaining particularly white-male social and economic privilege. Considering Ann's points that "each person, from the earliest moments, becomes her or his own empiricist" and "every experience shapes our own theory of how the world works" (Weick, 1999, p. 328), theorizing is used to consider how some empiricists' accounts and theories are overlooked or dismissed. This is a central concern of social work and thus a common practice by social workers. It includes incorporating the claims of those who are marginalized and discredited and forming counterclaims to dominant constructions.

While our theorizing acknowledges the actualities of the constraints many of us work under—real barriers to others' and our own emancipation—theorizing and everyday inquiry and action is carried out with the intention to overcome those barriers. It is used to follow Ann's direction, "to turn our attention to the humblest activities of social caretaking and offer our boldest ideas about strengthening the social web connecting us all" (Weick, 2000, p. 401).

One More Thing . . .

As I was gathering my notes and bundling up to walk across campus at the end of class one evening this winter, I overheard two students talking as they left the room. As I listened I was struck by how the problem they shared was so common and accepted. The first student said, "Yeah, it is never done. You come in and there is another case, and another." The second, agreed and added, "It never ends. You just keep doing it; there is always more." I remember talking about casework in those same ways. I also remember hearing my mom talk about caring for a family and home using such words. It was how the women talked about their work in the nursing assistant training program that I studied and is familiar in a way that Ann Weick describes guilty knowledge.

Indeed, we have our work cut out for us; certainly, this social caretaking—the work designated and associated with what is woman—is set up so that it is never done. Maybe the forces arranging guilty knowledge keep us busy and in place, give us reason to go through the same paces day after day with no end, diminish our attempts to speak a social work in terms that are closer to our experience and the lives of the people we come to know through our work, and prohibit us to speak and be heard as people who have something to say.

If forces arranging guilty knowledge are indeed that powerful, then I wonder how this piece is able to complicate social care, or how it is in some way able to appropriate the language of science to make claims about social work practice, or further, how it is able to respond to Ann's call for bold expressions of caretaking. That is, performing social caretaking and theorizing as I suggest here is difficult when the forces of history that diminish care and separate care from complex deliberation (noted here as theorizing) insist upon actions to obey those forces—to obey a history that diminishes and marginalizes care.

Having said that, there is something to carrying out social caretaking and talking forcefully about guilty knowledge that I alluded to earlier and want to speak to more directly in closing. Simply, I have attempted to heed Ann's words and stay close to her meaning as I wrote what I wrote here about theorizing. Embedded in my action of what might be called writing forcefully is listening *care*fully. For me, heeding Ann's challenge is to treat her message about social care with worth. I think that this is no small matter: the place that listening with intention has in the production of caretaking knowledge, crediting claims toward social care, and taking guilty knowledge seriously. And at least as important to me about this caring-scholarly endeavor that nonetheless is set toward privileging what I had to say, is how carefully I listened to Ann. Most important is that this piece takes what she had to say seriously.

Notes

1. To make sense of the histories I refer to here, I rely heavily on Michel Foucault's archaeology (1975) and genealogy (1979) and particularly Adrienne S. Chambon's (1999) interpretations for social work (pp. 54–55).]

2. Dorothy E. Smith (1999) added everynight to her analysis of everyday life, acknowledging that unpaid and poorly paid labor often requires work into the evening and that those with fewer resources remain aware of institutional power into the hours commonly considered private.

References

Atmore, C. (1999). Victims, backlash, and radical feminist theory (or, the morning after they stole feminism's fire). In S. Lamb (Ed.), *New versions of victims: Feminists struggle with the concept* (pp. 183–211). New York: New York University Press.

Bingham, S. G. (Ed.) (1994). *Conceptualizing sexual harassment as discursive practice*. Westport, CT: Praeger.

Butler, J. (1997). *The psychic life of power: Theories in subjection*. Stanford, CA: Stanford University Press.

Chambon, A. S. (1999). Foucault's approach: Making the familiar visible. In A. S. Chambon, A. Irving, and L. Epstein (Eds.), *Reading Foucault for social work* (pp. 51–81). New York: Columbia University Press.

de Montigny, G. A. J. (1995). *Social working: An ethnography of front-line practice*. Toronto, Ontario, Canada: University of Toronto Press.

Foucault, M. (1975). *The birth of the clinic: An archaeology of medical perception*. New York: Vintage.

Foucault, M. (1979). *Discipline and punish: The birth of the prison*. New York: Vintage.

Smith, D. E. (1987). *The everyday world as problematic: A feminist sociology*. Boston: Northeastern University Press.

Smith, D. E. (1990a). *Texts, facts, and femininity: Exploring the relations of ruling*. New York: Routledge.

Smith, D. E. (1990b). *The conceptual practices of power*. Boston: Northeastern University Press.

Smith, D. E. (1999). *Writing the social: Critique, theory, and investigations*. Toronto, Ontario, Canada: University of Toronto Press.

Solomon, B. (1999). *An illusion of difference: Reconstituting women on welfare into the working poor*. (UMI No. DA9964517). Dissertation Abstracts International, A: The Humanities and Social Sciences, 2000, 61, 3, Sept., 1186-A–1187-A.

Solomon, B. (2001). The ins and outs of welfare-to-work: Women as they enter and exit a nursing assistant employment and training program in upstate New York. *Sociology and Social Welfare*, *28*(3), 157–186.

Solomon, B. (2002). A social constructionist approach to theorizing child welfare: Considering attachment theory and ways to reconstruct practice. *Journal of Teaching in Social Work, 22*(1/2), 131–149.

Solomon, B. (2003). A "know it all" with a "pet peeve" meets "underdogs" who "let her have it": Producing low-waged women workers in a welfare-to-work training program. *Journal of Contemporary Ethnography, 32*(6), 693–727.

Solomon, B. (in press). "Go it alone" poverty in a small city: Pockets of poor housing, the scrutiny of "busy bodies," and difficulty accessing support. *Journal of Poverty.*

Weick, A. (1999). Guilty knowledge. *Families in Society, 80*(4), 327–332.

Weick, A. (2000). Hidden voices. *Social Work, 45*(5), 395–402.

CHAPTER 6

A Dialogue

Can a Conservative Profession Like Social Work Have an Emancipatory Practice?

MEL GRAY and RICHARD POZZUTO

Summary: Mel

Social work arose as a response to poverty. While poverty obviously predates social work, there were a number of agents noticing, trying to understand and address poverty, and their practices undoubtedly influenced the beginnings of social work. These included the church and utilitarians, and they are examples of groups that appear to have been driven by moral imperatives rather than the market economy. The private charity movement had arisen in 1860 in London as a response to extreme weather. A movement for personal services among the poor also developed. By 1869, operating from a perspective of Christian Socialism, the Society for the Organisation of Charity and the Repression of Mendicancy (later the Charity Organisation Society [COS])—strong believers in efficient administration and personal services for the poor—developed to coordinate such services, and it had a major influence on government. While not all its actions may have been constructive, knowledge and context should be considered and its intentions acknowledged. It should be credited for its ability to influence government to take measures to eliminate poverty seriously, though it was against the poor laws, which originated much earlier to assist those who could not work and as a response to acts of the monarchy. Social work shifts and develops along professional lines circa 1915 with Flexner's speech, and this professional emphasis contributes to a maintenance rather than change agenda. While social work's emancipatory ideals, such as those practiced by Jane Addams, are still evident in the way social work theoretically defines itself, this is not an accurate reflection of the daily work carried out by the individual. In fact social work's universal value system also sends conflicting messages in other areas, including culture and diversity. Additionally, there seems to be an interplay between social work's conservatism, its attraction to technical rationalism, its desire to carve out a professional niche, and current economic rationalist work imperatives. In defining emancipatory practice as a collective and generative activity, social work may have the opportunity to develop differently in the developing world.

Summary: Richard

Social work arose from the results of the newly developed market economy, a system that resulted in social dislocation because economic rules and norms become market, rather than culturally, driven. While there are always different groups and interests in any movement, COS developed from the propertied class's fear of the working-class developing. While COS (and earlier charitable organizations) may have had some moral imperatives for its work, one of its main focus was on keeping some control over the developing working class. COS may be viewed as a progressive movement in relation to its movement away from feudalism and its influence on government policy, but also took an individual liberal perspective, neglecting other models such as Marxism. Modern-day social work must acknowledge itself as part of current class arrangements. Social work remains a conservative profession, demonstrated by its ready adoption of the technical problem-solving approach.

This dialogue was inspired by ideas evoked in the intellectually charged atmosphere created by the Transforming Social Work gatherings in Vermont where, despite the participants' different intellectual and geographical locations, we found that we shared a common narrative, though a different interpretation of social work's history. In true social constructionist style, this dialogue helped us appreciate the way in which our different contexts and experience shaped and influenced our views and interpretations of social work's history and how the weight of the past influenced our views on social work's perceived transformative potential in the present. In our subsequent E-mail communications we began to talk about these differences and similarities through reading and commenting on one another's work. As we progressed we realized that we appeared to disagree ideologically on the roots of social work. Thus we began to talk about this, and our conversation eventually turned to the idea of emancipatory practice and whether this was possible within a conservative profession such as social work. In tracing social work's historical development and current practice, we agreed that it was indeed a conservative profession with pretensions to emancipatory practice. Thus in this chapter we argue that an emancipatory practice is possible within the limits of the profession, and we identify trends that give social work hope for the future. By emancipatory practice we mean a movement away from traditional notions of liberation (usually associated with release from a singular oppression or oppressor) toward a much broader and more holistic view that encompasses individual, community, and global responses to "oppressive forces." By acknowledging the multiple restrictive forces from individual thought to social arrangements, and the effects of time, culture, and context, the focus becomes a collective process of ongoing change, where there are no universal solutions to social problems, only universal goals of "establishing meaningful and satisfying relationships," "eliminating unnecessary repression," and economic inequality.

Introduction

Neither Mel nor I am sure that dialogues have any definite beginning or end points. Sometimes the participants change, but the dialogue continues. Other times dialogues begin internally and become external, perhaps continuing again internally. They can be passed from generation to generation and transcend the life span of any particular individual. At any rate, we cannot identify the beginning of the dialogue. Perhaps the topic had been on our minds. Perhaps it was sparked by some aspect of the gathering in Vermont.

During the course of the gathering, Mel and I learned that we shared an interest in social transformation. We sought to participate in that transformation in both our private and professional lives. At some point the topic of our conversation moved to the possibilities of our profession, social work. What follows is a reconstruction of the dialogue from that point.

MEL Well, Richard, if we are questioning whether emancipatory practice is possible in social work because we think it is too conservative, surely our first task is to establish why we think social work is a conservative profession.

RICHARD I agree, and to do this we really need to go back to social work's historical development. From my point of view social work, as a unique practice, developed out of the conditions resulting from the establishment of a market economy. Polanyi's (1957) perspective has a lot to say about social work. The roots go back to the charity organization and settlement movements. The first COS began in London, in part, as a result of the propertied class's fear of the poor and wage laborers.

MEL I'm not sure I fully agree, but let's take them one at a time. First, could there be another interpretation? The usual one is that social work arose as a response to poverty.

RICHARD You know as well as I do there was poverty long before the founding of social work, and there were mechanisms for addressing poverty long before social work as well. I believe if you want to understand the origin of social work as a named, identified, specific activity, you have to look at transformations in the society that occurred at a particular point in history. I'm back to the development of a market economy.

MEL If poverty predates social work as an actual social practice, that doesn't mean that social work didn't try to respond to the poverty present at the time it came to be. What is interesting to me is what happened between the time social work enters the scene in the early 1900s and the middle of the 14th century when feudalism was nearing its end and wages were coming into use. The latter was a symbol and a means for the emancipation of labour from serfdom. Are you familiar with de Schweinitz (1961)?

While there were organized nongovernment ways of attempting to deal with "early" poverty, certainly in Europe, as elsewhere, the church had developed mechanisms for addressing poverty, so, too, was there a period of social reform resulting from the work of early social researchers, most of whom were utilitarians (Boyle, 2000; Reisch & Andrews, 2001).

RICHARD Slow down a little. I think we can agree that most social phenomena are quite complex and that often, if not always, if we look closely enough, any change will have both positive and negative aspects. As with everything, there are going to be varied opinions and perspectives.

MEL We are of like mind on that.

RICHARD Let me go a step further, then back to what you said about feudalism. If we take a look at social changes, we are going to find varying groups with different interests having their own ideas about the "proper" functioning of society. These interests are dynamic, and the allegiances are dynamic and multifaceted. I think they change with social circumstances and may contribute to the creation of social circumstances.

MEL All right, but what is your point?

RICHARD My point is simply this: It's really a mistake to look for simple answers, simple driving forces, and uniform perspectives about all this. You could look at wages, for example. I think they were a mechanism for "emancipating labor" from serfdom. And getting wages for labor is not necessarily the same thing as being a wage laborer. To me a wage laborer is somebody who sells labor activity through a market, and that market determines the value of the labor. During the period you referred to there was something called wage guarantees. So wages were not dependent solely upon a market. Sometimes they were even indexed to the cost of bread. Also, there were some aspects of feudalism that worked as well as or better than our current economic arrangements. I am not referring to the aspects of "ownership" of serfs but more to what Tönnies (1957) referred to with his idea of *gemeinschaft*, which he called an older form of spontaneous community based on mutual aid and trust.

MEL I'm not sure I want to go that far back. We both acknowledge there were significant economic and social changes occurring prior to and around the time that social work was developing, don't we?

RICHARD Yes. We seem to agree. Do we agree that the economy, defined as mechanisms for getting and distributing goods, is useful in understanding the evolution of social work?

MEL All right. Provisionally.

RICHARD What we need to add to this is the notion of culture and some grasp regarding the economy as an aspect of culture or something other than culture. Polanyi (1957) argues that prior to the development of a market economy, the "rules," if you like, for getting and distributing goods resulted from cultural practices. The economy was embedded within the culture. A market economy reverses this. The rules of getting and distributing are based upon the "laws of the market," which, in turn, drive social relations. Industrialization greatly increased productive capacity, but the earlier notions of mutual dependence and mutual aid were not significant factors in distribution. A new form of poverty resulted, scarcity in the context of plenty, and cultural dislocation. I believe it was to this that social work attempted to respond.

MEL It depends where we see the "culture" coming from. I have been reading about the utilitarians like Jeremy Bentham and his disciple James Mill and their relationship to the early reformers like Edwin Chadwick. Chadwick introduced sanitation reforms in Britain believing that the main reason people became paupers was disease. His report, I think the *Report on the Sanitary Conditions of the Labouring Population* (in Boyle, 2000), was based on the study of 77,000 paupers of whom 14,000 had been made poor by catching fever. It led to the first Public Health Act in 1847. James Mill was, of course, the father of John Stuart Mill, author, among other things, of *Political Economy* and *The Subjugation of Women* (in Boyle, 2000). He was a lifelong supporter of the vote for women. What united the utilitarians, besides achieving the greatest good for the greatest number, was counting or measuring things, and it was this culture that led to increasing legislation and eventually paved the way to the concept of the welfare state. They all agreed that government needed reform. Utilitarians were more enamoured with ideas and numbers than with people.

RICHARD Your point is well made about the contributions of the utilitarians. Something was also lost, however. The greatest good for the greatest number loses the possibility of the greatest good for the whole, for the community . . . as I was trying to say earlier, good or bad, progressive or regressive are not really mutually exclusive terms.

MEL Okay, but the utilitarians were the precursors of the welfare state and the reforms for which the COS were working. There was a direct relationship between the utilitarians and COS reformers. Charles Booth, a friend of

Canon Barnett, was married to Mary Macaulay (Beatrice Webb's cousin) whose father became secretary to the Board of Health following Chadwick's departure. Under Mary's influence, Booth refused to accept the prevailing view of poverty caused by idleness, gluttony, drink, waste, profligacy, betting, and corruption, noticing that many of the despised poor led considerably more God-fearing lives than he did. Booth painstakingly researched and documented the extent of poverty in London, through detailed house-by-house descriptions of streets, and invented the idea of the "poverty line." He deigned to suggest that alcohol was a symptom not a cause of poverty, giving a measure of 14% of poverty being due to alcohol addiction, which, he believed, related more to the emancipation of women.

RICHARD I agree. There were some real contributions. I agree also that it is not only the poor who recognized the problem of poverty.

MEL I guess this is where Polanyi's (1957) interpretation, and yours, comes in. Seebohm Rowntree's research in York began to confirm Booth's figures. When Booth presented his figures confirming the need for old-age pensions, the massively influential COS—Booth's sworn enemy for their patronizing philanthropy—called it the "most outrageous and absurd scheme yet promulgated"[in Boyle, 2000, p. 124). Ironically, 20 years after their fallout, Beatrice Webb and Charles Booth served together on the Commission on the Poor Laws. Booth's research had clearly shown the structural causes of poverty and the need for social change, but he was disillusioned by the way in which his findings were being used to gain political mileage by the likes of the Webbs. Though he was a keen statistician, the quality of his encounters with the poor in London's East End were poorly reflected in hard numbers. Despite Booth's increasing lack of faith in numbers and his foresight in recommending social assistance, which became a reality in 1908 (see de Schweinitz, 1961, p. 205), Beatrice and Sidney embraced the idea of counting with missionary zeal, seeing this as their chance to succeed on the public stage. Thus quantification became an obsession that led to the foundation of the London School of Economics.

RICHARD Okay, so we are agreed—though we come to it from different angles—that economics and the development of a market economy play a major role in the evolution of social work. So back to the economic argument. In a market economy, workers and employers are not tied to each other in a set of mutual obligations based on culture and tradition as they were within a feudal economy. And the value of the worker was a function of a "market for labor" rather than of culture and tradition. In effect workers had greater freedom but less security, and there was greater independence for the nonpropertied. Since this threatened the authority of the propertied class, fear was a major factor in the founding of the COS. Would you agree?

MEL I'm not sure I agree with the "fear" idea. This is the beginning of charity—there was a genuine desire of the rich, many of whom were religiously motivated, to help the poor, and they thought they were doing the right thing even though they were highly moralistic. It is interesting to see history revealed from a new perspective. However, we cannot totally devalue the values of early reformers and charity workers, even if we do not like them or because Polyani (1957) comes along with a new theory about it.

RICHARD Mmmm, but remember, religion is not apolitical. Certainly Weber ties Protestantism and capitalism together.

MEL Okay, religion and politics and economics can be interrelated. However, as I said, we cannot totally devalue the values of early reformers and charity workers, even if we do not like them.

RICHARD We see this differently. The original name for the COS was the Society for the Organisation of Charity and the Repression of Mendicancy. I believe its primary goals were the organization of charity and the repression of mendicancy, that is, begging. There is a difference between organizing charity and making charity more effective. There is also a difference between eliminating begging and eliminating the need for begging. As I see it two things were going on. Charity was interfering with the effectiveness of the poor laws to control a developing underclass, and the propertied class was still shaken by the transition of the "naturalness" of a feudal system to the contractual relations of its industrializing society. I do not believe the elimination of poverty was the prime focus of the COS. This is not to say that the members of the COS intended to punish or abuse the poor.

MEL I agree that the elimination of poverty might not have been a prime focus. What was more important was the COS's view of, and the pressure it placed on, government to develop measures that would lead to the elimination or, at least, the reduction of poverty. I think we have to see a complexity of factors at work here.

RICHARD Yes, I'm not trying to say there is a single motivation, neither am I saying that political economics holds all the answers. Behind economics, as you rightly point out, is the obsession with counting and the way early COS leaders, like Webb, supported the evolving "economic emphasis" over the compassionate understanding that people like Booth came to know.

MEL So we are agreed that the COS used a combination of conservative and emancipatory approaches, perhaps arising from both fear and compassion. While the COS was concerned about moral degradation, perhaps because of its religious mission, it was also altruistic, and this informed its belief that it was doing the right thing in helping the poor.

RICHARD I think that depends upon which group you are talking about. Bernard Bosanquet (1997) was a major spokesperson for the COS. He wrote an eloquent elaboration on social Darwinism as the foundation of the work of the COS. This same foundation was an attack upon socialism as contradicting the guiding principles of social Darwinism and, hence, actually harming "society." This leads me in a roundabout way to the conclusion that a main interest of the COS was aiding the development of a class of wage laborers. The Settlement House Movement had a different perspective.

MEL I'm not sure I agree with this interpretation. Maybe we need to take more of an in-depth look at people influencing organised charity. While philanthropy has a long history, this "organised charity movement" comes into its own in London in 1860–61, a time of extreme hardship due to extremely cold weather causing a flood of new requests for emergency relief with which the poor law system was unable to cope. De Schweinitz (1961) is a great source on this early history. Thus private charity gained prominence, and the first organised effort at poverty relief was the London Society for the Relief of Distress. By the end of the 1860s, reaction set in. It came from an influential part of the ruling class concerned about the operation of public relief as well as the management of private charity. At the same time, influenced by Christian Socialism, came the growing movement for personal services among the poor. Thus began the work of Octavia Hill, whose father had been a close associate of Chadwick. She developed a project to renovate slum dwellings for the purpose of renting them to families with low incomes. The rent collectors would be cultured women who would thus gain the opportunity to help poor families to better ways of life. Helen Bosanquet (in Boyle, 2000), in her documentation of the history of the London COS, recorded this as an acceptable way of bridging the divide between rich and poor.

RICHARD Try as I might, Mel, I can't agree with your interpretation. The COS was not the first organized effort at poverty relief. The private efforts, basically through the churches, were quite organized. They were not coordinated with each other. The COS tried to put charity under a single authority, the COS. And Octavia Hill may have been well intended, but there was a large element of social control in her program. She had strict rules that had to be followed if one remained within her projects. "Cultured women" collecting the rent as a way of bridging the cultural gap? Which way was the influence flowing?

MEL Well, bear with me a bit. The need for organised charity and services among the poor led to the formation of the Society for Organizing Charitable Relief and Repressing Mendicancy in 1869. You mentioned them. It soon became known as the London COS, which de Schweinitz (1961) believed *disregarded almost entirely the influence of social and industrial opportunity and conditions*. Hence, even if the COS did support the way society was going, I'm not sure it was aware of the implications of its actions. I would doubt that it had a hidden agenda of making people wage labourers to promote capitalism.

RICHARD Okay, so let's carry your argument further: If there was no hidden agenda and the COS was acting for the good of England, what exactly was informing its thinking? Did it have an egalitarian perspective? Did it see citizenship and property as closely linked? Did it see a relationship between economic success and moral forthrightness along with religious favor?

MEL I think the COS operated from a Christian socialist perspective. It was part of the ruling class and a generation of do-gooders who were responding to the social conditions of the poorer classes. The COSs came to have a major impact on the operations of government in public assistance in both Great Britain and the United States, spreading there in 1877.

RICHARD That is my point. The COS was influential. It had a major impact on the operations of government in both Great Britain and the United States. That impact was, and is, a conservative impact. It takes an individualistic, liberal perspective and purports to deal with social problems. There is little social about it.

MEL Perhaps, but it was the COS that got the government involved with social welfare. This certainly was and is better than the vicissitudes of the market.

RICHARD Nevertheless, its activities, in conjunction with a large number of other activities, perpetuated the class system. The poor law was a legislative act intended to force people to become wage laborers. The COS tried to make this law effective. In that sense it did facilitate a class of wage laborers. In another sense the COS was progressive in that it assisted in the movement away from feudal society toward industrialization. The issue is the form of industrial society it favored.

MEL I disagree, Richard. Your claim that the poor law was a legislative act intended to force people to become wage labourers is not true. The poor laws began to take shape in the 1500s when the government was forced to play a role in poor relief during Henry VIII's reign as a result of his expropriation of the monasteries and their properties, which he turned over to his followers. I suppose the class system comes from having a monarchy in the first place. Prior to that the church had done a sterling job of caring for the poor. The 1601 Law of Settlement, introduced during the reign of Elizabeth, was to do a great deal of damage in the emerging wage labour system because it tied workers to the parish where they were born and severely limited their opportunities to find work. This makes some sense of Adam Smith's idea of the free circulation of labourers.

The poor laws then were a series of laws and amendments designed to deal with the government administration of relief despite opposition from "employers" that this reduced the "worker's" desire to work. In large part, the poor laws, especially the creation of the workhouse in 1834, attempted to address the problem of those who couldn't (through sickness and ill health) and wouldn't work.

RICHARD It's not that simple. The poor laws are not all one "thing" with a single direction. I agree with your assessment that the Law of Settlement was a major impediment to the development of a wage labor system. At that time the balance of political power did not favor a wage labor system. The Settlement Act had a lot to do with connectedness to the land and mutual responsibility. Maybe that was good. Maybe it was bad. The Reform of Local Government Act of 1832 provided significant political power to industrialists, manufacturers, and merchants. Here the balance of power shifts. Also, we see a different role for the poor laws. The 1834 poor law replaced the 1601 act. I'm suggesting the 1834 poor law had as its purpose the reinforcement of market principles.

MEL Are you suggesting that we can use 1834 as a dividing point?

RICHARD Roughly.

MEL Okay, then let's go back to my question. The people involved with the COS thought they were being good, socially and morally responsible citizens—is there anything wrong with that?

RICHARD That's a hard question. Is there anything wrong with their intent? To a degree but not entirely. Is there anything wrong with the result? Yes. Do I have to come up with a single answer?

MEL You're dodging my question again, Richard. Let's rephrase it a little. Could they have been expected to do any better given the period in which they lived?

RICHARD I don't know what you can actually expect from people if you are living within the historical period. It is a lot easier, as you said, with hindsight. From a current standpoint, a more reflective stance would have been nice. I do not know how difficult that would have been. We are talking about the late 1800s. There was a great deal written that provided alternate perspectives. Marx had already published the *Communist Manifesto*. Regardless of the "correctness" of Marx, he certainly pointed out some issues. The syndicalist movement was alive in France (Joll, 1980). Robert Owen had attempted some social reforms. Proudhon (1840/1994) had questioned the nature of property, and Bakunin (1974) was also published. There were alternative models.

MEL That may be, Richard, but I still think you are confusing the early charity movement with social work and overlooking the sincere attempts of charity workers to respond to people's suffering. The profession of social work only emerged in the early 1900s, while the poor law period, the charity organisation and settlement movements, the friendly visitors, charity workers, and settlement workers were all precursors to social work as it later developed, possibly after the famous Flexner speech. It was after 1915 that social work's modern professional form began to take root. Also, the charity organisation movement was part of the general push for the state to assume moral obligation for its citizens. Both Mary Richmond and Jane Addams were in accord on this.

RICHARD You are right. I've been talking about the COS. The COS is not exactly the social work profession. From my reading it seems that social work in the United States, at least, likes to claim the COS as one of its progenitors. I'm not sure how wise that is.

MEL I think at the time social work took on a similar shape in most Western countries where it was introduced. It became increasingly connected to government service provision and followed Mary Richmond's lead in its increasing desire to professionalize. It was on this point that she and Jane Addams disagreed. These trends in the development of social work led it to be more heavily involved in system-maintaining than system-changing processes in society, but was this necessarily a bad thing? After the poor law came the welfare state and this, in part, was due to the contribution of social workers placing pressure on government to take responsibility for the welfare of its citizens, which is suggestive of emancipatory practice.

RICHARD Yes, but during the mid-1800s through the early 1900s it was not clear that a market economy would prevail. There were other possibilities. Certainly there was a syndicalist and socialist, Marxist or not, alternative. With the entrenchment of a market economy these alternatives were less likely. It makes sense that social work contributed to the development of state welfare. This is to the profession's credit. Had it taken a different course earlier, there may have been different options by 1915.

MEL Still, Richard, as I see it, the COS was founded to address poverty and to dispense charity and later became involved in community organisation, particularly service coordination. The friendly visitors did not do social work as we know it today. They were the precursors of modern-day social workers. However, they were idealists who believed in ideas of citizenship, community, the common good, and limited state intervention. Jane Addams's strong sociological orientation grounded her settlement workers and early reformers in emancipatory practice based on sound social justice goals and changing and improving society. Remember, she received the Nobel Peace Prize. Social justice, by its very nature, calls for emancipatory practice, that is, practice that is empowering and gives people opportunities for self-development and economic involvement. Increasingly social work has defined itself as working with marginalized and oppressed groups in society and with processes of social inclusion and social development. However, for the most part, this is not what social workers are doing on a daily basis. It cannot be said that social work, collectively as a profession, has any major impact on society. If all the social workers in the world downed tools for a day, what would happen? Would society suffer a major blow? Probably not. It is more likely that the individuals and families with whom they have built close relationships would suffer. Perhaps Howard Goldstein (1988) was right all along and we should be fighting for the humanistic alternative, the small changes that make an impact day by day rather than the grand scheme system making and changing goals.

RICHARD Mel, I agree that society would not fall apart if every social worker stopped working for a day. I also agree that the people they work with would probably suffer. But there is also another vantage point. There are a lot of unintended consequences of the actions of social workers. In the United States the activities of social workers often contribute to the delineations of class. If you have contact with a social worker who is responsible for determinations regarding entitlement programs, they tell you, and others, clearly what your social class is. It is a subtle way of maintaining current social arrangements. I am saying that the actions of social workers are part of the construction of the social world. Many of these actions are around class distinctions.

MEL Are you implying then that social workers entrench class distinctions?

RICHARD Not at all. In the United States most mental health services are provided by social workers. Mental health issues are not class specific, though I would be surprised if upper-income people were not more likely to see psychologists or psychiatrists rather than social workers. Medical social work may be a better example of social work that is not class specific.

MEL So, Richard, do you think we have reached a conclusion about social work being a conservative profession?

RICHARD I think we have in arguing that conservatism is associated with moderation, resistance to change, caution, and a favoring of traditional views and values that radical social workers described as the maintenance of the status quo.

MEL Even the Webbs and other early social reformers seen as precursors to social work did not advocate revolutionary change. The Webbs were socialists but not revolutionaries and were far more radical in wanting to overthrow the poor law than were the COS led by Octavia Hill, who saw their role as social investigator and assessor of requests for charity. This was a public administration type of role that firmly embeds a public-private relationship in dispensing social assistance (see de Schweinitz, 1961, p. 148). To this day this is the model of those who have sought to align social work with the social processes of stability and re-creation as opposed to generative processes of creating new and different social arrangements.

RICHARD Yes, the COS promoted change of a different kind. It was more conservative than the politically minded Webbs.

MEL So, then do you see the COS as conservative even though it promoted drastic social change?

RICHARD Context is important. You've been making that point. You could see COS as seeking stability as well as promoting change. The point is that social work was not found supporting the emerging labor and socialist movements that protested against the inequality and unfairness of the capitalist system, and this was the reform issue of the day!

MEL Yes, I wouldn't argue with this. Social work has never given up this liberal, consensus-based, democratic perspective that assumes common interests among varying classes and cultural groups. Do you agree with this argument?

RICHARD Yes. I think this fits the United States, but I am not sure that social work rests on the same assumptions in every nation. How do you see it?

MEL I believe social work is a diverse profession that simultaneously gives conflicting messages. It offers a value system that it sees as universalisable, which is essentially Western and based on Judeo-Christian principles while at the same time valuing multiculturalism and diversity. However, if people do not see individual autonomy and self-determination as worthwhile goals, we then see a need to raise awareness and conscienticize them into this Western way of thinking. Some societies value the collective, and some cultures hold incompatible beliefs. One can't be tolerant and universalise values at the same time. Maybe it's time we let go of the professional model and rather tie social work to need. After all, it was this influence that led to a dominant focus on empirically based clinical or casework practice and to helping aimed largely at changing individuals or at helping them to adjust to their environment.

RICHARD Sure, the professionalisation of social work was not without its consequences. This is in large part what gets social work into difficulty now. Professional practice in large measure can be equated with technical problem solving.

MEL I agree, but social work is also a discipline.

RICHARD I don't see it as a discipline, although it is more than technical professional training.

MEL I think it is a discipline because it involves intellectual activity.

RICHARD It does involve intellectual activity, but I believe a discipline implies political neutrality. I may have a positivist notion of a discipline. For me it has the connotation of advancing knowledge for the sake of advancing knowledge.

MEL You think knowledge is neutral?

RICHARD No, but that is a different issue. Ideas and systems of understanding are tied to class interests and represent a form of power that maintains social organisation. Within the life span of social work there have been the possibility of two transitions. The first was the transition from a premarket to a market society, already discussed. The second transition has to do with the development of a global market economy. Some of the same issues from the founding of social work are relevant today within a different context. There is opportunity and there is the possibility for emancipatory practice.

MEL What is meant by emancipatory practice?

RICHARD You have been using the term. That is not exactly a transparent question. But, be that as it may, I think that emancipatory practice is generative. In part it creates in thought what is later to be created in a shared, lived experience. What can be created in thought is dependent upon what is visible, that is, problematized. How it is conceptualized, and the language used, both internally and externally, to discuss the issue. Also emancipatory practice assumes little to be natural in the sense that it is God-given and immutable. This notion of emancipatory practice is consistent with the view of life as a creative process. I think we share that. Therefore, it has to do with creative relationships and challenges to systems of thought that perpetuate unnecessarily restrictive relationships. In a way it is both something that is done and the way it is done. The essential point here is that our notion of social work being conservative is tied or related to our understanding of what social work is supposed to be about, namely, emancipatory practice. It is about creating what is possible in terms of establishing meaningful and satisfying social relationships. More abstractly, it is about eliminating unnecessary repression and minimizing alienation. It is about creating a way of life that is meaningful and satisfying. It is a process that changes over time.

MEL I have been grappling with the question about whether engaging in political activities necessarily means working for social justice. I think I was making an erroneous assumption that it was. Why is this important for our question on whether a conservative profession can have an emancipatory practice?

RICHARD All political activity is not intended for social justice as I believe we would define it. You can find attempts today for groups to establish more repressive governments.

Back to social work though, I believe the value of social justice gives the mandate for emancipatory practice, but the structural makeup of the profession militates against this. The Central Council for Education and Training in Social Work (CCETSW) in the United Kingdom and the Council on Social Work Education (CSWE) in the United States are really powerful and they reinforce what I understand as the conservative line.

MEL Some points I see as relevant are that most social workers work for government; many nongovernment organisations where they are employed are equally conservative; economic rationalism is superceding concerns about welfare and social justice and social work has to conform with this. And faith-based charity being pursued by Bush is going to make social work even more conservative. Do you agree?

RICHARD Yes, I think we have established social work's conservative nature, but what we are now trying to do is see whether it is progressive; that is a term I am not fully enamored with. Social work as identified with the COS was progressive in the sense that it facilitated the transition from the premodern to the modern. On the other hand, this implied a significant piece of social control. At that time it may have been necessary, but it is outdated now, and social work continues to apply the aspects of modernity that correspond to the notion of central authority, experts, singular answers, focus on techniques, and the reduction of big questions to technical issues. Maybe I have not said that in a way that makes sense.

MEL Maybe our question was too ambitious, Richard. Like you, I share your concerns with social work's emphasis on technical rationality, reductivism, measurement, and certainty. For me, its humanistic, intuitive, communicative, compassionate, and artistic side is seriously undervalued, and maybe the conservatism about which we speak has more to do with carving boundaries and identities than with political ideology. Social work's preoccupation with finding universal definitions and values, global education standards, evidence-based practice, and a common identity has always overshadowed its concerns with people's suffering and with finding innovative ways to alleviate poverty and its attendant social problems. Still, today, most students are more interested in individual problems than in the more complex social ones.

RICHARD Yes, I agree. For social work to have an emancipatory practice I believe you have to take a bottom-up or grounded perspective. At the level of individual social interactions, social workers can model the type of interactions that we believe are life engendering. This requires that social workers see themselves as much more than technicians. If we add to this a respect for self-determination, we can, as social workers, facilitate the construction of a social world that we believe is more life engendering.

MEL Sure, and our analysis as social workers also has to focus on social relations. We are social beings. We are born into an ongoing social world. Our lives are meaningful only within that context. What we overlook is that it is through social relations that we solve problems and create new possibilities. When we as a profession individualize our analysis, we isolate ourselves from our collective possibility. An emancipator practice needs to keep these factors in mind.

RICHARD I agree. Maybe we have established that social work does have conservative beginnings and that the predominant focus in social work intervention is still system maintenance.

MEL I agree. I am not convinced that social workers readily adopt broader system-changing roles or methodologies. Maybe that kind of social work is not appropriate in the highly industrialized Western world where the professional model holds sway, and maybe this won't change until social work grows in importance in the developing world. Or then again, maybe it is a product of the modern world and will have to grow into something else to maintain its relevance in a globalised world. Imagine what will happen when international conferences are conducted in Chinese or Spanish with translation into English! Maybe that's when the culture will change. Who's to say?

RICHARD Essentially, emancipatory practice is about creating a just culture in any culture. Language has a lot to do with it in a wide variety of ways. I also believe that any understanding of "justice" is culturally specific. We could look at that as a paradox or we could take a more dialectic, process approach. Also, for an emancipatory practice we need to look at two aspects of practice. There is the "issue" that is being addressed. Let's say that is in the present. There is a set of actions that are taken to address the issue. If we stretch it a little we can view them as also being in the present, and from one perspective they focus on the issue. Of course, we are concerned about the usefulness and results of these actions as related to the issue. These actions also provide the foundation for future actions. They become the "stuff" of our social world. They are the context for our future. Focusing not on the issue but the social pattern assumed between worker and client, or created between worker and client, we see we are creating the world we are going to live in. These actions can legitimize current social arrangements; they can in small ways problematize them. The actions can open new ways of understanding for both the client and the worker.

MEL Is this unique to social work?

RICHARD No. Not at all. Social work is only one small piece of creating the world we live in, as you suggested earlier. I am suggesting it can contribute to the creation of a meaningful social existence or it can, in small ways, make life more difficult. An emancipatory practice is not so much an emancipation "from" something. It is not even an act that can be completed. It is more emancipation "to" something, which involves participation in a continual emancipatory process.

MEL I like this notion of being part of a historical process. I suppose social work itself is also continually evolving, as are social structures. So we are continually part of a web of interdependent forces in constant interaction with one another that constitute the whole. It is almost impossible then to take one part and isolate it for analysis. For one thing, Richard, things don't stand still long enough and really can only be understood retrospectively when the whole pattern emerges. So if we think of emancipatory as emergent and generative, then maybe, in a sense, even a conservative profession like social work can have an emancipatory practice. What do you say?

RICHARD I say enough. I need time to think through some of this stuff.

MEL I can agree with that. Vermont is beautiful in the fall.

RICHARD And I can agree with that.

References

The following are readings that are relevant to the discussion. Some authors have been mentioned in the text. Others have been relevant to the development of the authors' perspectives.

Abel, E. K. (1998). Valuing caring: Turn-of-the-century conflicts between charity workers and women clients. *Journal of Women's History*, *10*(3), 32–52.

Abrams, P. (1982). *Historical sociology*. Ithaca, NY: Cornell University Press.

Addams, J. (1911). *Democracy and social ethics*. New York: Macmillan.

Arblaster, A. (1984). *The rise and decline of Western liberalism*. New York: B. Blackwell.

Bakunin, M. (1971). *God and the state*. Freeport, NY: Books for Libraries Press.

Bakunin, M. (1974). *Selected writings*. New York: Grove Press.

Baum, G. (1996). *Karl Polanya on ethics and economics*. Montreal, Canada: McGill-Queen's University Press.

Berger, P., & Luckmann, T. (1967). *The social construction of reality*. New York: Doubleday.

Bosanquet, B. (1997). Socialism and natural selection. In D. Boucher, *The British idealist* (pp. 50–67). Cambridge, UK: Cambridge University Press.

Boyle, D. (2000). *The tyranny of numbers*. London: Harper-Collins.

Camilleri, P. (1996). *(Re)constructing social work: Exploring social work through text and talk*. Aldershot, Hants, UK: Avebury.

de Schweinitz, K. (1961). *England's road to social security*. New York: Barnes.

Flexner, A. (1915). Is social work a profession? *Studies in Social Work*, 4, 576–590.

Foucault, M. (1980). *Power/knowledge: Selected interviews and other writings*. New York: Pantheon Press.

Fraser, N., & Gordon, L. (1994). A genealogy of dependency: Tracing a keyword of the U.S. welfare state. *Signs, 19*(2), 309–336.

Fromm, E. (1941). *Escape from freedom*. New York: Farrar & Rinehart.

Goldstein, H. (1988). Humanistic alternatives to the limits of scientific knowledge: The case of ethical dilemmas in social work practice. *Social Thought, 19*(1), 47–58.

Gramsci, A. (1971). *Selections from the prison notebooks of Antonio Gramsci*. New York: International Publishers.

Joll, J. (1980). *The anarchists*. Cambridge, MA: Harvard University Press.

Jones, G. S. (1971). *Outcast London: A study in the relationship between classes in Victorian society*. Oxford, UK: Clarendon Press.

Marcuse, H. (1964). *One dimentional man*. Boston: Beacon Press.

Margolin, L. (1997). *Under the cover of kindness: The invention of social work*. Charlottesville: University Press of Virginia.

Marx, K. (1964). *Economic and philosophic manuscripts of 1844*. (Edited with an introduction by Dirk J. Struik). New York: International Publishers.

Mendell, M., & Salee, D. (Eds.). (1991). *The legacy of Karl Polanyi: Market, state and society at the end of the twentieth century*. New York: St. Martin's Press.

Mowat, C. L. (1961). *The Charity Organization Society*. London: Methuen & Co.

O'Brian, M., & Penna, S. (1998). *Theorizing welfare: Enlightenment and modern society*. London: Sage.

Ollman, B. (1976). *Alienation: Marx's conception of man in capitalist society*. New York: Cambridge University Press.
Owens, R. (1963). *A new view of society and other writings*. New York: Dutton.
Polanyi, K. (1957). *The great transformation*. Boston: Beacon Press.
Proudhon, P. J. (1994). *What is property?* New York: Cambridge University Press.
Reisch, M., & Andrews, J. (2001). *The road not taken: A history of radical social work in the United States*. Philadelphia, PA: Brunner-Routledge.
Sartre, J. P. (1956). *Being and nothingness*. New York: Philosophical Library.
Schön, D. (1983). *The reflective practitioner: How professionals think in action*. New York: Basic Books.
Seigfried, C. H. (1999). Socializing democracy: Jane Addams and John Dewey. *Philosophy of the Social Sciences, 29*(2), 207–231.
Stearns, P. (1971). *Revolutionary syndicalism and French labor: A cause without rebels*. New Brunswick, NJ: Rutgers University Press.
Stone, D. (2002). *Policy paradox: The art of political decision making* (rev. ed.). New York: W.W. Norton.
Thompson, E. P. (1964). *The making of the English working class*. New York: Pantheon Books.
Tönnies, F. (1957). *Community & society*. East Lansing: Michigan State University Press.
Walkowitz, D. J. (1999). *Working with class: Social workers and the politics of middle-class identity*. Chapel Hill: University of North Carolina Press.
Watson, F. D. (1971). *The charity organization movement in the United States*. New York: Arno Press.
Webb, S. A. (2000). The politics of social work: Power and subjectivity. *Critical Social Work, American Electronic Academic*

Journal, 1(2), http://www.criticalsocialwork.com/00_2_politics_webb.htm

Wolff, R. P., Moore, B., & Marcuse, H. (1965). *A critique of pure tolerance*. Boston: Beacon Press.

CHAPTER 7

Constructive Social Work Practice in an Age of Uncertainty

NIGEL PARTON

I met Mary K. O'Connor (from the School of Social Work at Virginia Commonwealth University) at the Constructing Social Work Practices conference in Tampere, Finland, in August 1997 (see Jokinen, Juhila, & Pösö, 1999). This was the first time I realized there might be others who might share my long-standing interest in drawing upon social constructionist perspectives for analyzing and contributing to social work theory, inquiry, and practice. Through Mary's active support and encouragement, I participated in the first Vermont gathering and have been involved ever since. Our meeting in the fall of 2001 took place in the immediate aftermath of the events of September 11th. We spent much of our emotional and intellectual energy trying to understand and come to terms with what had gone on and its possible implications. It is this that provides the backcloth for my chapter.

In many respects the events of September 11, 2001, can be seen to have irreversibly changed global economic, social, and political life. The events seemed to both exemplify and intensify many of the elements that had come to characterize the nature of human experience, particularly in the Western world, in the final years of the previous millennium where concerns about risk and uncertainty had become increasingly pervasive (Urry, 2002a; 2002b). The events of September 11th clearly illustrated the central statement of Prigogine's (1997) argument in *The End of Certainty* that we now live in "a fluctuating, noisy, chaotic world" (p. 12) where nothing can be taken for granted and where in a world of complex structures and systems, events can produce unexpected and, apparently, unconnected effects. This is the world that social work now inhabits.

In this chapter I will thus be arguing that the social, political, and organizational contexts in which social work is now operating have become increasingly complex, fluid, and uncertain and that few of the problems it is expected to address can be seen to have any easy or unambiguous solutions. I will argue that perspectives that are sympathetic to postmodern, constructionist, and reflexive ways of thinking and acting have much to offer in this increasingly fluid and uncertain world. While the focus of my analysis will be developments in England, I suggest it has relevance to much of the Western world, particularly North America.

At the center of my analysis will be an attempt to address a major conundrum. For while the world has taken on many of the characteristics associated with postmodernity in terms of its complexity, fluidity, and uncertainty, mainstream policy and practice has responded in even more modernist and rationalist ways. How has this come about and with what implications? The way change has been introduced has very much been a top-down process (Jordan, 2000). There has been an intense focus on performance and efficiency targets, together with an emphasis on centralized and formulaic regimes of inspection, audit, and scrutiny (Newman, 2001). While many of the more liberatory and radical elements of social work theory and practice have received official endorsement, for example, partnership and empowerment, they have been transformed into a variety of mechanisms for the increased regulation of both social workers and the people with whom they work (Langan, 2002). As Stepney (2000) has argued, there seems little doubt that practitioners experience these initiatives as increasing managerial control. Moreover, "the emphasis on technical recording, systematic information gathering, performance indicators, all tend to reinforce mechanistic practice rather than creativity and innovation" (Stepney, p. 12). Social work, particularly in the statutory sectors, has become little more than labor in the service of economy, efficiency, and effectiveness.

The chapter has four substantive sections. I begin by outlining the way the nature of social work developed from the mid-19th century onward through to the late 20th century. I then discuss the situation in which social work now finds itself in England at the beginning of the 21st century. I then critically analyze the growing influence of the evidence-based practice movement (EBP) and demonstrate that its narrow and circumscribed version of "evidence" is neither appropriate nor helpful in the current climate. Finally, however, I suggest that it may be on the terrain of evidence that we need to demonstrate the relevance of perspectives and practices that are explicitly postmodern and constructionist in approach. A primary aim should be to "extend the evidence base" of social work theory, inquiry, and practice (Hall, Juhila, Parton, & Pösö, 2003; White and Stancombe, 2003).

The Nature and Emergence of Social Work

What I have argued previously (Parton, 1991, 1994, 1999, 2000) is that the emergence of *modern* social work was associated with the transformations that took place from the mid-19th century onward in response to a number of interrelated anxieties about the family, and the community more generally. It developed as a hybrid in the space, "the social" (Donzelot, 1980), between the private sphere of the household and the public sphere of society. It operated in an intermediary zone. It was produced and reproduced by new relations among the law, social security, medicine, the school, and the family. The emergence of the social and the practices of social workers, who were to become its major technologists, was seen as a positive solution to a major problem for the liberal state (Hirst, 1981), namely, how can the state establish the health and development of family members who are weak and dependent, while promoting the family as the "natural" sphere for the care of those individuals and thus not intervening in all families? Social work developed at a midway point between individual initiative and the all-encompassing state. It provided the compromise between the liberal vision of unhindered private philanthropy and the socialist vision of the all-pervasive state that would take responsibility for everyone's needs, and hence potentially undermine individual initiative and family responsibility.

One of social work's enduring characteristics is its essentially ambiguous nature (Martinez-Brawley & Zorita, 1998). Most crucially, this ambiguity arises from its commitments to individuals and their needs on the one hand, and its allegiances to and legitimation by the state in the guise of the court and its statutory responsibilities on the other. Social work occupies the space between the respectable and dangerous classes, and between those with access to political and speaking rights and those who are excluded (Philp, 1979; Stenson, 1993). It fulfils an essentially mediating role between those who are actually or potentially excluded and the mainstream of society. This ambiguity catches the central but often submerged nature of modern social work as it emerged from the late 19th century onward.

Part of what social workers have traditionally sought to do is to strengthen the bonds of inclusive membership and try to nurture reciprocity, sharing, and small-scale redistribution between individuals in households, groups, and communities. Social workers have also been concerned with the compulsory enforcement of social obligations, rules, laws, and regulations. The two elements have been intertwined, and invariably the latter provides the ultimate mandate for the former—it is in this context that social work involves both *care* and *control, emancipation* and *regulation*. However, over the last 25 years the regulatory has increasingly become its dominating rationale, so that the ambiguity, which has traditionally lain at its core, appears to have become submerged or even lost, particularly in local authority statutory agencies. As I will argue, social work in England has become so associated with the state that its historical roots and the variety of different philosophies, traditions, and interests that have informed its development have become marginalized.

The Contemporary Nature of Mainstream Social Work in England

Since the late 1970s significant changes in the organization, practice, and culture of all public services in England have occurred. Beginning with the election of Margaret Thatcher in 1979, the primary impetus for such change was initially driven by attempts to rein in public expenditure and introduce some of the disciplines of the private sector via the quasi market, the purchaser-provider split, and the growth of a contract culture. However, the changes have moved far beyond simple attempts to exert tighter fiscal control. Not only have we witnessed the emergence of neoliberal ideologies of microgovernment, political discourses concerned with accountability and performance, and attempts to improve economy, efficiency, and effectiveness, but we have also seen a growing emphasis on the need to make the actions of professionals and the services they provide far more "transparent" and "accountable" (Power, 1997). What has occurred is a significant shift toward giving managers the right to manage, instituting systems of regulation to achieve value for money, and thereby producing accountability to the taxpayer and the paymaster on the one hand and the customer and the user on the other (Clarke, Gerwirtz, & McLaughlin, 2000).

While these changes were originally introduced under the auspices of the Conservative administration, since 1997 the changes invoked by the New Labour government have been even more rapid and intensive. In particular, the promulgation of a whole range of new performance targets, inspection regimes, and continual attempts to maximize "best value" and ongoing effectiveness regimes has had the effect of both rationalizing on the one hand and centralizing on the other. As Stephen Webb (2001) has suggested, there is currently "a double discursive alliance of *scientism* and *managerialism* in social work which gears up to systematic information processing operations to produce regulated action. We thus have the assimilation of a form of 'scientific management' in social work" (p. 74). What seems to have happened is that in the current context for the state, there is a paradox of the simultaneous demand for certainty together with the denial of its possibility; it is assumed that professionals cannot provide certainty and are, in any case, not trusted to do so. The net result seems to be that the various changes introduced act to sidestep this paradox and to substitute *confidence* in systems for *trust* in individual professionals (Smith, 2001). This is most starkly illustrated by the numerous public inquiries into the deaths of children who have been under the supervision of, or have been referred to, social workers. The official response to these apparent failures has been to increase the procedural requirements placed upon practitioners in child welfare cases and the promulgation of a variety of detailed systems for the assessment, monitoring, and review of cases and the work carried out (Parton, 2006). Thus while the wider environment seems to be turning more uncertain, fluid, and contingent, the microworld of the practitioner is being subjected to a whole variety of processes of standardization and regularization.

Two key assumptions underpin developments. First, it is recognized that society is experiencing enormous changes, particularly arising from the economic and social impacts of globalization. As a consequence, many of the traditional institutions such as the community, the family, and religion are undergoing considerable changes such that many of the values and structures that had been in place since the late 19th century can no longer be taken for granted. At the same time, however, and second, it is assumed that research and technological developments, particularly in information and computer technology, mean that social workers are in a good position to respond to the new challenges if only this new knowledge and technology can be harnessed and used. Rather than leaving the use and application of this knowledge to the discretion of professionals, increasingly it is embedded in the guidance, procedures, and computerized systems that have been introduced since New Labour came to power.

Under New Labour the changes go under the broad banner of "Modernizing Social Services" (Department of Health, 1998a). The changes are primarily concerned with regulating local authority departments through a series of supervisory and monitoring bodies, with setting new standards and targets with which to measure performance, for agencies to enforce these, and with establishing a new system for placing social workers under the guidance of new regulatory bodies.

Managers continue to play a key role but are now not simply concerned with managerial control but are seen as being in the vanguard of taking these new visions forward. In contrast to the Conservative changes, this version of managerialism is presented as empowering and emphasizing partnership (Glendinning, Powell, & Rummery, 2002). It purports to speak for service users so that any resistance to managerialism by social workers is easily attacked as being elitist. Rather than managerialism being seen as simply being concerned with the power of managers to enhance cost effectiveness and efficiency, New Labour sees its managers as operating toward a much higher order. As Newman (2001) has argued, the key aspects of modernizing managements' higher purposes have been presented as the updating of services to match the expectations of modern consumers, empowering citizens and communities and social inclusion. However, the public sector is enjoined to deliver these new services within the discourses of quality management, customer service, and user involvement—all of which require not simply continual improvement but also the need to break traditional models of both service provision and professional self-interest. Public social services are to become more like the private sector with an emphasis on entrepreneurialism and modern commercial practices.

In many respects, the repositioning of the central state and the local state can be seen as having many of the characteristics of "McDonaldization" (Ritzer, 1998, 2000) and franchising. As John Harris (2003) has suggested, this New Labour vision of how modernization translates into local authority departments is based upon strong central government control of the agenda to be implemented locally. Like the corporate headquarters of a modern business, New Labour has defined social work's objectives at the national level, set outcomes to be achieved locally, and monitored the results in considerable detail. The emphasis on local leadership, entrepreneurialism, and a strong performance culture with regard to standards and quality has been pinned to the achievement of targets set by central government. For example, in 1998 the objectives for local authority social services included that by 2001 there should be a reduction to no more than 16% in the number of children looked after in children's homes and foster homes that had three or more placements in one year, and that there should be a reduction of 10%

by 2002 in the proportion of children who were reregistered on the child protection register from a baseline for the year ending in March 1997 (Department of Health, 1998b).

Harris (2003) argues the approach is close to a public sector model of franchising, for franchise holders, although legally independent, must conform to detailed standards of operation designed and enforced by the parent company, in this case central government. In this franchising arrangement there is limited operational autonomy, and the consequences of having the franchise taken away, if performance is not seen as up to scratch, are considerable. The introduction of performance league tables, similar to those in soccer, and the allocation of annual star ratings for good and bad performance all point to this, where the best performing departments are given three stars and the worst no stars. It now appears that those local authorities that perform well—gaining a maximum number of stars—will be given much greater freedom from central government strictures. It is in this context that notions of quality take on a particular significance, as illustrated by *A Quality Strategy for Social Care* (Department of Health, 2000). "Delivering high quality social care services is essentially a local responsibility. The *Quality Strategy* will set a national framework to help raise local standards, but this will only be achieved through local policy and implementation" (Department of Health, 2000, para. 18). Elements of the design of the quality system were set out in the *Quality Strategy* and included national service frameworks, national standards, service models, and local performance measures, against which progress within given timelines for accomplishment would come into operation. While the process can be seen as increasing rationalization and centralization, it is also clear that the responsibility for delivery is with local service providers.

In the workplace itself, the process of McDonaldization is based on applying the principles of efficiency, calculability, predictability, and control to the processing and serving of a limited range of products. McDonaldized systems are seen to function efficiently by following a predesigned process to produce a given end. By breaking down the process into a series of discrete and clearly specified tasks, a standardized, regulated, and therefore efficient process of production is designed. Calculation, counting, and quantifying are key features, and the importance of predictability for the consumer, and the company or the government, is that the product and service will be the same both over time and in different places (James, 2004).

Evidence-Based Practice (EBP)

The other key element I wish to draw attention to in this new era for social work practice is the increasing emphasis on the importance of evidence-based practice. An important element in the rationale of the *quality movement* in social work and social care has been the argument that practitioners adopt a more rigorous application of critical appraisal skills to their practice. They should draw upon clear guidelines and protocols developed from research findings. EBP is the doctrine that professional practice should be based upon sound research evidence about the effectiveness of any assessment or intervention. At a superficial level it is very difficult to argue against something that seems so commonsensical. Two key assumptions underlie the strategy. The first defines "sound evidence," which may be relied upon to contribute to the classification of an intervention as effective or ineffective, as evidence derived from studies conducted in a certain way held to be "scientific." The approach is based on that developed within medicine and is typified by the influential "hierarchy of evidence" seen as definitive of what constitutes sound scientific research, where the strongest evidence is seen to emanate from at least one systematic review of multiple, well-designed, randomized trials. The principle that underpins the hierarchy is that of validity, that is, the elimination from research findings of bias arising from any difference between those treated by the intervention being researched and patients and clients not so treated.

The second key assumption underpinning EBP is based on the notion that the most useful, though not necessarily exclusive, method for disseminating sound research evidence is via appropriate guidelines (Taylor & White 2002). It is recognized that practitioners cannot be expected to read every research study relevant to their practice and that such guidelines are meant to be accessible and authoritative. The logic of the guidelines is essentially algorithmic, that it guides its users to courses of action, dependent upon stated prior conditions. In general, while such guidelines do not claim to determine professional action completely, professional discretion is considerably limited, particularly when the formulaic evidence is literally embedded in the computerized systems that practitioners are required to operate. For example, when carrying out an assessment, certain information is required so that the assessment cannot be completed until all the data required by the system are inputted and in the format/categories specified.

Clearly, however, the emergence of EBP is closely associated with some of the policy and practice changes discussed above. Its growth and official legitimation has taken place in a context where there are considerable concerns about risk and uncertainty, and growing concerns about professional expertise and effectiveness and the impact on users. EBP seems to provide a coherent and practical approach to overcoming some of these problems and at the same time reinforces a number of the concerns around the increased emphasis on accountability, transparency, and monitoring. The hierarchical preference for randomized, controlled trials in EBP is interesting. Such an approach is premised on the *inference* of cause-effect relationships from past statistical relationships between interventions and outcomes *aggregated* from the findings of a range of research studies. It is, therefore, less concerned with causative processes in individual cases or situations than with establishing what interventions are *likely* to be effective, irrespective of why. In this sense the model is *probabilistic* (that is, one where the cause-effect relationships are inherently uncertain) and *empiricist* (that is, one where knowledge can only justifiably derive from past experience). In drawing its findings from *aggregate* data, these may not be appropriate in any *particular* situation.

However, as Liz Trinder (2000) has demonstrated, the development of EBP in relation to social work is at a very rudimentary stage. In many respects the knowledge base and professional standing of social work is very different from that of medicine, where the approach originated. Even so, the language of EBP has become increasingly powerful and in this respect can be seen as a key contributor to the growing dominance of the rationalistic and managerialist approaches I have discussed. In some respects it has the effect of legitimating and providing a rhetorical backcloth for such developments. While I am not, in principle, against the notion of EBP, my concern is that it has been used in a quite specific way that has the impact of reinforcing the political instrumentalism and aspirations for greater central control that are being implemented by the modernization agenda. It is consistent with attempts to manufacture a sense of certainty in an increasingly uncertain world.

It is my view that EBP should take on a support role, rather than be promoted to the front line in the development of practice knowledge, as seems to be the case currently. For, increasingly, it has been recognized that the relationships between research and decision makers—whether these be politicians, policy makers, or practitioners—is much more subtle and complex than the EBP approach often assumes (Packwood, 2002; Young, Ashby, Bozaz, & Grayson, 2002). Research is better understood as just one of the factors that might play a role in decision making.

Recent commentators have argued that it is much better to talk in terms of *evidence-informed* practice, rather than *evidence-based* practice and see the most appropriate approach as being characterized as an *enlightenment model* (Packwood, 2002; Young et al., 2002). Here research is seen as standing a little distant from immediate practice concerns; the relationship is much more indirect. The focus is less likely to be the decision/problem itself, but the *context* within which the decision might be taken, providing a frame for thinking about it. The role of research is attempting to *illuminate* the landscape for decision makers and its aim becomes one of primarily clarifying issues and informing debate and less one of problem solving. Research thus takes on the role of contributing to the democratic process, rather than being embedded in narrowly focused decision-making processes. In the process it is recognized that research evidence is likely to be contested and subject to debate.

Rather than simply be concerned with critiquing the narrow focus of approaches that currently dominate the EBP movement, I would argue a key strategy is to try to "extend the evidence base." For clearly, debate is likely to be more reasoned when research is part of the equation than if research is not available in the first place. In the context of social work, research on processes as well as outcomes of interventions is equally, if not more, relevant in order to aid our understanding and inform what we do and how we do it (Hall et al., 2003; White and Stancombe, 2003). We should not dismiss the emancipatory potential of research (Humphrey, 1997; Stake, 1997). Clearly research can provide insights into the nature of society, how it is changing, as well as the important social structural factors that have an impact on everyone's day-to-day life. Evidence-based practice does not have to be based on the clinical trial or the random controlled test of comparative evaluations. The accumulation of evidence is vital to demonstrate how social divisions, for example, have an impact on the lives of clients. In some respects, evidence and different types of research could well provide a vital vehicle for critically commenting upon and resisting some of the centralizing and dehumanizing elements of contemporary policy and practice, that is, reducing practitioners to organizational functionaries and community members to "service users." As ever, the key issue is invariably related to power and knowledge and, crucially, who asks the questions and with what import. Not only can research encourage *enlightenment* and *emancipation*, it can act to *empower* the most powerless. It can help to provide information and insights that otherwise would not become available. Not only can research challenge some of the assumptions of those currently holding power but it can give voice to those who were previously silenced. For example, there is now a growing methodological literature on research with children that extends across a range of research styles, including, for example, experimental and survey research as well as ethnographic and qualitative work (Alderson & Morrow, 2004; Christensen & James, 2000; Morrow & Richards, 1996), and these are having the effect of articulating children and young people's voices, views, and experiences and their implications for policy and practice in quite new ways (see Hallett & Prout, 2003; Parton & Wattam, 1999). Simply because research can have negative and unintended consequences does not mean that it cannot have positive impacts as well. What I am suggesting is that in the process of trying to deconstruct EBP we can also act to try and provide opportunities for new forms of research and thereby extend what is understood as the evidence base.

Constructive Social Work and Reflexive Judgment

It is in this changing social and professional context that I have attempted to develop the notion of *constructive social work* (Parton, 2002, 2003; Parton & O'Byrne, 2000). It has been created as an explicit counterweight to some of the developments in official policy and practice that I have outlined in this chapter. As I have argued, the predominant response to the growing risk, uncertainty, and fluidity of current times in social work since the 1970s has been to construct ever more sophisticated systems of accountability for practitioners and users, and thereby attempt to rationalize and scientize increasing areas of social work activity with the introduction of complex procedures and systems of audit, together with a narrow emphasis on evidence-based practice—where it is assumed the world can be subjected to prediction and calculative control. My concerns have been twofold. Not only do these developments misconstrue the nature of recent changes, and thus carry considerable risk of a range of unintended consequences, they are in great danger of failing to build on the range of skills that have traditionally lain at the core of social work, particularly those related to process and where the ability to negotiate and mediate with creativity has been of central relevance.

The term *constructive social work* was chosen for two reasons. First, *constructive* reflects the wish to try to provide a perspective that is explicitly positive, for the core idea of *construction*, from the Latin to the present day, is that of *building* or *putting together*. Second, however, the term was chosen to reflect our attempt to draw on approaches that had developed over the previous 20 years, associated with social constructionist, narrative, and postmodern perspectives. In such perspectives an understanding of language, listening, and talk is seen as central, and meaning and understanding are matters of negotiation between the participants.

There are a number of ideas informed by social constructionism that are drawn on for developing constructive social work (Burr, 2003; Gergen, 1999). First, constructionism insists that we develop a critical stance toward our taken-for-granted ways of understanding the world, including ourselves. It *problematizes* the "obvious," the "real," and, crucially, the "taken for granted"; it challenges the view that conventional knowledge is based upon disinterested observation and that we can therefore separate subject and object, the perceived and the real, and it cautions us to be ever suspicious of our assumptions about how the world appears and the categories that we use to divide and interpret it. Second, because the world is the product of *social processes*, it follows that there cannot be any given, determined nature to the world "out there." Third, social categories are seen as historically and culturally specific and therefore vary over time and place. Particular forms of knowledge are not only the products of their history and culture and are thus artifacts of it, but there are therefore numerous forms of knowledge available. We cannot assume that our ways of understanding are necessarily the same as others and are any nearer "the truth."

Fourth, our knowledge of the world is seen as being developed between people in their daily *interactions*. These *negotiated* understandings can take a variety of forms that thereby invite different actions. Crucially, language and all other forms of representation gain their meaning from the ways in which they are used within *relationships*. Fifth, as our practices of language are bound within relationships, so are relationships bound within broader patterns of practice—rituals, traditions, and so on—for as we describe, explain, or otherwise represent ourselves and the world, so do we fashion our future. If we wish to make changes, therefore, we must confront the challenges of generating new meanings, and of becoming what Kenneth Gergen (1999) calls "poetic activists" (p. 49). *Generative discourses* provide ways of talking, writing, and acting that simultaneously challenge existing traditions of understanding and at the same time offer new possibilities for change.

A central emphasis of constructive social work is thus upon process, plurality of both knowledge and voice, and the relational quality of knowledge and language. It is consistent with the core values and traditions of social work and proceeds on an assumption that clients, no matter what their circumstances, have significant resources within and around them in order to bring about positive change. This argues that social work is as much, if not more, an art as it is a science, and proceeds on the basis that practice should be understood as much as a *practical-moral* activity as a *rational-technical* one. It is affirmative and reflexive and focuses on dialogue, listening to and talking with the other. An ability to work with ambiguity and uncertainty, both in terms of process and outcomes, is key. The principle of indeterminacy suggests the fluid, recursive, and nondetermined way that social situations unfold. The general thrust is thus that social life is replete with possibilities and that the linguistic social bond proposed is more open to alteration and expansion than is often assumed. But the principle does not underestimate that the clients of social work are usually the most constrained and marginalized of those in our society.

Drawing on the work of Kant (1952), Scott Lash (2000) differentiates between what he calls *determinate judgment* and *reflexive judgment*; it is reflexive judgment that is seen to lie at the core of the contemporary fluid, risk culture of the postmodern. However, determinate judgment, which lies at the core of a narrow EBP approach, is seen as the sort of judgment that aims for objective validity—it is the model of physics and mathematics. Its conditions of possibility are the categories of logic. In contrast, reflexive judgments do not operate from given rules of logic but operate on the basis of *finding* the rule. Unlike the propositional truths that are determinate judgments, reflexive judgments are seen as estimations that are based on "feelings" of pleasure and displeasure but also on feelings of shock, overwhelmingness, fear, loathing, as well as joy. Determinate judgment is perceived as drawing on various technico-scientific processes in an attempt to map and then control external and objectively recognized dangers; whereas reflexive judgment is described as involving more imaginative and intersubjective approaches to uncertain or contested areas of knowledge—with interpretation and negotiation replacing calculation and prediction. While determinate judgment is linear, reflexive judgment is nonlinear. Knowledge is seen as precarious and uncertain—probabilistic, at best; more like, according to Lash (2003), "possibilistic."

It is thus much more appropriate to see that what is required in the contemporary contexts of social work is the encouragement of this reflexive judgment as opposed to the determinate judgment. The increasing complexity and fluid nature of the world means that the world is less predictable, therefore less regularized. This is not to say that the practitioner is likely to be in control in these situations. It is to suggest, however, that there is far more room for maneuvering than may at first appear. As Lash (2000) suggests, "reflexive judgment is always a question of uncertainty, of risk, but it also leaves the door open to much innovation" (p. 52). In the process, the individual practitioner is encouraged into a much more interdependent stance, with the notion of proactive "rule finding" displacing the dependence on the rules and norms of bureaucratic procedures and guidance. Issues around the nonlinear, complex nature of contemporary decision making and the culture in which professional practice takes place is not recognized in the "modernizing" agenda of New Labour and other advanced liberal regimes.

It is in this context that I have attempted to develop this notion of constructive social work, which is not simply concerned with critiquing the contemporary dominant dogmas but with providing a positive contribution for creatively taking forward our notions of theory and practice in and of social work. The notion of reflexivity lies at its core. What the work of Lash and others (Froggett, 2002) suggests is that issues around the emotions and aesthetics are key and that the way our feelings interrelate and inform our judgments should not be underestimated. However, rather than see these as being impediments simply to be eradicated or overcome—as is the case with the rational-technical approach of the dominant forms of EBP and

New Labour's modernizing agenda—they are seen as lying at the core of what needs to be recognized and worked with. The continual attempt to place one's premises into question and to listen to alternative framings of reality in order to grapple with the potentially different outcomes arising out of different points of view and experiences are seen as key to developing social work theory, inquiry, and practice.

References

Alderson, P., & Morrow, V. (2004) *Ethics, social research and consulting with children and young people*. Ilford: Barnardo's.

Burr, V. (2003). *Social constructionism* (2nd ed.). London: Routledge.

Christensen, P., & James, A. (Eds.). (2000). *Research with children: Perspectives and practices*. London: Falmer Press.

Clarke, J., Gewirtz, S., & McLaughlin, E. (Eds.). (2000). *New managerialism, new welfare?* London: Sage.

Department of Health. (1998a). *Modernising social services: Promoting independence, improving protection, raising standards* (Cm 4169). London: The Stationery Office.

Department of Health. (1998b). *The quality protects programme: Transforming children's services* (LAC[98]28). London: Author.

Department of Health. (2000). *A quality strategy for social care*. London: The Stationery Office.

Donzelot, J. (1980). *The policing of families: Welfare versus the state*. London: Hutchinson.

Froggett, L. (2002). *Love, hate and welfare: Psychosocial approaches to policy and practice*. Bristol, UK: Policy Press.

Gergen, K. (1999). *An invitation to social construction*. London: Sage.

Glendinning, C., Powell, M., & Rummery, K. (Eds.). (2002). *Partnerships, New Labour and the governance of welfare*. Bristol, UK: Policy Press.

Hall, C., Juhila, K., Parton, N., & Pösö, T. (Eds.). (2003). *Constructing clienthood in social work and human services: Interaction, identities and practices*. London: Jessica Kingsley.

Hallett, C., & Prout, A. (Eds.). (2003). *Hearing the voice of the child: Social policy for a new century*. London: Routledge Falmer.

Harris, J. (2003). *The social work business*. London: Routledge.

Hirst, P. (1981). The genesis of the social. *Politics and Power, 3*, 67–82.

Humphrey, B. (1997). From critical thought to emancipatory action: Contradictory research goals? *Sociological Research Online*. Retrieved October 23, 2005, from http://www.socresonline.org.uk/socresonline/2/1/3.html

James, A. L. (2004). The McDonaldization of social work—or "Come back Florence Hollis, all is (or should be) forgiven." In R. Lovelock, K. Lyons, & J. Powell (Eds.), *Reflecting on social work: Discipline and profession* (pp. 37–54). Aldershot, Hants, UK: Ashgate.

Jokinen, A., Juhila, K., & Pösö, T. (Eds.). (1999). *Constructing social work practices*. Aldershot, Hants, UK: Ashgate.

Jordan, B. (with Jordan, C.). (2000). *Social work and the third way: Tough love as social policy*. London: Sage.

Kant, I. (1952). *The critique of judgement*. Oxford, UK: Oxford University Press.

Langan, M. (2002). The legacy of radical social work. In R. Adams, L. Dominelli, & M. Payne, (Eds.). *Social work: Themes, issues and critical debates* (2nd ed.) (pp. 209–217). Basingstoke, UK: Palgrave.

Lash, S. (2000). Risk culture. In B. Adam, U. Beck, & J. van Loon (Eds.), *The risk society and beyond: Critical issues for social theory* (pp. 47–62). London: Sage.

Lash, S. (2003). Reflexivity as non-linearity. *Theory, Culture and Society, 20*(2), 49–57.

Martinez-Brawley, E. E., & Zorita, P. M. B. (1998). At the edge of the frame: Beyond science and art in social work. *British Journal of Social Work, 28*(2), 197–212.

Morrow, V., & Richards, M. (1996). The ethics of social research with children: An overview. *Children & Society, 10*(2), 90–105.

Newman, J. (2001). *Modernising governance: New Labour, policy and society*. London: Sage.

Packwood, A. (2002). Evidence-based policy: Rhetoric and reality. *Social Policy and Society, 1*(3), 267–272.

Parton, N. (1991). *Governing the family: Child care, child protection and the state*. Basingstoke, UK: Macmillan/Palgrave.

Parton, N. (1994). Problematics of government, (post)modernity and social work. *British Journal of Social Work, 24*(1), 9–32.

Parton, N. (1999). Reconfiguring child welfare practices: Risk, advanced liberalism, and the government of freedom. In A. S. Chambon, A. Irving, & L. Epstein (Eds.), *Reading Foucault for social work* (pp. 101–130). New York: Columbia University Press.

Parton, N. (2000). Some thoughts on the relationship between theory and practice in and for social work. *British Journal of Social Work, 30*(4), 449–464.

Parton, N. (2002). Postmodern and constructionist approaches to social work. In R. Adams, L. Dominelli, & M. Payne (Eds.), *Social work: Themes, issues and critical debates* (2nd. ed.) (pp. 237–246). Basingstoke, UK: Palgrave.

Parton, N. (2003). Rethinking professional practice: The contributions of social constructionism and the feminist "ethics of care." *British Journal of Social Work, 33*(1), 1–16.

Parton, N. (2006). *Safeguarding childhood: Early intervention and surveillance in a late modern society*. Basingstoke, UK: Palgrave/Macmillan.

Parton, N., & O'Byrne, P. (2000). *Constructive social work: Towards a new practice*. Basingstoke, UK: Palgrave.

Parton, N., & Wattam, C. (Eds.). (1999). *Child sexual abuse: Responding to the experiences of children*. Chichester, NY: Wiley.

Philp, M. (1979). Notes on the form of knowledge in social work. *Sociological Review, 27*(1), 83–111.

Power, M. (1997). *The audit society: Rituals of verification*. Oxford, U.K.: Oxford University Press.

Prigogine, I. (1997). *The end of certainty*. New York: The Free Press.

Ritzer, G. (1998). *The McDonaldization thesis*. London: Sage.

Ritzer, G. (2000). *The McDonaldization of society* (New Century ed.). Thousand Oaks, CA: Pine Forge Press.

Smith, C. (2001). Trust and confidence: Possibilities for social work in high modernity. *British Journal of Social Work, 31*(2), 287–305.

Stake, R. (1997). Advocacy in evaluation: A necessary evil? In E. Chelimski & W. R. Shadish (Eds.), *Evaluation for the 21st century* (pp. 472–486). Thousand Oaks, CA: Sage.

Stenson, K. (1993). Social work discourse and the social work interview. *Economy and Society, 22*(1), 42–76.

Stepney, P. (2000). Implications for social work in the New Millennium. In P. Stepney & D. Ford (Eds.), *Social work models, methods and theories* (pp. 9–14). Lyme Regis, UK: Russell House.

Taylor, C., & White, S. (2002). What works about what works? Fashion, fad and EBP. *Social Work and Social Science Review, 10*(2), 63–81.

Trinder, L. (2000). Evidence-based practice in social work and probation. In L. Trinder & S. Reynolds (Eds.), *Evidence-based practice: A critical appraisal* (pp. 138–162). Oxford, UK: Blackwell Science.

Urry, J. (2002a). The global complexities of September 11th. *Theory, Culture and Society, 19*(4), 57–69.

Urry, J. (2002b). *Global complexities*. Cambridge, UK: Polity.

Webb, S. (2001). Some considerations on the validity of evidence-based practice in social work. *British Journal of Social Work, 31*(1), 57–79.

White, S., & Stancombe, J. (2003) *Clinical judgement in the health and welfare professions*. Maidenhead, UK: Open University Press.

Young, K., Ashby, D., Bozaz, A., & Grayson, L. (2002). Social science and the evidence-based policy movement. *Social Policy and Society, 1*(3), 215–224.

CHAPTER 8

En-Voicing the World

Social Constructionism and Essentialism in Natural Discourse—How Social Work Fits In

FRED H. BESTHORN

Flying into the picturesque New England town of Burlington, Vermont, for a gathering of social work colleagues, I was awestruck by the beautiful landscape as it cascaded beneath me—heavily forested with an infinite variety of deciduous and evergreen trees, low rolling hills, and clearly visible streams and small pastoral farmsteads. I felt connected, momentarily swept away to a peaceful, dreamlike place. Much of my experience is with the treeless, wide-open flatlands of the central plains. Although I have grown to cherish the prairie through the years, this new place was a whimsical escape from the monotony of unencumbered vastness.

My second trip to Vermont was quite different. As the plane settled gently into its final approach, I was struck, for a flash, by how things had changed. Now, instead of a lush, green, vegetative carpet, there was an unfolding smattering of oxidized red and leeching swatches of saffron yellow and burnt orange meandering through a purplish, blue-green aura. My first reaction was of horror! What had happened to this verdant landscape? Had the land been stripped of trees, exposing the sun-bleached under crust of tainted soil? Was it now laid waste by chemical staining and worse? I was reminded of places from childhood—the Kansas oil patch where raw crude oil was inadvertently spilled or intentionally dumped onto the land. These places always succumbed to slow death, as first vegetation and then the soil itself died. After a month or two baking in the unremitting heat of a Kansas summer, the ground looked tormented, almost as if were groping for a final breath amid a waxy, white lamina that, in the sentient world, harkens approaching death.

This fleeting awareness seemed ghastly, unbelievable! But, of course, I was humored by my observation. In truth, I'd arrived at the most stunning time of year as I caught the first glimpse of fall, in all its astonishing color and majesty. It was my perception that had changed, not the essential character of the landscape beneath me. This was still the same place I had visited the year before. These experiences of flying into Vermont once again raised important philosophical questions that have captivated me for years and that increasingly matter to social work as it seeks to integrate novel approaches to theory, teaching, and practice in a new millennium. My excursion to Vermont was to attend a yearly gathering of social work scholars sharing a common commitment to open dialogue around alternative ways of knowing and being in the world. The Transforming Social Work conference was an opportunity to think about how our understandings of reality emerge—how cognition, history, and culture interface with what we think we know about the world. These yearly discussions, and especially the openness with which we agreed to disagree with one another over difficult questions, inspired and provoked lingering ideas that had emerged once again on that very first trip to Burlington. This chapter is a direct result of those discussions and that experience.

I call myself a social constructionist. I'm committed to ideas suggesting that much of what we know or think we know is a construction emerging from our unique historic, dialogic, and discursive cultural context. I question the privileged voice of the grand metanarratives of Western social, economic, political, and scientific thought that identifies the *Truth*—what counts as reality, who is able to define it, and who has access to knowing it. I have contested with vigor the hubris of those claiming the final word on a matter, or those whose stories or interpretations claim to have *finally* captured events as they truly are.

Yet, I'm also a devoted naturalist. I've dedicated my professional life to bringing ecological consciousness—*better yet, earth consciousness*—into social work theory and practice. This follows in the footsteps of important ecological forebearers of the profession. For example, the ecological approach of Carol Germain (1978, 1979, 1980, 1991) evolved as an early attempt to bridge the gap between general systems theory and the growing trend to conceive of the world in ecological terms. Her approach understood human behavior as inseparably linked with the environment—interdependent, complementary, and constantly changing (Germain, 1978). In an attempt to articulate this ecological perspective for practice, Germain and her colleague, Alex Gitterman, joined forces to apply the ecological metaphor to direct social work practice. For Germain and Gitterman (1980):

> The environment is dynamic and complex. It comprises many kinds of systems, each with its characteristic structure, level of organization, and spatial and temporal properties. The social environment comprises human beings organized in dyadic relations, social networks, bureaucratic institutions, and other social systems including the neighborhood, community, and society itself. The *physical* environment comprises the natural world of animals, plants, and

> land forms, and the built world of structures and objects constructed by human beings. The social and *physical* environments are related to each other in complex ways [italics in original]. (p. 137)

Thus, our profession is steeped in the language and praxis of ecological frameworks—person-in-environment, the life model, ecological perspectives—and yet, with but few exceptions, has largely muted the distinct elements of the natural environment in its discourse. Recently, however, new generations of social workers are calling us to give principled and detailed attention to the natural environment as part of an expanded person-environment perspective (Besthorn, 2002a, 2004a, 2004b; Besthorn & Saleebey, 2003; Coates, 2003; Kahn & Scher, 2002; Rogge, 2000; Wolf, 2000). Indeed, the profession is coming to realize that as citizens and professionals we may only ignore the natural environment to the great peril of ourselves and the clients we serve. The recent catastrophic environmental disasters in the Gulf Coast region of the United States with hurricanes Katrina and Rita and the horrific tsunami event in the Indian Ocean that claimed thousands of lives are just two of a growing number of stark reminders that the world community is reaching a critical threshold in its relationship to the natural environment.

The dilemma, of course, is identifying with both positions. As a social worker committed to our time-honored professional ethos of person-environment, this is not merely an intellectual exercise for me. I have experienced the deep embodiment of dialoging with nature, of hearing its voice while at the same time being deeply awed by the ineffable, invisible, and transcendent character of its interaction with the human world. And, as a social worker steadfast in my constructionist leanings, I've known the disenchantment that comes with realizing the oppressive manifestations and abuses of privileged narrative. I savor the thought of deconstructing and changing the advantaged regimes of truth and power that have subjugated or annihilated huge portions of both human and nonhuman worlds. Two positions have historically characterized this tension. One is sometimes referred to as *essentialism*—the idea that reality generally and nature specifically have inherent structures and patterns of their own. These structures and patterns are relatively stable and independent and are not an outcome based upon what humans perceive about them. *Constructionism*, on the other hand, flows from the idea that reality and nature are the outcome of the economic, social, and linguistic conventions of the human communities that create them.

This chapter first seeks better understanding of the constructionist and essentialist debate within the context of environmental philosophy. It asks if there is a basis for thought and action that balances these different orientations. We must never succumb to a false belief that difficult axiological, ontological, and cosmological questions do not matter to the nitty-gritty world of social work practice. They matter profoundly for they have vital implications for what we value and what we do. As suggested, our profession is historically committed to person-environment approaches. We have lavished our language with repeated references to ecological constructs and increasingly have come to see our role in a serious and deepening environmental crisis (Besthorn, 2001, 2002a, 2002b, 2003; Coates, 2003; Kahn & Scher, 2002; Rogge, 2000; Tangenberg & Kemp, 2002; Zapf, 2002). But, if social work's emerging conceptualization of the deeper significance of natural environment is only one construction among myriad possibilities, then it can be argued that no one construction is better than another and it can be further reasoned that there is no sure basis for professional action at all. Of course, as with most things, any action proposal depends, in part, on what values are being promulgated. But, those who then argue for bigger SUVs, greater economic progress, more consumer goods, and weaker environmental protection laws are seen as legitimate in their positions as those who argue for wilderness protection, cleaner air, and uncontaminated water.

Second, I examine the prospect of creating a more balanced constructionist/essentialist approach by exploring the idea that nature speaks. That is, nature has a vocative character that we are intersubjectively involved with such that it joins with us as we coconstruct a reality that honors earth systems and the human habitats that depend upon them. Seminal to this deeper ecological consciousness for social work is the conviction that nature has inherent value and an authenticity unto itself. The natural environment matters for social work because it is real and not simply created by some collective agreement to a given discourse or set of textual assertions about it. Finally, this chapter also offers some modest proposal for enhancing social work's person-environment perspective and some tentative ways this may enhance practice.

The Constructionist Framework

Social work scholar Mary Katherine Rodwell (1998) suggests that the constructionist worldview is part of a cognitive, linguistic, and sociocultural postmodern movement to dethrone the privileged position of logical positivism by infusing an idea of embedded knowledge in localized contexts. In so doing, constructionist metatheory seeks to reinvigorate human agency by liberating it from the totalizing narratives of privileged worldviews. Constructionist ideas aim to emancipate narratives that have been subjugated by powerful Eurocentric, androcentric, and heterocentric stories and language. Some authors have drawn subtle differences between major variants or subsets of the constructionist framework. For example, some delineate between constructivism and constructionism, while others refer to the language of critical constructivists or radical constructivists (Franklin, 1998; Greene, Jensen, & Jones, 1996; Guidano, 1991; Mahoney, 1991; Middleman & Wood, 1993; Morrison, 1997; Robbins, Chatterjee, & Canda, 1998; Rodwell, 1998; Saleebey, 1993, 2001, 2004). It is not the intent of this chapter to engage in a detailed discussion of these disparate descriptors. But for purposes of clarity, I will use the term constructionism or social constructionism unless I am specifically referring to a constructivist frame of reference. It is recognized that there are sometimes subtle and perhaps even profound differences between these terms, but the interested reader will find comprehensive critical reviews of these issues in different social work and social scientific literature (Franklin & Nurius, 1998; Kleinman, 1988, 1997). I agree with Rodwell (1998) that it is probably most useful to view these constructs "as a fuzzy set of frameworks with mainly indistinct boundaries" (p. 20). They are diverse and sometimes contradictory, but they all contribute to our understanding of what it means to *be* in the world. The intent here is to see if core themes of constructionism have been applied too uncritically to all manner of reality, especially the natural world and not just to what has to do with social conditions and human experience.

Briefly stated, constructionism asserts that humans are active participants and coconstructors with each other in creating and comprehending experience. What we call material and social reality is only real to the relative extent that we name it as real or, in collective relationship, coevolve some agreement on its meaning. The significance of reality is neither ultimate nor unchanging and generally comes to be endorsed though a negotiation among a given collective. Much of what we understand the world *to be* comes from our words, stories, opinions, and beliefs and the words, stories, opinions, and beliefs of those who surround us (Saleebey, 2001). That is, we make meaning of the material world or any phenomena occurring in the world through our uniquely human interpretive lenses. We construct our worlds through a complex mix of conceptualizations, perceptions, values, explanations, language experiences, narratives, dialogues, and conversations—all of which occur in relationship to others.

Several social work scholars have suggested similarities among the variants of postmodern constructionist frameworks (Franklin, 1998; Rodwell, 1998). Although it is unlikely that there could ever be absolute agreement of opinion on these central features, it has been suggested that there are a number of shared characteristics. First, humans are a meaning-making species, and human agency is the critical component in this meaning-making enterprise. Human beings have a decisive, species-specific role coupled with their superior cognitive/linguistic skills for the interpretation of reality. In this sense, humans differ from other sentient members of the natural world, who must rely predominantly on instinct or short-term learning rather than language, memory, symbolic images, and constructed artifices in order to negotiate their spatial relationship to the world. Second, constructionists assert a primary, human-mediated, dialogical view of the world. This assumes human language, negotiated through individual human cognition and collective social discourse, becomes the avenue for making meanings. It suggests that reality is both socially (narratively, sociohistorically, culturally) and psychologically (self-schemas, neural feedbacks, feed-forward mechanisms) constructed by distinct and frequent arbitrative interchanges between two or more individuals, each having language and a point of view. This reflexivity of meaning making leads to permeable and fluid identities of self and world, leaving open the possibility of the reconstruction of all proximal and distal realities. Third, constructionist frameworks generally reject the idea of objective reality existing in space and time, which is somehow passively received through one's perceptional mind/brain processes. Rather, they assert the viability of multiple interpretations of reality (behavior, relationships, and events) and, to some degree, the importance of tacit knowing to access this intersubjective experience of reality. What matters is not *Truth* in any objective sense but rather *truth*. Truth, in this latter sense, only becomes relevant as it nourishes meaning and action. Fourth, constructionist perspectives accept the existence of some essentialist phenomena that exist beyond self-referential construction. However, they tend to affirm that there is no way to know these objectively because "the operations of human cognitive structures and processes and the nature of language and social processes, in particular, make it impossible for us to know an objective reality completely" (Franklin, 1998, p. 61). Finally, constructionist frameworks have been criticized at one time or another for either their relativism or uncritical anthropocentrism (Rodwell, 1998).

Fabricating Nature

Social constructionism has had a profound impact on my understanding of social work and its epistemological and ontological perspectives on a host of human developmental concerns. Like many of my constructionist social work colleagues, I am deeply indebted to these perspectives for bringing to consciousness what Gergen (1985) calls *radical doubt* about the *taken for granted* world. I am convinced that the emancipatory aims of constructionism are noble and, indeed, revolutionary, and that it has contributed in profound ways to the critique of oppressive narratives and a revitalization of human agency in a too often commodified and homogenized world. In this regard, Saleebey (2001) notes that constructionist models have been a necessary and liberatory corrective counterbalance to a long history of dominating social paradigms. He writes:

> Many people(s) have had their meaning and understanding of the world forced on them from the outside. The use of

coercion, threat, violence, or simply the power of the media can swarm our own sense of our experience. For too long in our society, people who are "outsiders," on the "margin," or of a very different culture have had their theories muted or distorted by others who have more power or who control social and political institutions as well as the media of communication. The power and freedom to making meaning, for individual or group or culture, is a priceless and delicate condition. . . . When we work with others who have lost credibility or conviction . . . we work to help them restore their own meaning. . . . In doing this we are invoking the power of language, and the powers of mind, in the project of coming to name one's own world. (pp. 10–11)

My deep concern with constructionist models is the consequences of a viewpoint that moves beyond, often uncritically, sometimes unknowingly, the *human coconstruction of social realities* to the much more troublesome idea of the *human construction of all reality*. This has become particularly so with regard to the natural world. Several of my social work colleagues find it perplexing that I still hold to an essentialist framework when it comes to my interest in and understanding of the natural world, especially as I seem so firmly embedded in a constructionist framework with regard to my understanding of the social world. Their point seems to be that if the way we represent the social world is always interpretive, discursive, and based on concurrences, then it would seem to follow that the whole world (in this case, they mean the natural world) is therefore constructed through interpretive discourse. Nature exists, if one can say it exists at all, only to the degree that our language collective organizes it. Saleebey (2001) quotes the descriptive words of Whorf in this regard:

We dissect nature along lines laid down by our native languages. The categories and types we isolate from the world

> of phenomena we do not find there because they stare every observer in the face; on the contrary, the world is presented in a kaleidoscopic flux of impressions which has to be organized in our minds—and this means largely by the linguistic systems in our minds. We cut nature up, organize it into concepts, and ascribe significances as we do, largely because we are parties to an agreement to organize it this way—an agreement that holds throughout our speech community and is codified in the patterns of our language. (as cited in Saleebey, p. 181)

This most far-reaching form of constructionism, what philosopher and environmental ethicist J. Baird Callicott (1997) calls *radical deconstructive postmodernism*, moves from the conclusion that representations of the world are mediated by our unique historical, cultural, and cognitive capacities to the conclusion that all natural reality is invented by words. The sine qua non of this position is that the natural world is constructed by agreed upon language conventions and, as such, is momentary, textual, and provisional and has no essential quality. This is what Callicott calls the *strong* position of constructionism. He further suggests that the *weak* constructionist position sees the natural world as having an essential quality, but humans can never understand it in any manner except through agreed upon cognitive and linguistic capacities. While different in magnitude, both positions suggest that nature has no essential reality or none that can be known but rather reflects creative discourse between the literate and imaginative capacities of languaged persons. Thus, for environmental philosophers Chaloupka and Cawley (1993) "nature, like everything else we talk about, is first and foremost an artifact of language . . . any attempt to invoke the name of nature . . . must now be either naive or ironic" (p. 5). In the nascent discipline of environmental ethics, constructionist philosophers "question the assumption that science is about nature as it exists outside of us" (Bird, 1987, p. 256). For them, nature is ordered discursively and has no inherent structures or patterns of it own.

These claims suggest a view of nature that is very different from the nature I have come to know. They suggest that there is no nature but rather *natures*. Numinous nature with its multifaceted and diverse array of potentialities beyond our ability to fully comprehend them (Marguilis, 1994; Rolston, 1997; Soule & Lease, 1995) becomes a subsidiary to a linguistically constructed nature. As constructionist environmental philosopher and historian William Cronon (1996) has argued, nature is no longer and perhaps never has had an *otherness* about it but rather serves as a mirror upon which humans project the multiple reflections that they wish to see. This implies a relativism that creates little ethical ground upon which to make determination of value in the natural world. In Cronon's words, the natural world

> is not a primitive sanctuary where the last remnants of an untouched, endangered, but still transcendent nature can for at least a little while longer be encountered without the contaminating taint of civilization. Instead, it is a product of that civilization, and *could hardly be contaminated by the very stuff of which it is made* [italics added]. Wilderness hides its unnaturalness behind a mask that is all the more beguiling because it seems so natural. (p. 9)

Cronon's comments seem to suggest that environmental problems such as resource diminution, ecosystem degradation, and toxic pollution are from this standpoint not problems in any conventional sense but are, rather, discursive debates of competing scientific and personal perceptions that require no sure action. This view implies environmental problems are really language problems: definitional, negotiated, and dependent on claim makers. Similarly, John Hannigan (1995) suggests, "it is rare indeed to find an environmental problem which does not have its origins in a body of scientific research" (p. 76). For him, acid rain, loss of biodiversity, global warming, ozone depletion, desertification, and dioxin poisoning are all examples of *problems* that are first and foremost a set of scientific and languaged observations.

From this viewpoint, environmental problems are not assaults to the ecological fabric of nature that can be detected, albeit imperfectly, through the use of scientific and conceptual tools (Kidner, 2000). Rather, environmental problems are constructed by these tools and cannot in any cogent sense exist independently of the ways we perceive them and the way we language them. The fact that it is difficult for science to fully assess ecological damage or definitively track the source of contaminants is seen as a clear indication that problems are fluid concepts that are culturally grounded and serially negotiated. Actions to reduce environmental contamination are often met with great skepticism by some constructionist environmentalists since there is no way to definitively *prove* harm. From this perspective *damage* is as much a linguistic construct as nature, ecology, and environment. All actions or no action become as legitimate as any other.

A recent series of events illustrates this reality. The decision by the current administration to begin large-scale cutting of the remaining vestiges of virgin U.S. forest lands in order to *protect* them from the ravages of fires is justified as just as legitimate approach to forest management as any other (Pegg, 2003). Similarly, forest conservationist Ted Williams (2000) writes impassionedly concerning the proliferation of what he calls "false forests" (p. 73) and the spurious philosophical justifications offered by some environmentalists and the logging industry that these managed forests are as valid a solution to the problem of clear-cutting as stopping the practice completely. After all, so the logic goes, it does not matter to nature since nature is simply *us and our activities*—birthed into linguistic existence. In fact, it has been argued that these kinds of decisions are better approaches since they are assumed to be the only course of action that provides both economic benefit as well as *protection* of forests. This kind of logic has become all too often coupled with a neoconservative policy agenda that relies upon a kind of pseudophilosophical mummery. Indeed, there is a broad cross-section of environmental policy and philosophy literature that speaks to the ways that the neoconservative, antienvironmentalist right has misused the subjectivist dimensions of the constructionist critique to either neutralize or debunk annoying environmental policy (Bender, 2002; Ehrlich & Ehrlich, 1998; Macnaghten & Urry, 1998; Murphy, 1995; Pope & Rauber, 2004). To those of us who spend a great deal of time fighting to protect and maintain the few remaining pockets of wild nature, the political misuse of constructionist philosophy has very significant implications. It is a *real* problem affecting *real* nature and is ironically counter to the values of many social constructionists who have labored long to unmask destructive practices by exposing underlying belief systems.

I do not quarrel with the contention that perceptions of nature are affected by culture, experience, and language or that unmediated connection with the natural world is improbable. I am pleased the constructionist critique has broadened and humanized the staunchly mechanistic focus of traditional science to include a much needed sociocultural dimension. I am glad constructionists remind us that narrow biological reductionism in describing the ecological world cannot be supported in a complex cultural world. But as Kidner (2000) observes, "just as the biological reductionism of an ecological approach is now rejected on good grounds, so *sociological* [italics added] reductionism shows no more promise" (p. 342). At the extreme periphery of constructionism, radical deconstructive postmodernism, to use Callicott's terms, falls into the same exceptionalist dualism that it hopes to deconstruct. It replaces one reductionism with the other. Sociological reductionism does no better a job of bridging the gap between culture and nature than has strict biologicalism and runs the risk of faring no better in protecting the environment.

If one is fair to argue, as many social workers are discovering and attesting to (Besthorn, 2001, 2002a, 2003, 2004a; Besthorn & Canda, 2002; Besthorn & McMillen, 2002; Coates, 2003; Rogge, 2000; Saleebey, 2004; Ungar, 2002), that the demolition of the natural world stems from human estrangement from nature, it is hard to conceive how environmental protection will arise out of a new framework that has the potential of perpetuating the same alienating tendency to reduce essential nature to a socially agreed upon construct. This notion embodies what philosopher Roy Bhaskar calls the *epistemic fallacy*—the view that "statements about being can be reduced to or analyzed in terms of statements about knowledge" (cited in Kidner, 2000, p. 343). From this vantage point, epistemology trumps ontology in the ordering of philosophical debate. Too often statements suggesting that *conceptions of nature are socially constructed* mutate, almost imperceptibly, into *nature is socially constructed* (Collier, 1994). When this shift in meaning occurs, a danger arises. Namely, making the assertion that threats to nature have no reality except as social constructions becomes much the same as saying threats may not exist at all, thus why bother being concerned? One would be hard pressed to find anyone making a categorical claim that damage to the world has not existed or does not exist. Yet, while many claim that the world is experiencing alarming rates of ecological harm, there is the associated assertion that we cannot be certain of this damage in any indisputable way since damage may be viewed differently depending on the historiocultural or sociocultural context in which one lives (Bailey, 2001; Helvarg, 2004; Huber, 2000; Lomborg, 2002).

As a social work scholar working extensively on how environmental factors impinge on our clients and our helping protocols,

I have consistently observed that this kind of imprecise reckoning occurs often and across many contexts. The current administration in Washington uses just this kind of justification to systematically dismantle decades-old environmental protections to the great and lasting harm of the most dispossessed among us (Pope & Rauber, 2004). This sort of unctuousness "reflects the tension between a detached academic stance which has already abandoned any felt commitment to or involvement in the natural world, and the intuited or directly experienced loss of the wild and the natural which, although we are often unable to articulate it, we deeply sense in nonintellectual ways" (Kidner, 2000, p. 344). Ecological destruction is not just a matter of how language constructs the world; it is a matter of deeply felt and observed experiences. We do know and feel in our deepest selves that the natural world is being inexorably transformed from lush woods and sweeping grasslands to a world of factories, highways, and housing tracts.

Global capitalism's transformation of natural places into sites of agribusiness and expanding industrial production, and the evolution of a *socially focused and highly anthropocentric constructed world* is consistent with this transformation (Bender, 2002). Indeed, attempting to identify viscerally with the natural order is, as American naturalist Aldo Leopold (1949) put it, "to walk alone in a world of wounds" (p. 38). In each succeeding generation people are therefore confronted with powerful social and emotional reasons for resigning themselves to the loss of the natural world and "withdrawing into a substitute fantasy world constructed with the aid of the electronic media" (Kidner, 2000, p. 344). The virtual replacement of natural history found in Disney World, the family fantasyland of Las Vegas, oceanic extravaganzas like Sea World, and sanitized natural fabrications found in places like Nashville's Marriott complex are only several of the tawdriest examples. Nature in the media-ized, computerized world appears to arise out of various technologically and spectacularly amplified perspectives which, in the absence of experiential contact with the natural world, forbid us from assessing the accuracy or thoroughness of those viewpoints and productions. Indeed, global capitalism offers powerful incentives for us to make this myopic substitution from nature to *un-nature*, from vital connection to virtual misperception. Global capital needs the real land, real trees, real animals, and cultivated space as physical raw material to fuel its productive fires. It needs a homogeneous consumer-driven world—consistent, conditioned, compliant, and complacent—willing to accept a verbal and virtual substitute for nature. Again, in the words of Kidner (2000):

> If nature, then, was not originally *constructed* by technology and language, it is in many ways in the process of being *reconstructed* by these means; and the metaphor of "construction" assumes the absence or obliteration of natural structure, so that the world is simply made up of (verbal or physical) "raw materials." This demolition of nature that frames and transcends human awareness, and its replacement by a "nature" that is defined and constructed by industrial and discursive activity from the fragments of the original nature, implies a corresponding definition of the person to fit a rational, commercial world—a redefinition which, in Arthur Kleinman's (1988, p. 42) words, has "deepened discursive layers of experience while paradoxically making it more difficult to grasp and communicate poetic, moral, and spiritual layers of the felt flow of living." (p. 345)

The Cartesian/Newtonian paradigm, buttressed in enlightened modernity, has always attempted to create a human realm that is separate and above the natural realm (Besthorn, 2002a, 2002b). Humans and nature are assumed separate, just as mind and body, fact and theory, and subject and object are assumed separate. In similar ways, the radical constructionist framework is for some a consistent next step to this same dualistic ordering of phenomena. The assumption that the human realm is separate from the natural realm is the *taken for granted* part of nearly all modern science, economics, and psychology (Besthorn & Canda, 2002; Besthorn & Saleebey, 2003). It seems just common sense to the uninitiated. Not only are humans thought to be separate from nature, they are ascribed as superior to it. Modernity *alleges* the absolute separateness of human/nature construct and then claims that humanity does not derive its existence and language from nature but rather prescribes them to nature. It is "a relative minor step to the position that nature itself exists only as an artifact of the superior, human domain" (Kidner, 2000, p. 347).

Language is the most important and potent component in maintaining this sense of separateness. Redefining natural reality on the basis of linguistic convention has many precursors in the history of domination. Examples include the demand by missionizing and colonizing groups that Western indigenous peoples speak English or the insistence of conquistadors that New World place names be designated in Spanish. Just as Cartesian modernity fashioned a cognitive disjunction between concepts and reality by creating a discourse of separateness, so can constructionism begin to craft a perceptual disjunction that first names, sorts, ranks and then "becomes and replaces, the order of the world that it is taken as representing" (Reiss, 1982, p. 35). The *world of meaning making* is placed above a *world of being*—a world of vital aliveness. As the substitution of manufactured human reality for natural reality continues, "language appears not so much as a human attempt to communicate with and describe those forms which exist beyond language, but rather as itself *constituting* reality" (Kidner, 2000, p. 348). We find ourselves in a world that Baudrillard (1981) describes as existing with no nature but rather as a world where our true nature is "the universe of communication" (p. 200). Numinous nature is effectively excluded from a world that is dominated by words and concepts. This anthropocentric bias keeps us from speaking with the world and keeps us from hearing the world speak to us. Talking *about* nature is a very effective way of not communicating *with* it. In the end, we find ourselves thinking of language and communication as only interhuman activities. But as famed linguist and systems theorist Gregory Bateson convincingly noted, there is a vast difference between language communication and biological communication: "Language depends on nouns, which seem to refer to things, while biological communication concerns pattern and relationship" (Bateson & Bateson 1987, p. 188).

Silencing Nature

As suggested, at the core of the constructionist framework is a potential for a distorted understanding of the process of meaning making. As a social worker deeply concerned with both human and nonhuman nature, I find that constructionist meaning making can be highly problematic in its exclusive focus on interhuman discourse. The central issue becomes finding a way to hear the voice of the natural world once again. It is ironic that the constructionist framework privileges languaging and discursive relationships in the human realm while at the same time marginalizing language and relationships in the most basic milieu humans depend on for existence: the natural world. The constructionist framework has the potential to mute the voice of the earth while reducing humanity's deeply sensate and relational capacities to communicate. Communication is reduced to rules of grammar and syntax and socially constructed linguistic conventions.

For me, as a social worker committed to the professional value stance that relationship matters, the solution lies not in rejecting constructionism but in finding a balance that expands the boundaries of reciprocal discourse to include the voices of nature in the way we understand ourselves and our place in *relationship* to the rest of the sentient world. Humanity is not ontologically separate from the natural world, nor have we constructed nature through our collective discourses as modern enlightenment philosophy and radical constructionism have tried to convince us. We are one voice in the world. We are sensate in the larger sensorial world. David Abram (1996), philosopher and ecologist, eloquently captures this sentiment:

> Our bodies have formed themselves in delicate reciprocity with the manifold textures, sounds, and shapes of an animate earth—our eyes have evolved in subtle interaction with other eyes, as our ears are attuned by their very structure to the howling of wolves and the honking of geese. To shut ourselves off from these other voices, to continue by our lifestyles to condemn these other sensibilities to the oblivion of extinction, is to rob our own sense of their integrity, and to rob our minds of their coherence. We are human only in contact, and conviviality, with what is not human. (p. 22)

It seems the most obvious thing to me that things speak. My experience, from childhood until now, has been a resounding recognition that we humans are not the only things in the world having voice. In fact, from the beginning of our evolutionary trek, we have been involved in an active communicative dance with the nonhuman world. Communication, in this sense, is not just the property of humans in relationship with each other. Human beings are not the only things having communicative agency. The dialogical agency of nature undercuts enlightenment dualism and balances constructionist anthropocentrism. I understand that to say that nature speaks, that the world is *envoiced*, may seem quite strange to the ear unaccustomed to hearing anything except human voices. But I am convinced there is firm theoretical and philosophical support for this perception. It is grounded in the phenomenological, hermeneutical, existential, theological, ecological, feminist, historical, literary, biological, and anthropological ideas of such luminaries of Western thought as Maurice Merleau-Ponty (1945/1962, 1964, 1968), Martin Heidegger (1927/1967, 1969/1972) Henry Bugbee (1958, 1962), Roy Bhaskar (1989), Paul Shepard (1994, 1995), Gary Synder (1990, 1994), David Abram (1995, 1996), Scott Friskics (2001a, 2001b), Albert Borgmann (1984, 1995), Katherine Hayles (1991, 1995), Christopher Preston (2000), Donald Worster (1995), and Donna Haraway (1988). For these scholars, and many more like them in both Western and Eastern philosophical traditions, we are at the most basic level, *situated knowers* in an *en-voiced* world of speakers. That is, we exist in a highly complex and interrelated world made up of cultural and languaged contexts, all of which are heavily influenced by biological and specific ecological contexts. In short, we are members not only of human communities but animate, sensate communities made up of a vast array of living and speaking beings.

If, indeed, the world speaks to us, why do we not hear it? Part of the explanation lies in our cognitively bound and poorly reasoned assertion that because we do not generally hear the world, the world must, therefore, be silent. Quite simply, modern culture increasingly occludes our ability to listen to the natural world. We live in an incredibly noisy, clamorous, technological, and mechanized world. Airplanes, televisions, automobiles, and the constant peeps and buzzes of a world fashioned to capture our attention drown out the voices of nature. Most people have been conditioned to uncover creative ways to avoid finding themselves alone in silence. The world of cell phones, miniature stereos, portable video games, and 24-7 radio ensures that, for most of us, silence will be forever banished from our waking existence.

In a noisy world where stillness is reviled while self-referential chest pounding is highly prized, genuine listening becomes a casualty. Modern *infotainment* culture discourages the practice of deep listening. It, contrary to the rhetoric of individuality and self-determination, is awash in self-imposed regularity, socially enforced uniformity, and consumeristic required standardization. The greatest sin is not to *fit in* while, paradoxically, the greatest desire is to *stand out* in the vast ocean of sameness. We often go to great lengths to trumpet distinctiveness in the way we look, what we wear, where we live, what we drive, and what we've done. The rueful search to find one's *15 minutes of fame* has become a kind of unconscious cultural tableau for those seeking some semblance of uniqueness and individuality.

The sad litany of youthful shooting sprees; the stalking, and in some cases, murder of celebrities; and the nearly constant barrage of pomposity and braggadocio of reality TV speaks of desperate people demanding to be recognized in a monotonous world of conformity—seemingly obsessed with escaping anonymity and avoiding the silence. It often seems that the rudest and loudest voice usually wins. The strident and boisterous *I* has become the undisputed imperial subject of Western society. With all this self-expression and self-assertion with a background of noisy glitz and glimmer, is anyone listening? We simply cannot talk and listen at the same moment. And, if we only rarely listen to one another, is it so surprising that we scarcely fathom listening to the natural world? This imbalanced emphasis on human voice distorts our notions of who we are, impoverishes our relational abilities, and forces us to inhabit a world characterized by, in the words of Friskics (2001a), a "grammar of monologue" (p. 403). In this context not only have marginalized peoples been denied voice because of their truncated ability to speak out loudly in a noisy, dominant culture, but nature itself, aside from the occasional earthquake, hurricane, and tornado, has become wholly passive, nominally silent, and utterly lacking in agency (Friskics, 2001a, 2001b). It should not astonish us that human relationships with nature are understood through either the modernist myth of a rational human subject studying, manipulating, and controlling inert matter or the constructionist narrative of languaging humans dialoguing and crafting nature from collective cultural agendas.

Yet the *grammar of monologue*—our inability to be silent and to listen to anything but ourselves—is not the only cause for our failing to find voice in nature. Most of us also have so little sustained and experiential contact with the natural world that we have few opportunities for hearing even if we were so inclined. We have become so accustomed to understanding the natural world in the way we might understand a washing machine, wristwatch, or computer—artifacts whose function it is to convenience us—that we find little compelling need or pleasurable desire, except in occasional photo-op excursions, to spend time in natural settings. Reducing the natural world to its functional equivalency or claiming it as a by-product of homolinguistic convention has the same relative impact. We transform eloquent, en-voiced fellow beings into "mute, plastic, natural resources . . . the object of our desires as a silent storehouse full of inert stuff—an inventory of lifeless stock" (Friskics, 2001a, pp. 400, 401). Nature becomes visual backdrop, oralgraphically created by self-referential human voices "freely creating world upon world of words . . . poured forth in conversation after conversation" (Cheney, 1989, p. 119).

En-Voicing the World

How then are conscientious social workers to understand engagement with the earth? Some will no doubt have dismissed this discussion as a jaded polemic—romantic, mystical, illogical—simply irrelevant to the grave, chaotic new world now confronting pragmatic social work scholars and practitioners. But, to do so would mean missing the critical importance that dialogue and dialectic play in the way we live in the world.

Dialogue always addresses us in ways that make claims on us and commission us to active reply. We are called upon to take responsibility in ways that are ethically decisive. Dialogue, at its most seminal level, is a call to care with respect and compassion. Dismissing this discussion would also mean to have missed an opportunity to transform the seeming silence and furtive quality of nature into an opportunity to learn a new language of the en-voiced world, less encumbered by the singularity of human centeredness and open to a fresh dialogue of ecological interrelatedness and vivified humility. Mircea Eliade (1972) makes a similar point in his international study of shamanism. He notes that "all over the world learning the language of animals . . . is equivalent to knowing the secrets of nature" (p. 98), and, one might add, our secrets as well.

Dialogic encounters with nature do not have to be seen as ridiculous aberrations completely outside temporal, rational experience. Nor should they be seen as misguided extrapolations of simple, anthropomorphic ascriptions to inanimate reality. Relegating these ideas to the realm of superstition or irrationality simply postpones the need to address them openly and critically. Rather, finding en-voicement with the natural world has a significance that can inform the social work profession and transform our personal lives. It revisits a sophisticated, atavistic phenomenology of nature that has been alive in ancient cultures for millennia. En-voicing the world through dialogue with it is based on several ontological premises: (1) all the phenomenal world is alive and inspirited—overflowing with *vis vitalis*—and this aliveness includes humans, cultural artifacts, and natural entities, both biological and inert, and (2) the nonhuman world is alive and articulate and able to communicate with the human world. Participation in this dialogue with nature means "we find the capacity to affirm our fellows and ourselves, receive intimations of the irreducible meaning of our being together, and recognize ourselves as both called upon and empowered to incarnate this value and meaning in our lives and actions" (Friskics, 2001a, p. 403).

Social Work and Nature

This work was not designed to be a chapter on practice, but some initial implications of this discussion for the way social work goes about its business is appropriate. Thinking and practicing with an eye toward dialoging with nature suggests a reordering of the way we conceive our traditional person/environment constructs and how we construe the idea of *relationship* within those historic models. Prominent in this reacquaintance with person-environment is the ability to integrate the many elements of land, geographical place, and physical space into a reconsideration of those things we consider having voice. Finding voice in a multiplicity of things in the natural world benefits practice because it broadens the array of natural helping systems available to promote client health and well-being. For example, in community work with children from troubled central city neighborhoods, social workers make effective use of Equine Assisted Therapy to acquaint children with the sights, sounds, smells, and voices of horses as these gentle animals speak to the deep, often hidden, sensitivity of a lonely, isolated child. Children often find the company and language of animals far more predictable and engaging than the troubled adults kids often find themselves having to accommodate (Besthorn, 2004a).

From the perspective of practice settings, dialoguing with nature suggests giving long and considered attention to the physical space where practice actually occurs. The helping agency is for many clients and staff a sterile, lifeless, and sometimes dangerous place. Our narrow conceptualization of the helping environment often precludes us from experimenting with the vocal, languaged, and tactile qualities inherent in the natural world and how they might be incorporated into the agency. While not specifically essentialist, one simple strategy to bring nature into practice settings was employed in an adolescent day-treatment program. The project sought to include as part of the ambient environment soft, subtle nature sounds and relaxing music through the facility's public address system. This replaced the raucous country/western milieu, and initial reports indicated, after some early resistance from clients and staff, a lowering of tensions and better *flow* (Saleebey, 2004) in the helping and service delivery process. The Eden Project's use of animals in nursing home settings to comfort and stimulate elderly residents shares a similar appreciation for the restorative qualities of the natural world (Nebbe, 1995).

From a macro perspective, hearing the voice of nature means taking an active role in bringing attention to efforts to silence nature's voice as well as the effect of rampant ecological degradation on the well-being of individuals and communities. When we can't conceive of the possibility of hearing the voice of earth, we fail to recognize its screams for us to pay attention. We also fall short in unmistakably hearing the plaintive wails of the most marginalized who daily face the aftermath of damaged environments and the pompous voices of the powerful claiming the poor must endure such inconvenience and suffering as the price of progress.

On a recent trip to India, I was confronted headlong with the reality that for great masses of people in this ancient land social problems are, at their heart, environmental problems. One could hear the cries of children and the almost audible growl of the few remaining trees in a *ragpickers'* community where women, children, and the disabled struggle to eke out an existence on top of a 50-foot-high garbage heap filled with the toxic remnants of both Indian and Western industrial society's progress. We literally strode across the top of this stinking colossus and watched children as young as three or four pick through the toxic, cadmium-laced remains of discarded computers that were dumped here en masse from so-called North American and European waste/refuse recyclers. The air was hot and terse with the sounds of despair, anger, and resignation.

In this place, Indian social workers developed a community action project of lower-caste women whose first task was to create living conditions that were safe and that gave residents access to sanitation, clean water, and breathable air. The second order of business was to plant trees and flowers. These efforts sought to bring back birds and insects to begin the process of healing those who otherwise lived their entire life in the drab brown stench of rotting refuse and decaying flesh. Finding a living green place to feel the pulse of nature was the top priority of this committed and ebullient group. The smell of poverty and environmental degradation is similar. It is a sickening sweet smell of putrefying animal fat, decaying soil, human sweat, and acrid urine. Social work must be, as are our Indian colleagues, at the vanguard of documenting environmental degradation and actively supporting community groups and legislation in dealing with these problems.

Conclusion

This discussion began with a review of essentialist and constructionist positions on the character of reality. It tied this discussion to the natural world and how humans both understand and move through natural space. The question for social work theory and practice is how the constructionist dilemma, as discussed here in the context of environmental philosophy, might inform our profession, which has had its own internal debate concerning both the promise and problem of constructionism. By finding a way to hear the voice of the natural world, we've concluded it seems completely possible to maintain a conceptualization of nature as external to our humanness and existing independent of cognition and language, while at the same time fully appreciating the ways humans perceive nature as deeply influenced by both cultural and cognitive factors.

If nature is to be another voice social work hears, then our understanding and use of the person-environment equation is enriched. We can marshal the healing powers of nature to help reduce stress and promote solace. We can create ambient spaces, in agency and community, which promote creativity, comfort, and collaboration—think of public gardens in this context. We can help people find their voice in relationship with the natural world when we construct that world as something vital and essential to a better quality of life. How we construct and construe nature, then, is critical for how we pursue our professional edict to strengthen the person and environment transaction.

In the end, when clearly articulated, both the essentialist and constructionist positions lead to a very similar place. Nature, whether by a multiplicity of cultural and perceptual influences or by the limits of our ability to fathom its infinite complexity and essence, shall for the most part remain a mystery to us. Perhaps the best we can do, as this chapter argues, is to bring the other's voice into the dialogue. Language does not define the human world exclusively and in the process deny the independent existence of anything outside of its construction. Dialogue, as we have come to narrowly think of it, is, indeed, not a monologue. Constructionism has sometimes confused the two.

Language can be seen as emerging from the land, from the full ecology of its sounds, sights, feelings, and movements rather than something humans impose upon it. Language, culture, and nature can interconnect in a new dance, which may help to redefine our uniqueness and commonality in relationship to others. Such an understanding of language and cognition integrated into the larger discourse of social work can bring us to a new place in membership in a global community full of new and previously unheard voices that beckon us and command our attention. Language does not have to act as a kind of unconscious collusion to keep us alienated from ourselves, others, and nature. The challenge to the constructionist debate is to make room for these new voices and to consider them in the dance of the universe rather than as novel, although new, reflections of our perceived divinity in the evolutionary order of things.

References

Abram, D. (1995). Merleau-Ponty and the voice of the earth. In M. Oelschlaeger (Ed.), *Postmodern environmental ethics* (pp. 57–77). Albany, NY: SUNY Press.

Abram, D. (1996). *The spell of the sensuous: Perception and language in a more-than-human world*. New York: Vintage Books.

Bailey, H. (2001). *Global warming and other eco-myths: How the environmental movement uses false science to scare us to death*. Washington, DC: Competitive Enterprise Institute.

Bateson G., & Bateson, M. C. (1987). *Angels fear: Towards an epistemology of the sacred*. New York: Macmillan.

Baudrillard, J. (1981). *For a critique of the political economy of the sign*. St. Louis, MO: Telos Press.

Bender, S. (2002). *Global spin: The corporate assault on environmentalism*. White River Junction, VT: Chelsea Green Publications.

Besthorn, F. H. (2001). Transpersonal psychology and deep ecological philosophy: Exploring linkages and applications for social work. *Social Thought: Journal of Religion in the Social Services, 22*(1/2), 23–44.

Besthorn, F. H. (2002a). Is it time for a new ecological approach to social work: What is the environment telling us? *The Spirituality and Social Work Forum, 9*(1), 2–5.

Besthorn, F. H. (2002b). Radical environmentalism and the ecological self: Rethinking the concept of self-identity for social work practice. *Journal of Progressive Human Services, 13*(1), 53–72.

Besthorn, F. H. (2003). Radical ecologisms: Insights for educating social workers in ecological activism and social justice. *Critical Social Work: An Interdisciplinary Journal Dedicated to Social Justice, 3*(1), 66–106. Retrieved March 1, 2003, from http://www.criticalsocialwork.com/CSW_2003_1.html

Besthorn, F. H. (2004a). Beetles, bullfrogs and butterflies: Contributions of natural environment to childhood development and resilience. In M. Ungar (Ed.), *Pathways to resilience: A handbook of theory, methods and interventions* (pp. 106–127). Thousand Oaks, CA: Sage.

Besthorn, F. H. (2004b). Restorative justice and environmental restoration—Twin pillars of a just global environmental policy: Hearing the voice of the victim. *Journal of Societal and Social Policy, 3*(2), 33–48.

Besthorn, F. H., & Canda, E. R. (2002). Revisioning environment: Deep ecology for education and teaching in social work. *Journal of Teaching in Social Work, 22*(1/2), 79–101.

Besthorn, F. H., & McMillen, D. P. (2002). The oppression of women and nature: Ecofeminism as a framework for a social justice oriented social work. *Families in Society: The Journal of Contemporary Human Services, 83*(3), 221–232.

Besthorn, F. H., & Saleebey, D. (2003). Nature, genetics and the biophilia connection: Exploring linkages with social work values and practice. *Advances in Social Work, 4*(1), 1–18.

Bhaskar, R. (1989). *The possibility of naturalism.* Hemel Hempstead, UK: Harvester Wheatsheaf Publishing.

Bird, E. A. (1987). The social construction of nature: Theoretical approaches to the history of environmental problems. *Environmental Review, 11*(3), 255–264.

Borgmann, A. (1984). *Technology and the character of contemporary life: A philosophical inquiry*. Chicago: University of Chicago Press.

Borgmann, A. (1995). The nature of reality and the reality of nature. In M. Soule & G. Lease (Eds.), *Reinventing nature? Responses to postmodern deconstruction* (pp. 31–46). Washington, DC: Island Press.

Bugbee, H. (1958). *The inward morning: A philosophical exploration in journal form*. State College, PA: Bald Eagle Press.

Bugbee, H. (1962). *Thoughts on creation: Essays in philosophy*. State College, PA: Pennsylvania State University Press.

Callicott, J. B. (1997). *Earth insights: A survey of ecological ethics from the Mediterranean basin to the Australian outback*. Berkeley: University of California Press.

Chaloupka, W., & Cawley, R. M. (1993). The great wild hope: Nature, environmentalism, and the open secret. In J. Bennett & W. Chaloupka (Eds.), *In the nature of things: Language, politics, and the environment* (pp. 4–18). Minneapolis: University of Minnesota Press.

Cheney, J. (1989). Postmodern environmental ethics: Ethics as bioregional narrative. *Environmental Ethics, 20*(3), 117–134.

Coates, J. (2003). *Ecology and social work: Toward a new paradigm*. Halifax, Nova Scotia: Fernwood Books.

Collier, A. (1994). *Critical realism: An introduction to Roy Bhaskar's philosophy*. London: Verso Publishing.

Cronon, W. (1996). Introduction. In W. Cronon (Ed.), *Uncommon ground: Rethinking the human place in nature* (pp. 1–11). New York: Norton.

Ehrlich, P. R., & Ehrlich, A. H. (1998). *Betrayal of science and reason: How anti-environmental rhetoric threatens our future*. Washington, DC: Island Press.

Eliade M. (1972). *Shamanism: Archaic techniques of ecstasy*. Princeton, NJ: Princeton University Press.

Franklin, C. (1998). Distinctions between social constructionism and cognitive constructivism: Practice applications. In C. Franklin and P. S. Nurius (Eds.), *Constructivism in practice: Methods and challenges* (pp. 57–94). Milwaukee, WI: Families International Press.

Franklin, C., & Nurius, P. (1998). *Constructivism in practice: Methods and challenges*. Milwaukee, WI: Families International Press.

Friskics, S. (2001a). Dialogical relations with nature. *Environmental Ethics, 23*(4), 391–410.

Friskics, S. (2001b). How does nature speak to our concern? The case of Montana's rocky mountain front. In L. Kaplan (Ed.), *Philosophy and everyday life* (pp. 201–226). New York: Seven Bridges Press.

Gergen, K. (1985). The social constructionist movement in modern psychology. *American Psychologist, 40*(3), 266–275.

Germain, C. B. (1978). General-systems theory and ego psychology: An ecological perspective. *Social Service Review, 52*(4), 535–550.

Germain, C. B. (1979). Introduction: Ecology and social work. In C. B. Germain (Ed.), *Social work practice, people and environments: An ecological perspective* (pp. 3–22). New York: Columbia University Press.

Germain, C. B. (1980). Social context of clinical social work. *Social Work, 25*(6), 483–488.

Germain, C. B. (1991). *Human behavior in the social environment: An ecological view*. New York: Columbia University Press.

Germain, C. B., & Gitterman, A. (1980). *The life model of social work practice*. New York: Columbia University Press.

Greene, G. J., Jensen, C., & Jones, D. H. (1996). A constructivist perspective on clinical social work practice with ethnically diverse clients. *Social Work, 41*(2), 172–180.

Guidano, V. F. (1991). *The self in process: Toward a post-rationalist cognitive therapy*. New York: Guilford Press.

Hannigan, J. (1995). *Environmental sociology: A social constructionist perspective*. London: Routledge.

Haraway, D. (1988). Situated knowledge: The science question in feminism and the privilege of partial perspective. *Feminist Studies, 14*(3), 575–599.

Hayles, K. (1991). Constrained constructivism: Locating scientific inquiry in the theater of representation. *New Orleans Review, 18*(1), 76–85.

Hayles, K. (1995). Searching for common ground. In M. Soule & G. Lease (Eds.), *Reinventing nature: Responses to postmodern deconstruction* (pp. 47–64). Washington, DC: Island Press.

Heidegger, M. (1967). *Being and time* (J. Macquarrie & E. Robinson, Trans.). Oxford, UK: Basil Blackwell. (Original work published 1927)

Heidegger, M. (1972). *On time and being* (J. Stambaugh, Trans). New York: Harper & Row. (Original work published 1969)

Helvarg, D. (2004). *The war against the greens: The wise use movement, the new right, and the browning of America*. Boulder, CO: Johnson Publishing.

Huber, P. (2000). *Hard green: Saving the environment from the environmentalists—A conservative manifesto.* New York: Basic Books.

Kahn, M., & Scher, S. (2002). Infusing content on the physical environment into the BSW curriculum. *The Journal of Baccalaureate Social Work, 7*(2), 1–14.

Kidner, D. W. (2000). Fabricating nature: A critique of the social construction of nature. *Environmental Ethics, 22*(4), 339–359.

Kleinman, A. (1988). *Rethinking psychiatry: From cultural category to personal experience*. New York: Free Press.

Kleinman, A. (1997). Everything that really matters: Social suffering, subjectivity, and the remaking of human experience in a disordered world. *Harvard Theological Review, 90*(4), 328–343.

Leopold, A. (1949). *The Sand County almanac: And sketches here and there*. London: Oxford University Press.

Lomborg, B. (2002). *The skeptical environmentalist: Measuring the real state of the world*. Boston, MA: Cambridge University Press.

Macnaghten P., & Urry, J. (1998). *Contested natures*. London: Sage.

Mahoney. M. J. (1991). *Human change processes: The scientific foundations of psychotherapy*. New York: Basic Books.

Marguilis, L. (1994). Living by Gaia. In J. White (Ed.), *Talking on the water: Conservations about nature and creativity* (pp. 57–78). San Francisco: Sierra Club Books.

Merleau-Ponty, M. (1962). *Phenomenology of perception* (C. Smith, Trans.). London: Routledge & Kegan Paul. (Original work published 1945)

Merleau-Ponty, M. (1964). *The primacy of perception*. Evanston, IL: Northwestern University Press.

Merleau-Ponty, M. (1968). *The visible and the invisible* (A. Lingis, Trans.). Evanston, IL: Northwestern University Press. (Original work published 1964)

Middleman, R. R., & Wood, G. G. (1993). So much for the bell curve: Construction, power/conflict, and the structural approach to direct practice in social work. *Journal of Teaching in Social Work, 8*(1/2), 129–146.

Morrison, N. C. (1997). Narratives of change: Teaching from a social constructionist perspective. *Journal of Systemic Therapies, 16*(1), 83–92.

Murphy, R. (1995). Sociology as if nature did not matter: An ecological critique. *The British Journal of Sociology, 46*(4), 688–707.

Nebbe, L. L. (1995). *Nature as a guide: Nature in counseling, therapy, and education*. Minneapolis, MN: Educational Media Press.

Pegg, J. R. (2003). *No new wilderness rule opens Tongass to loggers*. Environmental News Service, March, 2003. Retrieved April 16, 2003, from http://ens-news.com/ens/mar2003

Pope, C., & Rauber, P. (2004). *Strategic ignorance: Why the Bush administration is recklessly destroying a century of environmental progress*. San Francisco: Sierra Club Books.

Preston, C. J. (2000). Conversing with nature in a postmodern epistemological framework. *Environmental Ethics, 22*(3), 227–240.

Reiss, T. (1982). *The discourse of modernism*. Ithaca, NY: Cornell University Press.

Robbins, S. P., Chatterjee, P., & Canda, E. R. (1998). *Contemporary human behavior theory: A critical perspective for social work*. Boston, MA: Allyn and Bacon.

Rodwell, M. K. (1998). *Social work constructivist research*. New York: Garland Publishing.

Rogge, M. E. (2000). Children, poverty, and environmental degradation: Protecting current and future generations. *Social Development Issues, 22*(2/3), 46–53.

Rolston, H. (1997). Nature for real: Is nature a social construct? In T. J. Chappell (Ed.), *The philosophy of environment* (pp. 42–67). Edinburgh, Scotland: Edinburgh University Press.

Saleebey, D. (1993). Notes on interpreting the human condition: A "constructed" HBSE curriculum. *Journal of Teaching in Social Work, 8*(1/2), 197–217.

Saleebey, D. (2001). *Human behavior and social environments: A biopsychosocial approach*. New York: Columbia University Press.

Saleebery, D. (2004). The power of place: Another look at the environment. *Families in Society: The Journal of Contemporary Human Services, 85*(1), 7–16.

Shepard, P. (1994). The unreturning arrow. In J. White (Ed.), *Talking on the water: Conversations about nature and creativity* (pp. 205–227). San Francisco: Sierra Club Books.

Shepard, P. (1995). Virtually hunting reality in the forests of simulacra. In M. Soule & G. Lease (Eds.), *Reinventing nature? Responses to postmodern deconstruction* (pp. 17–30). Washington, DC: Island Press.

Soule, M. E., & Lease, G. (Eds.). (1995). *Reinventing nature? Responses to postmodern deconstruction*. Washington, DC: Island Press.

Snyder, G. (1990). *The practice of the wild*. San Francisco: North Point Press.

Snyder, G. (1994). Hanging out with raven. In J. White (Ed.), *Talking on the water: Conversations about nature and creativity* (pp. 137–156). San Francisco: Sierra Club Books.

Tangenberg, K. M., & Kemp, S. (2002). Embodied practice: Claiming the body's experience, agency, and knowledge for social work. *Social Work, 47*(1), 9–18.

Ungar, M. (2002). A deeper more ecological social work practice. *Social Service Review, 76*(3), 480–497.

Williams, T. (2000, May/June). False forests. *Mother Jones*, pp. 72–79.

Wolf, D. (2000). Social work and speciesism. *Social Work, 45*(1), 88–93.

Worster, D. (1995). Nature and the disorder of history. In M. Soule & G. Lease (Eds.), *Reinventing nature? Responses to postmodern deconstruction* (pp. 65–85). Washington, DC: Island Press.

Zapf, M. K. (2002, June). *The spiritual dimension of person and environment: Perspectives from social work and traditional knowledge*. Paper presented at the First Canadian Conference on Spirituality and Social Work, Toronto, Ontario, Canada.

CHAPTER 9

Art Works

Between Social Critique and Active Reenchantment

ADRIENNE CHAMBON

In this chapter* I attempt to work through a question that has been central in the Transforming Social Work meetings in Vermont: How do we speak "truths" to one another? What place(s) do we occupy, and what voice(s) can we speak with in social work in light of the sociopolitical configuration of these times? How do we tell, how do we write, how do we see, how do we listen? What approaches can be helpful and exciting if we want to engage actively with social realities?

I have chosen as a point of entry a project on the creation and re-creation of social ties that was part of the social service and community response to refugee newcomers—a research and training project I conducted with colleagues in Toronto in partnership with the Canadian Centre for Victims of Torture (CCVT) (Chambon, McGrath, Shapiro, Abai, Dudziak, & Dremetsikas,

*I wish to thank the *Social Sciences and Humanities Research Council of Canada* for funding; Nadya Martin for introducing me to the writings of Maxine Green; Ruth Dean, Deborah Knott, Dennis Saleebey, and Stan Witkin for their helpful suggestions.

2001). I wish to convey some of the learning from this project by using a particular language that, though it is not devoid of an argumentative construction, draws on literary and artistic works to bring up some points.

Some of the early thoughts and images that sustain this work were presented in the arts and social work group that came together in one of the early Vermont meetings. This was one of the first audiences in which the participants experimented with imagination, enthusiasm, half-thoughts, beginnings. This has been a wonderful source of support. Throughout the years, the arts, in various formats (narrative and poetry, theater, music, visual arts) have been an ongoing, if not growing, strand of the Transforming Social Work meetings—present at times as one of the objectives, other times, as an inspiration, a language, a mode of communication.

In this chapter, I focus on images and themes associated with disruption and displacement, transit and passages in refugee lives. The art connection is an easy one in regard to the CCVT, and it is congruent with the centre's activities. In our early contacts, the research team was invited by agency staff to attend the play *Come Good Rain*, which was written and performed by Ugandan playwright George Seremba. The play tells the story of Seremba's growing up under a repressive regime, his arrest, his torture, and his flight out of the country. Following the performance, CCVT staff members led a discussion with the audience. Additionally, arts-based activities are routinely held at the centre, some having an explicit therapeutic aim (art therapy), others sustaining community functions and celebrations. In our research and training materials, we used art works that had been created at the centre.

I have selected certain stories, poems, images from a film and from a video installation because they speak to the substance and process of the many conversations we held throughout all the years of the project with refugees, clients, staff members, and volunteers. Their focus is on forced displacement (not on torture). These literary and art works are filtered through associations and resonance with my personal and social lives. This feels like risky writing, but it is an attempt to represent situations other than is usually done in social work.

The Limits of Academic Critique in Social Work

MEDIA-BASED STORIES

Earlier, I wrote that it troubled me when social workers reproduce, most often unwittingly, established canons in discussing social issues. Structurally, social work is intensely responsive to (if not downright embedded in) contemporary concerns (Chambon, 1994). Thus, it is very easy for social workers to restate, as if they were our own, the terms of understanding that are privileged in other arenas, whether political, journalistic, bureaucratic, or economic. In particular, we tend to dismiss as unimportant the evidence that the media and their multiple relays are one of the important fabricators of representations. Although the nature and performance of media discourse have been criticized from within the communication field for aiming to shock, to disturb, to provoke horror and disgust among viewers, nevertheless, we, as social workers, draw upon such sources in designing our courses, in giving talks, in writing papers. We might do well to consider that the reporting of war and atrocities is tied to the media's commercial success, and that the forms of reporting make the events seem strangely haphazard, confusing, chaotic, and lacking justification. This is largely attributable to decontextualizing and dehistoricizing the "stories," accentuating the psychological features while downplaying the socioeconomic circumstances (Perlstein, 2004; Sontag, 2003).

Further, the repetition and recycling of horrendous images result in numbing the audiences that are being bombarded day after day, hour after hour, with accounts of death and devastation. Sontag (2003) argues that the sheer profusion of stereotypical accounts and imagery conveys to the viewers that whatever the circumstances, the settings, the national contexts, nothing has changed and nothing can change. The events reflect the nature of human beings, of political regimes, of global processes of exploitation. Such stories are foreclosed and inevitably demobilizing. By playing echo to these forms, social work shuts down the possibility of understanding situations in alternative social work ways.

CRITICAL ANALYTICS

Another type of limitation stems from academic practices. Here, we encounter an old cruelty linked to the meticulousness with which critical analytics takes things apart, objectifying social processes while casting aside the realm of personal commitments and of feelings. One of the outcomes of a certain kind of intellectual critique is then distancing, disillusionment, or "disenchantment from the world," as Bourdieu (e.g., 1998) repeatedly said. By persistently stripping the caring activities of their generous but problematic assumptions and focusing adamantly on their controlling effects, the literature on governmentality (e.g., Burchell, Gordon, & Miller, 1991; Rose & Miller, 1992) that I myself draw on, suggests the negation of professional practices and encourages the loosening of professional ties.

Subjective analytics do not fare so much better in this respect. In some of my work, I have grappled with the mode of exposition that I am using. In my wish to convey, as much as analyze, the dehumanizing effects of contemporary professional practices, I have tried to describe institutional operations intimately (Chambon, 2000, 2001). Such reflexive accounts are able to evoke up close and with greater intensity the strength of Liliputian strings, these so-named standards to which we are curiously attached. Initially, this mode of writing brings forth a sense of excitement because it shows the common institutional mechanisms and predicaments that enclose practitioners and clients. From this perspective, workers share with clients (and clients with workers) comparable forms of alienation, deprivation, disappropriation. Thus, we can think of a potential of new alliances between clients and workers. Yet, even then, this mode of writing does not move us very far toward a position of hope and possibility. I have found that it becomes unbearable to take apart, segment after segment, the minute actions of the social worker filling in a report, checking a preestablished form, increasing the pace of meetings where no one truly meets anyone, counting and accounting for the number of minutes of interactional speech, "processing" a meeting into data. In the act of telling about them, these institutional gestures are thrust upon the teller.

There lies a peculiar risk: to stay constrained in the very act of writing within the limits that shrink reality. Such writing tends to leave me, and most likely many readers, burdened with the weight of the world.

Changing Forms of Representation

In his October 2000 editorial in the journal *Social Work*, Stan Witkin urged us to consider alternative ways of writing: "The way we write is important, very important to how we learn and what we know" (Witkin, 2000, p. 389). Decrying the historical split between the sciences and the humanities, Witkin reminded us that in a humanities perspective, language "might be used to express, explore, analyze and create" (p. 389). He added: "If writing is a form of practice and inquiry, then alternate forms of writing are like different methodologies in their ability to generate different social realities" (p. 391). Witkin clearly identified that social work faced a challenge of representation. He urged us to invite "subjects" as real people in our texts, and to begin to author(ize) meaning in the way we voice our views so that we can expand our movements.

British sociologists John Law and John Urry (2004) state that "the disciplines of the social are themselves social practices that simply form another part of the social world" (p. 391). Historicizing knowledge, they argue that social science methods cannot maintain the position they held at their origins, in the 19th century, and necessarily evolve. This is also true of the physical sciences. The American sociologist Immanuel Wallerstein's (2004) collaboration with the chemist Ilya Prigogine helped him understand how the concepts of complexity and unpredictability over time have become common knowledge in chemistry. Therefore, Law and Urry contend:

> Social inquiry and its methods are productive; they (help to) *make* social realities and social worlds. They do not simply describe the world as it is, but also enact it. . . . These are performative. By this we mean that they have effects; they make differences; they enact realities; and they can help to bring into being what they also discover. (pp. 390–393)

After citing feminist theoretician of science Donna Haraway, they conclude with the question: "Is it possible to imagine social science method as a *system of interference*?" (p. 397). They then begin to formulate the following suggestions:

> the possible need to imagine a fluid and decentred social science, with fluid and decentred modes for *knowing the world allegorically, indirectly, perhaps pictorially, sensuously, poetically, a social science of partial connections* [italics added]. (p. 400)

Howard Goldstein repeatedly invited social workers to move out of the disembodied territory of abstractions and to confront dilemmas in living. In writing on the ethics of education, he raised the important questions, "Learning to be a social worker in a time of drastic change. How does this occur? What does one need to know?" And critically, "How does one learn?" (Goldstein,

1998, p. 241). He saw social work as a performing art (p. 247) and continuously advocated for turning to the arts and to literature to address social work's main philosophical concerns.

In *Releasing the Imagination: Essays on Education, the Arts and Social Change*, educator Maxine Green (1995), who had an important influence on Goldstein, wrote that it is now vital to counter social numbing and the closing of relational and social possibilities. "The emphasis on technical education, the perspective of standards, achievements, benchmarks reinforces repetition of the already known. This makes us feel even more helpless, and remain unresponsive. This approach results in 'freezing' our imagination. Ideas of possibilities are trapped in predictability" (p. 124).

In regard to the media, she added:

> Today's media present audiences with predigested concepts and images in fixed frameworks.[. . .] Our young, like us, their elders, inhabit a world of fearful moral uncertainty—a world where it appears that almost nothing can be done to reduce suffering, contain massacres, and protect human rights. The faces of refugee children in search of their mothers, of teen-age girls raped repeatedly by soldiers, of rootless people staring at burned churches and libraries. (p. 124)

She, too, concluded by saying:

> We need to recognize that events that make up aesthetic experiences are events that occur within and by means of the transactions with our environment that situate us in time and space. Some say that participatory encounters with paintings, dances, stories, and all other art forms enable us to recapture a lost spontaneity. Breaking through the frames of presuppositions and conventions, we are enabled to recapture the processes of our becoming. [. . .] [We are] made aware of ourselves as questioners, as meaning makers, as

> persons engaged in constructing and reconstructing realities with those around us. (p. 130)

Several attempts have been made in this direction. I will mention one here, Jane Gorman's (1993) article, "Postmodernism and the Conduct of Inquiry in Social Work." Using her voice as an embodied author, Gorman carefully catalyzed emotional resonance, imagery, and literature to demonstrate the relational challenges of working with fragile clients in a mental health center, and in conducting research. Reporting on her own work with great sensitivity made for a different kind of writing. Her article was moving, rigorous, caring, and highly inspirational to a number of readers.

Explorations

In recent years I have been exploring ways of communicating social experiences, what I call "ways of telling" through art forms and art practices with a view to expanding our approaches to knowledge. In an earlier publication with Allan Irving (Chambon & Irving, 2003), I explored the art works of Mark Rothko, Cindy Sherman, and Helena Hietanen to discuss how the works of these artists address emotional complexity and turbulence, social stereotypes and strategies to displace them, and the beauty and strength of ordinary materials and daily gestures, the latter remarkably converging with Ann Weick's (2000) "Hidden Voices" article in *Social Work*. This questioning is not unique to our field. The art world has been invited, similarly, to explore a "reenchantment of art" (Gablik, 1991) as a way of avoiding saturated commentaries and foreclosed narratives.

Fundamentally, I have become more deeply aware that the nature of trauma does not lend itself easily to verbalization, and that imagery and stories, if not allegories, work powerfully well in this context. This chapter represents an extension of the project. This time, however, it draws upon images and texts from outside the study. Yet, some strands remain and serve as pathways to these new thoughts and images. The strands or traces of the project are indicated with a different type style, italic, whose shape signals the movement of words in time.

A DIFFERENT KIND OF WRITING

Embodied ties connect me to refugees in a very immediate manner. Several images have come to me over time in thinking about my intense engagement with the CCVT. *The project required that each one of us introduce ourselves and our connection to the work, that we situate ourselves to one another, and locate our commitment.*

I think of myself as a stateless person, a young child, nationless within borders, tucked inside those seams, the daughter of a refugee. Multiple languages have always been spoken around me recalling multiple referents. These places are unseen, inaccessible. When I turned 10, and with a change in our family situation, we received traveling papers. We crossed the ocean and moved to New York. Before, as long as we did not step outside the contours of that nation that I learned to draw with colored pencils at school, as long as I did not stray outside its shores, I could move about, but not more than that.

BRIDGES

The CCVT has been offering art therapy for a number of years. Mary Sanderson, who had established the program, invited the participants to draw a number of figures, in particular, a bridge that would represent their journey, past and present. Many painted a bridge that arched over water. Some told the story of their crossing. Some depicted a group of people on one side, with a single figure on the other. Many structures were interrupted, unfinished in a state of construction or else in disrepair, waiting endlessly for patching up. Some bridges floated in the air. Some were drawn above a chasm. Many could not be crossed.

Leaving Atlantis is a video created by Julia Winckler, social worker and now photographer, and video artist Nerea Martinez de Lecea (2002). Using images, texts, songs, and sounds, the work "explores the experience of having become uprooted from one's place of origin" and "is based on the central themes of loss of home and cultural displacement" (Winckler, 2004). I saw it, along with Julia's other memory work, *Spuren/Traces*, exhibited at the Maison Heinrich Heine at the Cité Internationale Universitaire in Paris, in May 2003. The video, *Leaving Atlantis*, opens with the dreamlike image of a wide bed with its tall, dark wooden frame and long white sheets trailing in the ocean, picking up water, becoming weightier, gently rising and falling with the waves, drifting away from the shore as night falls, slowly, getting darker. The water is cold, the trace of a warm body is vividly present in the rumpled white sheets. Where is home?

A couple of lines from a poem came back to me as I worked with the CCVT. They are from a series of poems for children written by the French surrealist poet Robert Desnos (1955), *Chantefables et Chantefleurs*. They are short compositions, stories and parables that wind themselves around the figure of an animal, a plant, or a flower. Some have been put to music. Several have been anthologized in school textbooks (Chabanne, 1996). The poems were bedtime readings for me. I chose two poems that speak of memory and amnesia, imprints on the body and on the soul. Next to the poems are my translations.

Desnos said that of all of his writings, these poems would outlive him and circulate for a while. He did not see these poems in print. He wrote them during the Second World War and died of typhus at the Terezien concentration camp in Czechoslovakia in 1945. It is the last lines of *The Zebra* that I thought of repeatedly as I was working with the CCVT, and which compelled me to look up his book again: "The prison cell upon his hide has left the imprint of its bars."

LE MYOSOTIS	FORGET-ME-NOT
Ayant perdu toute mémoire	Having lost its memory
Un myosotis s'ennuyait	The forget-me-not felt bored
Voulait-il conter une histoire?	Whenever it wished to tell a story,
Dès le début, il l'oubliait	From the onset, it had forgotten all
Pas de passé, pas d'avenir	With no past no future
Myosotis sans souvenir	Forget-me-not with no remembrance

LE ZÈBRE	THE ZEBRA
Le zèbre, cheval des ténèbres	The zebra, horse of darkness
Lève le pied, ferme les yeux	Raises his hoof, shuts his eyes
Et fait résonner ses vertèbres	With the joyful sound of his neighs
En hennissant d'un air joyeux.	Under the bright sun of Barbary
Au clair soleil de Barbarie,	He then strides out of the stable
Il sort alors de l'écurie	Grazes on the pasture field
Et va brouter dans la prairie	The blades of witchcraft
Les herbes de sorcellerie	But the prison cell upon his hide
Mais la prison sur son pelage,	Has left the imprint of its bars
a laissé l'ombre du grillage	

PORTRAITS

It was Julia who introduced me to the work of Attie (1998a). *Portraits of Exile*, created by American artist Shimon Attie, in collaboration with Mathias Maile, was staged in Copenhagen in June and July 1995. It was part of the European *Sights Unseen*: a series of nine boxes, 1.6 m x 1.8 m, covered with transparent (Duratrans) material, were placed on the water of the Børsgraven Canal in Copenhagen and exhibited for a period of six to seven weeks. The boxes were submerged under a meter of water and lit from the inside so they could be seen by night and by day. In each box was the face of a refugee. Relying on archival documents, Attie had selected black-and-white photographs of refugees who escaped in 1943 when the Danish government openly supported the policy of assisting refugees in reaching Scandinavia, which they mostly did by crossing this canal. Not all faces were from that period. Among the nine, there were also contemporary photographs taken 55 years later of asylum seekers from the former Yugoslavia.

These faces with names were not locked in a museum, housed inside some walls, tucked into a file, entombed in an archive. The boxes floated close to the bank, in a row, at equal distance from one another, anchored to the bottom of the canal. They were in an open, temporary state, moving about, affected by the changing light of the day. They were there when the evening lights burned brightly, they were silhouetted in dark waters at night, they reflected the clouds and the sky during the day. As one walked close to the water at a soothing pace, these lit objects, these faces, appeared one by one, each different.

Close up, one saw that additional images had been overlaid on the faces. On his forehead one man carried the image of the boat that took him across the border. The face of a woman was partly covered by the stamp of her passport. The brutal, bureaucratic stamp pounded on a corner of her chin, on a birth date, left a bluish mark. The materiality of her journey and the impossibility of her journey were shown simultaneously.

We are face to face. I look down, she looks up. Her face is lined with age. Upon these lines, the lines of her passport. Her stamped face is not sealed. It moves gently in the water, its wrinkles sink and surface. She is not submerged, as Primo Levi (1986/1989) distinguished between the "drowned" (*sommersi*) and the "saved." We look at each other in a prolonged silence. Who am I, staring in such a way, searching for what? What am I looking for? The fiction of the representation attracts and repels me once I decipher the objects. These lit boxes of faces and stamps float at an unsafe distance, a moving distance.

The floating faces remind me of the Fayum portraits from Egypt, named after the region where they were initially found, a lake area south of Cairo, west of the Nile River. These portraits of men, women, and children, painted on precious wood or on linen cloth, were placed on the mummies as funeral portraits that accompanied the dead to the other side. Superimposed on the actual face of the deceased, these life-size portraits of middle-class and lower-income classes, were made during the lifetime of the person. Far from being stylized, hieratic representations, they were meant to be identical to the living. Painted with delicate colors made of pigments and wax, they still seem lifelike with their uneven features, showing delicate moods and character. Created during the post-Hellenistic era when Egypt was controlled by the Roman Empire (first to fourth centuries AD), they show a strong Greco-Roman cultural influence. Departing from the Egyptian tradition of depicting human figures in profile, the Fayum portraits were painted facing the viewer. These portraits were not meant to be looked at. They are the ones looking out, facing their passage, serious, quizzical, determined, sad, showing signs of fatigue. As if we had just drawn a curtain and taken a momentary glimpse of them.

Among the many commentaries made of the Fayum portraits (e.g., Bailly, 1997), an article (Ryan, 1998) in the Egyptian newspaper *Al-Ahram*, following an exhibit at the Museum of Cairo, speaks of the writer's startling surprise in contemplating these personalized portraits after more than 2,000 years. The realism of the art, along with the fadings and running colors that convey movement and fluidity, erases the distance in time, bringing these portraits into the present. He says:

> Make no mistake, these are real people, and disturbingly so because they remain, across the millennia, recognizable. And it is the moment of recognition that provides the first shock. The idiom is just too modern for such ancient

> objects, too impressionistic, too fleeting to have survived. These faces frown, foreheads wrinkle, eyes fix the spectator with a mournful gaze. (Ryan, 1998, p. 1)

Author and art theoretician John Berger (2002) further suggested that the discovery of these paintings is particularly poignant to us because our period is characterized by vast movements of migration and displacement and filled with great uncertainty. He wrote, "And so they gaze on us, the Fayum portraits, like the missing of our own century" (p. 60).

FACING INSTITUTIONS AND POLITICS

Shimon Attie was criticized in some quarters for collapsing past and present photographs in a single exhibit, as if he neutralized the remarkable rescue of refugees that took place in 1943 by combining it with the troubling situation of today. In a graduate seminar at the New York Institute of Photography, Attie (1998b) pointed out that he had carefully chosen the location of his installation, not far from the Danish Parliament building and the Department of Foreign Affairs, those places of power where decisions are made about who is to stay, who is to go. He argued that such a public installation could not simply be the object of a celebration, since a resolution to these recurring situations had not yet been found. The legislations that are currently being passed in different parts of the world, including in Denmark, seem to be taking back what was once accomplished. Who cared then, who cares now?

Italian film director Nanni Moretti interjected a powerful scene in his film *Aprile* (1998), which interrupts the flow of the rest of the film, that depicts situations of domestic life. In that unique scene, Moretti is documenting one of those recurring events. A boat has been stopped close to the Italian shore with Albanians attempting to land and seek asylum in Italy. The sequence departs from the habitual media imagery. It is at once more muted and more extreme. It shows a large ship gliding slowly, coming closer to the shore, with a compact group of men, women, and children hanging on to the deck, pressed tightly together. It is difficult to imagine that so many people can actually stand on a single ship. The film turns abruptly silent. The scene is soundless, in stark contrast to the bustle of the other scenes. Transfixed, suspended in that stillness, holding our breath, we look on at the ever slow movement of the tall ship, or maybe it is the effect of the camera zooming in. We stare at this group of humans that stand together, exhausted, with a serious expression on their faces. They do not know what the outcome of their journey will be; neither do we. Will they be allowed to disembark? Will they be turned back?

Moretti's mute image goes against the serialized images of small boats capsizing that we have been shown and told about over and over again (not that these do not exist), and that reiterate in looplike fashion the theme of victimization (Wright, 2002). He shows us a more solid, somber reality, determination and indeterminacy brought together in a prolonged image that cuts the viewer's breath, making all sound vanish.

Recently, the CCVT drafted a statement in response to the security and immigration legislations that were being proposed by the Canadian government. Developing a response for a globalized world, the statement attempts to lean on national and international charters, signed agreements on human rights, and stated values of democracy.

POETICS AND POLITICS

At the end of April 2004, CCVT staff circulated an E-mail informing us that the speakers from Rwanda who were supposed to be in Toronto the first week of May and were scheduled to give a presentation at the centre had been denied entry into Canada. Their visas were not delivered to them in time, though their visit had been planned for several months. The announcement came the day before the event and ended with two short sentences: "The event has been cancelled. No future date has been set."

Uruguyan writer Eduardo Galeano was in exile during the country's military regime between the 1970s and 1985, for close to 10 years until it was safe enough to go back to Latin America. On the task of the writer, he said in an interview (Sherman, 2000): "Working to unmask reality, to unveil it. *Ayudar a ver*: To help to see. That is the main function of art." He added,

> As for writers, they must be honest individuals who don't use literature as a commercial tool, but rather as a way of expressing the words that must be said. That, for me, is fundamental. The words that deserve to be said are the ones that are born of the need to say them. That is all I ask of people who write; the rest is less important.

In the same interview, he added:

> I write only when I feel the need to write, not because my conscience dictates it. It doesn't just come from my indignation at injustice: it is a celebration of life, which is so beautifully horrible and horribly beautiful.

The Book of Embraces by Eduardo Galeano (1989/1991), in its English translation by Cedric Belfrage, was given to me by Mulugeta Abai, director of the CCVT, who liked this work a lot. The centre had received a box full of copies of this volume, which had been awarded the Lannan Prize for Cultural Freedom.

In *The Book of Embraces*, Galeano achieves an appealing blend of tones, debunking totalitarianism, colonial rule, and military regimes, offering extreme gentleness, humorous reversals, and passionate encounters. Personal and political, his writing awakens us joyfully, outrageously from our slumber.

In the book Galeano cites several graffiti scribbled by ordinary people on the walls of South American cities, which he read as he walked by.

From "The Walls Speak" (p. 101):

> In Buenos Aires on La Boca Bridge: *Everybody makes promises and nobody keeps them. Vote for nobody.*
>
> In Caracas, during a time of crisis, at the entrance to one of the poorest barrios: *Welcome, middle class.*
>
> In Bogotá, around the corner from National University: *God lives.*
> And underneath, in a different hand: *By a sheer miracle.*
>
> And also in Bogotá: *Proletarians of all lands unite!*
> And underneath, in a different hand: *(Final notice.)*

In "Forgotten Dreams" he offers beauty and ideals with great tenderness:

> Helena dreamed she had left her forgotten dreams on an island.
>
> Claribel Alegria gathered Helena's dreams together, tied them up with a ribbon, and put them away for safekeeping.
>
> But her children discovered the hiding place and wanted to try on Helena's dreams. Claribel told them very crossly: "*Don't even touch them.*"
>
> Then she called Helena on the phone and asked her: "*What should I do with your dreams?*" (p. 47)

Reflecting Back

I have attempted to draw sidelines to our research, or perhaps lifelines. They do not provide a comprehensive network of images, linking every finding and relational feature of our work with the CCVT. They provide a number of openings to that work for ourselves and in communicating with others.

The works I chose "came to me" by association with the content and form of many conversations I took part in at the CCVT. They deal with questions of memory and traces of things passed, of being in between worlds, metaphorically, also physically. They address displacement, lack of home, seeking home. They include institutional decisions that shape the course of persons' lives: crossing a border or not; obtaining a passport or being sent back; knowing and not knowing what will be one's fate. They convey personal and group experiences.

Neither pure enchantment nor pure analytics. The artists were careful in documenting events, people's lives, and situations, which they could then transpose into a representation. Winckler and Martinez de Lecea's video segment (2003) conveys a condensation of fantasies in a dreamlike manner that is more "real" than a realistic scene. This requires an extensive knowledge and familiarity with the issue. Desnos's imprint of the prison bars on a zebra's hide can be juxtaposed to a particular institution of power, such as the site of Attie's exhibit, connecting then explicitly personal experience with legislative ruling. The faces floating in the river provoke the strolling person to no longer view the canal as an innocuous body of water, but to consider the historical traces of how it has been used, how it has saved lives, to wonder about the actual people who have crossed it, and to further wonder about the future of current families who are facing the same situation.

In his autobiographical film, Moretti (1998) inserted the boat sequence, which becomes the source of a question: To what extent do we consider social situations that are common to groups of people (but that we do not share at the moment) to be part of our lives? What is our life made of? The boat scene positions the viewer, the filmmaker, and actor as subjects observing the large ship, and the group of people seeking asylum as other subjects whose posture and expression raise a serious question. In showing their faces taut and worried, the filmmaker conveys simultaneously the distance to them and human proximity. The men, women, and children seeking asylum are not shown as victims. They are not subjected to terror. The scene is not horrific, but it is seriously troubling. We can look at them, they can look at us. Beyond empathy, we are faced with an open and unresolved person-to-person address (Levinas, 1995/1999), a human and political dilemma.

What these works achieve, including the poems and their mixed genres, is to derail the possibility of a fundamental divide between "them," the other, and us. This is in deep contrast to the models espoused by the media, a point that Susan Sontag (2003) makes in regard to journalistic conventions in *Regarding the Pain of Others*. She argues that among the rules for creating images of war, there are differences opposing European and North American with "distant others, colonized":

> This journalistic custom inherits the centuries-old practice of exhibiting exotic—that is, colonized—human beings. [. . .] The exhibition in photographs of cruelties inflicted on those with darker complexions in exotic countries continues this offering, oblivious to the considerations that deter such displays of our own victims of violence; for the other, even when not an enemy, is regarded only as someone to be seen, not someone (like us) who also sees. (p. 72)

The aim of the works that I discussed is not empathy with the immigrants and refugees We do not become them, nor can we. Yet, while we are not them, they are not outsiders, excluded, or abnormals, as Foucault (1999/2003) would put it.

The kinds of works I have called upon act as an address in the present. They are undistinguishably political and poetic. They are not about elsewhere, in a faraway land, unless we choose to read them that way. As Galeano (1989/1991) put it in "The Culture of Terror":

> Blatant colonialism mutilates you without pretense: it forbids you to talk, it forbids you to act, it forbids you to exist.

> Invisible colonialism, however, convinces you that serfdom is your destiny and impotence is your nature: it convinces you that it's *not possible* to speak, *not possible* to act, *not possible* to exist. (p. 159)

These poets, artists, do not provide solutions or a unitary resolution. They use forceful images, not melodramatic ones. The floating bed empty of people in the vastness of the ocean, with the personalized comfort of bed sheets, dispels a unidimensional vision of pain and terror. The beauty and softness of the image render the reality all the more unbearable. Perhaps this careful, thoughtful shift and tremor between the archival document and its fantasied image breaks frame from the collective numbing of what Hélène Cixous (1993) calls "a deadness." These movements string life through us and them, with knots and splicing. In this 1993 work, entitled *The School of Dreams*, Cixous relates to powerful types of writing that are life sources to her. One makes her feel the texture of life: "It doesn't tell a story, it makes us feel, taste, touch life" (p. 59). The other breaks conventions, throws images at us that stun us: "All great texts begin in this manner that *breaks*: they break with our thought habits, with the world around us, in an extreme violence that is due to rapidity" (p. 59).

Applications in Service Provision and in Social Work Education

I am proposing that social work, with its emphasis on people's lives, daily circumstances, institutional and political conditions, can actively position itself closer to practices and knowledge in the arts. Some concrete applications of this approach have been at the heart of service provision for refugees who are survivors of torture and of war. Working with images and through art has been a long-standing activity at the CCVT. Art therapy has been made available to children and to adults who have lost so much in their past lives, and who, as newcomers to Canada, find themselves between places and without a shared experience with others. More generally, arts-based forms of intervention are commonly used in trauma-related services, including services for war veterans. They are also increasingly used in the health field, particularly for women and in health programs.

Not only clients or service recipients/participants benefit from arts-based approaches. Evocative forms of knowing, including metaphors and art works, were identified at the outset as a core dimension in the training materials and workshops that our research team developed in partnership with the CCVT. Materials and exercises were created to stimulate reflection on the part of staff who had not experienced such trauma firsthand. It was felt that an analytical type of training would not be effective without an evocative dimension. A series of workshops supported by government funding was designed and delivered to settlement workers and related staff, in various cities in the province of Ontario. Indeed, professional education and training require that a thoughtful attention be paid to the means of transmission of knowledge and of representation.

In the graduate courses in social work that I teach, I include evocative materials and generally invite students to engage with this dimension of knowledge in order to begin to grapple with complex ideas and the significance of various interventions. In a master's-level course I developed, Intersecting Narratives of Self, Institution and Community, I encourage students to create evocative materials around narratives of self and the other. A handful of doctoral students typically participate in the course.

Beyond specific examples of service provision, training, and education, each one of us is invited to consider evocative and/or arts-based approaches as a means to expand our ways of knowing and of communicating with one another with a view to making social issues more visible to ourselves and to wider society.

References

Attie, S. (1998a). *Sites unseen: European projects. Installations and photographs*. Burlington, VT: Verve Editions.

Attie, S. (1998b). Shimon Attie: Sites unseen. Transcribed presentation and interview by L. A. Langwell, conducted in June at Annual National Graduate Seminar, New York Institute of Photography. Published in *Institute Journal*. Retrieved August 9, 2004, from http://www.thephotographyinstitute.org/

Bailly, J-C. (1997). *L'Apostrophe muette: essai sur les portraits du Fayoum*. Paris: Hazan.

Berger, J. (2002). The Fayum portraits. In J. Berger, *The shape of a pocket* (pp. 53–60). London: Bloomsbury.

Bourdieu, P. (1998). *Practical reason: On the theory of action*. Cambridge. UK: Polity Press.

Burchell, G., Gordon, C., & Miller, P. (Eds.). (1991). *The Foucault effect: Studies in governmentality*. London: Harvester Weatsheaf.

Chabanne, J-C. (1996). Présence de Robert Desnos dans les manuels de l'école élémentaire. In L. Flieder (Ed.), *Poétiques de Robert Desnos* (pp. 83–100). Fontenay/Saint-Cloud, France: ENS Éditions.

Chambon, A. (1994). Postmodernity and social work discourse(s): Notes on the changing language of a profession. In A. Chambon & A. Irving (Eds.), *Essays on postmodernism and social work* (pp. 61–75). Toronto, Ontario, Canada: Canadian Scholars' Press.

Chambon, A. (2000, August/September). Social work knowledge in Canada: A contested terrain. Paper presented at The Ethos of Welfare: Metamorphoses and Variations of Governmentality conference, University of Helsinki, Finland.

Chambon, A. S. (2001). Recomposition transversale des savoirs: Le cas du travail social au Canada anglais à la fin des années 1990. In P. Artières & E. da Silva (Eds.), *Michel Foucault et la médecine: Lectures et usages* (pp. 301–324). Paris: Éditions Kimé.

Chambon, A., & Irving, A. (2003). They give reason a responsibility which it simply can't bear: Ethics, care of the self and caring knowledge. *Journal of Medical Humanities, 24*(3), 265–278.

Chambon, A., McGrath, S., Shapiro, B., Abai, M., Dudziah, S., & Dremetsikas, T. (2001). From Interpersonal links to webs of relations: Creating befriending relationships with survivors of torture and of war. *The Journal of Social Work Research and Evaluation, 2*(2), 157–171.

Cixous, H. (1993). The school of dreams. In *Three steps on the ladder of writing: The Welleck Library Lectures at the University of California, Irvine* (S. Cornell & S. Sellers, Trans., pp. 55–108). New York: Columbia University Press.

Desnos, R. (1955). *Chantefables et chantefleurs: à chanter sur n'importe quel air*. Paris: Gründ.

Foucault, M. (2003). *Abnormal: Lectures at the Collège de France, 1974–1975*. Edited by V. Marchetti & A. Salomoni (Eds., English Series), A.I. Davidson, transl. by G. Burchell. New York: Picador. (Original French work published 1999)

Gablik, S. (1991). *The reenchantment of art*. New York: Thames and Hudson.

Galeano, E. (1991). *The book of embraces* (C. Belfrage, Trans., with M. Schafer). New York: W. W. Norton.(Original work published 1989)

Goldstein, H. (1998). Education for ethical dilemmas in social work practice. *Families in Society, 79*(3), 241–253.

Gorman, J. (1993). Postmodernism and the conduct of inquiry in social work. *Affilia, 8*(3), 247–264.

Green, M. (1995). *Releasing the imagination: Essays on education, the arts, and social change*. San Francisco, CA: Jossey-Bass.

Law, J., & Urry, J. (2004). Enacting the social. *Economy and Society, 33*(3), 390–410.

Levi, P. (1989). *The drowned and the saved* (R. Rosenthal, Trans.). New York: Vintage International. (Original work published 1986)

Levinas, E. (1999). *Alterity and transcendance* (M. B. Smith, Trans.). New York: Columbia University Press. (Original work published 1995)

Moretti, N. (Writer/Director). (1998). *Aprile* [motion picture]. Rome: Sacher Productions.

Perlstein, R. (2004, August). If journalists listened to media scholars. *University of Chicago Magazine, 96*(6), 34–37.

Rose, N., & Miller, P. (1992). Political power beyond the state: Problematics of government. *British Journal of Sociology, 43*(2), 173–205.

Ryan, N. (1998, August 13–19). Whispers in the dark. *Al Ahram Weekly,* 390. Retrieved August 19, 2004, from http://weekly.ahram.org.eg/1998/390/index.htm

Sherman, S. (2000, November 30). Words that must be said. Interview with Eduardo Galeano. *Atlantic Unbound*. Retrieved May 2, 2004, from http://www.theatlantic.com/unbound/interviews/ba2000-11-30.htm

Sontag, S. (2003). *Regarding the pain of others*. New York: Farrar, Strauss and Giroux.

Wallerstein, I. (2004). *The uncertainties of knowledge*. Philadelphia, PA: Temple University Press.

Weick, A. (2000). Hidden voices. *Social Work, 45*(5), 395–402.

Winckler, J. (2004). Retrieved August 23, 2004, from http://juliawinckler.com

Winckler, J., & Martinez de Lecea, N. (2003). (Writers/Directors/Producers). *Leaving Atlantis* [video installation]. Created and produced, Brighton, UK.

Witkin, S. L. (2000). Writing social work. Editorial. *Social Work, 45*(5), 389–394.

Wright, T. (2002). Moving images: The media representation of refugees. *Visual Studies, 17*(1), 53–66.

CHAPTER 10

Inhabiting the Off-Frame
Social Workers as Connoisseurs of Ambiguity

ALLAN IRVING

> I am steering by the torch of chaos and doubt.
> —Artist Sam Francis

In the early 1990s I found myself intellectually, emotionally, and spiritually in Dante's dark wood, somewhat lost, inhabiting haunted playgrounds of the mind. I realized I was in the off-frame of photography, dwelling in absences, places/texts that were marginal, uncertain, ambiguous. The hard shell of Enlightenment certainty had been shattered, and since then I have been on a long and continuous journey to escape its terrors, oppressions, exclusions, and intellectual thuggery. Other worlds, some bright, some mystical, some unencumbered by "research and method," all indeterminate and provisional, began to whisper and glint with possibility. Many new feelings and thoughts now resonated, including the words of the eccentric science fiction writer Philip K. Dick (Star, 1993) who remarked that although his days might start out in certainty, soon the onset of doubt would flow in and color his mind and emotions.

I wanted to abandon words like research, method, measurement, truth, and order and replace them, to the horror of my colleagues (I was teaching in the faculty of social work at the University of Toronto at that time), with words such as *wandering, unknowing, perspectivism, untruth,* and *chaos*. I craved quiet choreographies of movement, thought, and feelings without an end "product" (such a dreadful word) and without destination.

Two developments have helped immeasurably on my long leave taking from the Enlightenment. The first was a return to reading the works of Friedrich Nietzsche and Samuel Beckett, two authors who had captivated my imagination in the 1960s, and beginning to read Michel Foucault. All three authors brought me to see that the world is too complex and uncertain to be changed by rationalistic projects, disinterested research, and the one big idea, such as Marxism. They persuaded me that the Enlightenment project lay in ruins with its wearying discourses of structures, binaries, categories, hierarchies, and grids of regularity. All for me now became thresholds, in between, liminal, tangential, fragmented, incomplete, and transformational. Everywhere, if one chose to look, the wounds and fissures in Enlightenment reason were beyond repair, the loss of blood too great, and we were in the presence of a dying god. Nietzsche (1979) wrote that truth was nothing more than a

> movable host of metaphors . . . a sum of human relations which have been poetically and rhetorically intensified, transferred, and embellished, and which, after long usage, seem to a people to be fixed, canonical, and binding. Truths are illusions which we have forgotten are illusions; they are metaphors that have become worn out and have been drained of sensuous force. (p. 84)

Beckett had a deep distrust of rational efforts to shape, explain, and dispel the chaos of human affairs: "The crisis started with the end of the seventeenth century . . . the eighteenth century has been called the century of reason. . . . I've never understood that: they're all mad! They give reason a responsibility which it simply can't bear, it's too weak. . . . one must make a world of one's own in order to satisfy one's need to know, to understand" (cited in McMullan, 1994, p. 200). Foucault (1997a) at his most poetic said:

> I can't help but dream about a kind of criticism that would try not to judge but to bring an oevre [*sic*], a book, a sentence, an idea to life; it would light fires, watch the grass grow, listen to the wind, and catch the sea foam in the breeze and scatter it. It would multiply not judgments but signs of existence; it would summon them, drag them from their sleep. Perhaps it would invent them sometimes—all the better. All the better. Criticism that hands down sentences sends me to sleep; I'd like a criticism of scintillating leaps of the imagination. It would not be sovereign or dressed in red. It would bear the lightning of possible storms. (p. 323)

I had finally found religion and it was postmodernism.

The second development, and it followed in a lovely way from the first, was getting to know Stanley Witkin in the social work department at the University of Vermont. Stan and Dennis Saleebey were playing with the idea of organizing a gathering of postmodern types who could come together for a few days in Burlington, Vermont, on the shores of Lake Champlain, and through dialogue and activities share common and uncommon thoughts and feelings about social work from a postmodern perspective. Joining this group was a wonderful experience and went a long way toward relieving the isolation of teaching in university social work programs where Enlightenment positivism and social science empiricism controlled the discourse, stifled creativity, and colonized and blocked the imagination for students and faculty. Being present at the Vermont gatherings sustained my conviction that it was crucial to continue working in ways I could to secure a release from the tidy shackles of modernism and its baleful constraints. The meetings were a balm to my intellectual loneliness and feelings of marginalization and fueled my desire to continue searching for portals of access to other social constructions outside the in-frame that I could bring into my classes and writing.

In photography the off-frame effect draws us to an absence, a place/text that has been averted; it is a marginal place of uncertainty and ambiguity. The in-frame, the photograph itself, is the dominant discourse, a place of certainty, what is considered important and continuous. Using the metaphors of the in- and off-frames and references to the postmodern novelist and playwright Samuel Beckett, I will explore postmodern avant-garde possibilities for a disrupting of the constructed stabilities and coherences of the framing of social work within the Enlightenment in-frame. The idea is to encourage social work to embark on different journeys, artistic ones that now reside in the off-frames, journeys that are beyond instrumental solutions, and to intimate that we no longer are required to participate in the realms of universal reason and objectivity. In ridding itself of Enlightenment remnants, social work can cross a border to off-frames of disquieting indeterminacy, to places/spaces that are magical, diverse, and sacred where stable meanings slide into ambiguity.

I was inspired by the Vermont gatherings to continue to think about ways to trouble the rational certitudes of modernity and to try in my teaching to engage in conversations, practices, and performances that bring forth ghosts and discourses that were banished by Enlightenment/modernity. The terrain opens up as we make our escape from the drone of statistics and leave the nonmediated facticity of the world as a historical relic. It is evident to the Vermont participants that modernity is coming undone, fracturing, splintering, and unraveling by questions it can no longer contain as a more unruly but exciting contingent temporality moves from off-frame status to disturb the assumptions of occidental progress and reason. Western universal truth and empirical knowledge fade as spent foundational categories and are now viewed as metaphorical constructions masking relations of power and strategies of oppression and marginalization. It is possible to replace the "rigors" of Cartesian and empirical methods with hermeneutic conversations that are dialogic in the Bakhtinian sense (see Irving & Young, 2002). All stories that we tell one another are surrounded by a multiplicity of interpretations, and as Stanley Fish (1980) has observed, interpretation is not the act of construing but the art of constructing.

The plays and novels of Beckett deconstruct many of the fundamental tenets of modernity and expose the apparent self-evident categories and rational criteria—the dominant social discourses—through which modernity and social work are organized. Beckett provides us with multiple perspectives, a discontinuous reality, the effacing of the boundaries between subject and object, the destabilizing of all positivist conventions, fluid subjectivities, an occupation of the space of "otherness," the scattering of meaning, decentering and disorientation, a world of contingency, chance, and fragmentation, all directed at moving us out of the in-frame of Enlightenment rigidities. Rather than courses on research and statistics, I argue for a social work curriculum that would draw extensively on the arts and humanities to open up alternative spaces to the often brutal, constricting, and certainty of forms of rationality and to consider instead a world of provisionality, where visions of both self-reflexivity and interconnectedness can flourish, where clouds of unknowing are not seen as needing immediate dispersal and all totalizing/universal constructs will vanish into the off-frame. Rather than see ourselves as scientist-practitioners why not as practitioners who are connoisseurs of ambiguity?

Before discussing briefly the work of Beckett, a discussion of the Enlightenment as it constructed social work is offered. The 18th-century ethos of rationalism and empiricism as it embraced ideas of a unified, stable, coherent self, a teleological sense of history and progress, and a belief in the foundations of universal knowledge all shaped the discipline and profession of social work as it took form in the 20th century. The longest-running "soap" in Western culture is the endless retelling of the story of a garden, a fall, and a restoration. It is the primal, archetypal story, the story of the Bible, Dante's *Divina Commedia*, Milton's *Paradise Lost* and *Paradise Regained*, and Marx's *Das Capital.* The 18th-century Enlightenment, staking everything on its promise of a rationalist redemptive method, its posing of a fallen world to be reclaimed and redeemed by the force of reason, is a version of this basic story, and is the perspective that has created and shaped social work. The fall is always a fall away from a golden age where everything is in a state of wholeness and integration to a disintegrated state of separation, strife, fracture, estrangement, and anxiety (Blackburn, 2000).

In the fallen condition of disunity and disharmony, a way back to wholeness was required and a way back was the Enlightenment projection of a rational epiphany (or a series of these), a world redeemed and reclaimed bathed in the golden Cartesian light of reason. But what if there is no prelapsarian world (a world that existed before the "fall"), and hence no fall? What if the story begins in a fractured, fragmented, and ruined condition and stays there? What if the Enlightenment/modernist idea of a moment of truth, a final metanarrative, that is some overarching explanation and ground for our beliefs never arrives? Then we have a different kind of story, one told by Nietzsche, Foucault, Beckett, and those who work the postmodern side of the street. More than any other writer Beckett conducted, from the 1930s to his death in 1989, a relentless tour of the finely sifted rubble of our post-Enlightenment ruins where there are no ontological or epistemological landmarks. There is no garden, no fall, and no restoration, only the purgatorial here and now, a perpetual present. By the end of Beckett's (1954) play *Waiting for Godot* we at least know that the truth will never arrive, for as one of the characters says: "All I know is that the hours are long, under these conditions, and constrain us to beguile them with proceedings which—how shall I say—which may at first sight seem reasonable, until they become a habit. You may say it is to prevent our reason from foundering. No doubt. But has it not long been straying in the night without end of the abyssal depths?" (p. 91). In Beckett's play *Endgame* (1957) one of his characters tells a story about visiting a friend in a mental hospital. For the visitor the view from the window of the patient's room was beautiful, overlooking fields and the sea. All the patient sees though are ashes. The ashes of the ruined enlightenment.

Enlightenment

Enlightenment/modernity's chief pallbearer is the enigmatic philosopher Friedrich Nietzsche. His assault on the naive Enlightenment faith in human reason, universal truth, and the possibility of secure, unassailable knowledge pulled no punches: "In some out of the way corner . . . of the universe there was a star on which clever beasts invented knowledge. That was the most arrogant and mendacious moment of 'universal history'" (Nietzsche, 1979, p. 79). In *The Gay Science* (1882/1974) he writes, "that delusion and error are conditions of human knowledge" (p. 163) and "over immense periods of time the intellect produced nothing but errors" (p. 169). And then the coup de grace: "We have arranged for ourselves a world in which we can live—by positing bodies, lines, planes, causes and effects, motion and rest, form and content; without these articles of faith nobody could now endure life. But that does not prove them. Life is no argument. The conditions of life might include error" (p. 177).

Nietzsche (1882/1974) condemned the insatiable desire of positivist modernity for certainty and that there existed a "world of truth" that could be grasped once and for all by "our square little reason" (pp. 288, 335). He mocked those who seemed content to have human existence "reduced to a mere exercise for a calculator and an indoor diversion for mathematicians." He called for us to cherish the "rich ambiguity" of human life and ridiculed those who maintained "that the only justifiable interpretation of the world should be one in which you are justified because one can continue to work and do research scientifically in your sense—an interpretation that permits counting, calculating, weighing, seeing, and touching, and nothing more—that is a crudity and naiveté, assuming that it is not a mental illness, an idiocy" (p. 335).

Not letting matters rest, Nietzsche (1882/1974) suggested that a scientific interpretation of the world might be "one of the most stupid interpretations of the world, meaning that it would be one of the poorest in meaning" (p. 335). For Nietzsche a mechanical scientific world would be one without meaning. And drawing an analogy to music he asked, "assuming that one estimated the value of a piece of music according to how much of it could be counted, calculated, and expressed in formulas: how absurd would such a 'scientific' estimation of music be! What would one have comprehended, understood, grasped of it? Nothing, really nothing of what is 'music' in it!" (pp. 335–336). Nietzsche emphasized the role that language plays in shaping human life. It is our languages, history, and the profound ability to create new, imaginative worlds, not our supposed ability to find truth, that marks us as truly human. For Nietzsche language imposes a shape on the way we think about the world at any given moment. Hegel saw history as a rational progression toward truth and reconciliation in the world (the high-water mark of Enlightenment/modernity) whereas Nietzsche simply saw societies changing their perspectives over time but never arriving at a more accurate picture of the world. What counts for Nietzsche is not the world we discover but the one we create.

Nietzsche pinpointed two fundamental problems with the positivist/empirical tradition. First, it disregards the role that language plays in creating and constructing a multitude of worlds, and second, it assumes that everyone perceives the world in the same way. This is Nietzsche's (1883–1888/1968) famous notion of perspectivism—that every view is only one among many interpretations possible: "facts are precisely what there is not, only interpretations" (p. 267). Alexander Nehamas (1985) suggests that Nietzsche regarded the world as an artwork, a kind of literary text. Just as literary texts can be interpreted in quite different and often incompatible ways, Nietzsche argued that the world is open to similar kinds of interpretation. In *The Will to Power* (1968) he remarks that "we possess art lest we perish of the truth" (p. 435). Nietzschean perspectivism certainly says that no particular point of view such as science is privileged, but that we have many ways of knowing. He urged us to abandon the desire to find a single context for all human lives. In achieving self-knowledge we are not discovering an essential truth within but forging a self-creation. Nietzsche exhorted us to create new meanings out of the contingencies of our existence; life is to be fashioned in the fluid process of becoming who one is. We can be poets of our lives. Toward the end of his life Michel Foucault (1997a) also talked about creating ourselves as works of art.

One of the central figures in the transition from modernity to postmodernity is the philosopher Ludwig Wittgenstein. His late 1920s work *Tractatus Logico-Philosophicus* was a last post-Hegelian attempt to construct an overall system of explanation for the world. Subsequently Wittgenstein completely repudiated system building and was experimenting with what he called language games, and the publication of *Philosophical Investigations* in the early 1950s remains to the present a great postmodern piece—fragmentary, tangential, and preoccupied with the rules of its own construction. Wittgenstein's attention to questions of language emphasized the context in which meaning is produced and rendered problematic all universal truth, knowledge, and meaning claims. Philosophical investigations pointed straight to the postmodern situating of the subject as a complex intersection of discursive and social forces: we are created in dialogue. Wittgenstein argued that the logic of our language changes over time. He suggested that the propositions about the world we usually consider philosophically and scientifically certain, the various assumptions that construct our systems of belief and their particular logic and the established rules by which our reason proceeds alter over time and are not fixed once and for all. He wrote, "the mythology may change back into a state of flux, the riverbed of thoughts may shift. . . . And the bank of that river consists partly of hard rock, subject to no alteration or only to an imperceptible one, partly of sand, which now in one place now in another gets washed away or deposited" (Wittgenstein, 1969, sections 97 and 99). For Wittgenstein and postmodern scholars who followed after him, an appeal to reason is never self-validating. All validation, "all justification must come to an end," he wrote, so that at the end of all our justifications we find not self-validating truths but a groundlessness. "The difficulty is to realize the groundlessness of our believing" (Wittgenstein, 1969, section 166).

For a good 15 years I have been reading and writing about postmodernism, sometimes about its relevance to social work, and yet it was only in fall 2004 that I really had a conversion to what I call extreme postmodernism, finally departing from modernism and the Enlightenment, which definitely places me in the off-frame. While walking to the university, it suddenly occurred to me that the whole notion of the rational and rationality is simply a fiction. Despite our endless attention to making the world rational in the Enlightenment sense of rational, that there exist universally neutral, ahistorical standards of rationality, and convincing ourselves that it is so, and we desperately seek this in social work, the world, our relationships, our work is always wildly irrational, fragmenting, disintegrating, dissolving, shearing off, shifting, strangely protean, discontinuous, slippery, indeterminate, impossible to arrest in stable postures of meaning, resistant to the seductive appeal of totalizing theories or any theory and comprehensive accounts of the phenomenal world. Everything, it seemed to me that morning, and this has remained with me the past several months, was distending into ever wider and feebler meanings. Malone, in Beckett's (1965) novel *Malone Dies*, compares himself to a dwindling heap of sand, and that fall morning I felt the destabilizing vertigo that ensues when familiar paradigms of knowing and what we thought we always believed warp, shift, and disappear. Foucault (1997b) wrote in "What Is Enlightenment" that "one has to refuse everything that might present itself in the form of a simplistic and authoritarian alternative: you either accept the Enlightenment and remain within the tradition of its rationalism . . . or else you criticize the Enlightenment and then try to escape from its principles of rationality" (p. 313).

I decided not to mention any of this to my colleagues, whom I feared would slap a number of DSM-IV disorders on me, and certainly would view my dislocations as a madness, which in many respects it is. I remembered a comment that the poet Rimbaud made, that to see the world differently, poetically, we needed to engage in a process of deranging all our senses. I also remembered reading in James Miller's fine intellectual biography of Michel Foucault how the philosopher, when asked by a group of Berkeley graduate students in the 1970s for some stable truths and definite answers to perplexing questions, replied that there were no truths and there were no answers. All we have is the uncontainable ruckus of the world. The more we look for order the more we are caught in its sticky webs of evasions, bluffs, and halls of mirrors. In 2003 I had seen a play in New York by Richard

Foreman, put on by his group known as the Ontological Hysteric Theater, that presents Foreman's work as a theater of heightened noticing. In the plays things are constantly falling apart, regrouping, and falling apart again, as Foreman tries to open the door to what is here, now in front of us, but all too often unseen. And I recalled the poet John Keats's idea of "negative capability" (Colvin, 1970, pp. 253–254), the ability to live among doubts, hesitations, and uncertainties, as among the most important of our values. Casting my mind back over all these writings I came to the conclusion, a self-diagnosis, that I wasn't mad, just truly postmodern. Of course many would argue that postmodernism is a form of madness, a point of view I am only too happy to accept.

Once when he was asked what he most valued in his work, Beckett answered, "What I don't understand" (Higgins, 1996, p. 19). Beckett often spoke of throwing away all intellectual solutions and moving away from the destructive need to dominate life. "It is not even possible to talk about truth," Beckett remarked, "that's part of the anguish" (Juliet, 1989/1990, p. 17). He had a great admiration for the mystics, for those who viewed the world and the self outside Cartesian logic: "I admire their disregard for logic, their burning illogicality—the flame that consumes the rubbish heap of logic" (p. 27). All Beckett's work takes us far beyond Cartesian dualism, and Enlightenment reason, away from the blinding glare of rationalism and empiricism into the night where things, in the process of decomposition, also reawaken our senses, as described in his novel *Molloy*: "And that night there was no question of moon, nor any other light, but it was a night of listening, a night given to the faint soughing and sighing stirring at night in little pleasure gardens . . . where there is less constraint. . . . Yes, there were times when I forgot not only who I was, but that I was, forgot to be" (Beckett, 1965, pp. 48–49).

For Beckett, Descartes' dualism contains a kind of madness that radically splits mind and body and presents experience in distinct realms—the necessary precondition for rationalism, empiricism, and science. Beckett's relentless deconstruction of the Cartesian paradigm and exploration of the postmodern themes of indeterminacy, contingency, and unfixed forms takes on a new intensity in a sudden revelation he had in 1946. This revelation shattered Beckett's remaining trust in empirical knowledge, when the need to know things intellectually collapsed for him. This vision is given life in his play *Krapp's Last Tape*: "[it was] clear to me at last that the dark I have always struggled to keep under is in reality my most unshatterable association until my dissolution of storm and night with the light of the understanding and the fire" (Beckett, 1958, p. 21).

This passage represents one of Beckett's intuitive flashes of a non-Cartesian beyond, a disruption of the wilderness of Cartesian dualism of distinct minds and bodies. In Cartesian epistemology the way to knowledge is through an observer standing in relation to the world, a subject (mind) in relation to an object. The Cartesian mind measures, sorts, and categorizes data, organizes material, and scrutinizes validity. Beckett's literary works undermine Cartesian dialectics and all certain knowledge. In his novel *Watt*, Beckett (1959) gives us a vision of the cogito, the knowing mind come to nothing. Subjectivity is so enfeebled that it is an absence, a presence that is gone, where even the certitude of inner existence collapses into nonbeing. The Cartesian self as self-presence, existing beyond all doubt as the foundational starting point for all certain knowledge, in Beckett becomes a nullity (Begam, 1996).

Throughout his life Samuel Beckett would admit to only four certainties: that he had been born, was living, would die, and for reasons unknown and unknowable could not keep silent. When asked if his plays deal with those facets of human experience that religion also deals with, Beckett said: "Yes, for they deal with distress" (Reid, 1968, p. 15). This is what social work deals with as well, whether it is the distress caused by oppressive social conditions or with people caught in webs of emotional and psychological turmoil. Reading Beckett can help us focus on distress and compassion and open a dialogue and discourse about how to construct and create communities of caring that alleviate distress. Reading Beckett helps us appreciate absences, loss, waiting, pain, suffering, compassion, uncertainty, the bleached margins of life—surely all more telling words for social work than research, statistics, methods—and helps us to understand how every encounter is one we construct out of the shards and fragments of existence. A question I have been pondering for some time now is whether a major literary figure such as Beckett can be a guide for us in constructing a quite different kind of social work practice. The answer I believe can be strongly affirmative since Beckett's novels and plays deliver us into a world of contingency, a world of imagination and story, a world not of finding but of making.

In a beautiful article, "Guilty Knowledge"(1999), published in *Families in Society*, an article all social work students could benefit from reading, Ann Weick talks about the "emotion-filled heart of practice" (p. 329), a practice of compassion, caring, and hope, embracing those who are hurt, confused, ill, in despair, attending to the almost mystical complexity of people's lives. She encourages us to extend and educate our imaginations and to create "room at the edges for alternative views to flourish" (p. 330) and to accept working in zones of uncertainty and unresolvedness. Rereading her article recently set my imagination alight with notions of ceremonies of patching, the need to ease the tightness of the chains pinching and constricting us, being attentive to intertextual undertows, endlessly deferring truth claims, opening ourselves to the call of different, marginal, transgressive voices, the desirability of working to forge a less comfortable social work—one that strives to embrace complexity, to break up the textual surface of social work discourse, to move from one provisional encampment to the next, to stand out against the dead air of social work like a solo violin playing out of tune, and to whisper to our colleagues and students that modernism is in ruins, beyond repair. Organize a wake if you like as long as it is Dionysian in nature.

I would like to conclude with a brief lecture I imagine giving to a social work class; I might call it Ceremonies of Patching, Rituals of Chaos: I suppose you would prefer order, argument, logic, something definite, perhaps truth. But unfortunately, if that is what you want, I'm now so far gone that I concur fully with postmodern novelist Donald Barthelme (1997) who says, "fragments are the only form I trust." Let's face it, truth and knowledge are fugitive things open to paralyzing doubt, breakdown, and transformation. Truth is only what circulates as such, knowledge as Michel Foucault taught us is only and always particular, local, shifting discourses of power; everything is a story, all texts are subject to an unknowable multiplicity of interpretations. Years ago the philosopher Friedrich Nietzsche demolished whole walls of the house of Western philosophy. In 1873 he proclaimed, "truth is nothing more than a mobile host of metaphors . . . a sum of human relations, which have been enhanced, transposed, and embellished poetically and rhetorically and after long use seem final, canonical, and obligatory. Truths are illusions about which one has forgotten that this is what they are, metaphors which are worn out and without sensuous power" (1873/1979, p. 84). No wonder for Nietzsche the history of truth is the history of an error. Now that truth is dead we are free to drop once and for all our flat, bleached, objective social work prose and turn our energies toward the artistic creation of ourselves and our communities.

Please, let's give up the modernist project, original texts, and solid foundations. What counts for me is not the world we discover but the world we create, for as Nietzsche (1968) says, "this world can be justified only as an aesthetic phenomenon." Do you think social work will ever get it? Unlikely! But let's not give up. Instead, let's go down the postmodern rabbit hole and endlessly subvert the hitherto unimpeachable authority and stability of reason. See reason as nothing more than an abandoned and rusting car—both are metallic cocoons of Western culture. Ease the tightness of the chains. Truth is now as ghostly as invention. The world, as playwright and novelist Samuel Beckett said, is a mess, like the etiolated sculpture of Alberto Giacometti, full of harrowing instability so why keep trying to tidy it up? Stop trying to order the chaos and instead find ways to inhabit it, adjust our expectations so we celebrate not meanings but momentary clarities, moments of radiance of how life could be.

Social work is no longer defined by a single evolving historical narrative, but by fragments, multiplicity, contradictory pluralities, antidoxa. Everything we say or write, as Nietzsche acknowledged, is really only the personal confession of its author and an involuntary and unconscious memoir. I confess without apology that I reject completely the Enlightenment ideal of the perfectability of the mind and society, the human condition, the absurd idea of a never ending progressing rationality. There simply is no historical telos as Marx claimed, no beginning, no end, only the intense present, clouds of unknowing, a crumbling Western episteme, notes of melancholy, and sad perplexities. No belief in a timeless, absolute reason, rather an allergy to instrumental reason; I'm appalled by the very idea of objectivity and objective values. Words that do appeal: transgression, disruption, disintegration, pluralism, chaos, debris, detritus, decrepitude, failure, disorder, instability. I have an ongoing, obsessive desire to go to Turin in Italy and go mad like Nietzsche, but I must stop before you call the cops or, much worse, a dean of social work.

Let's think without foundations or not think at all, but first let's contest an imperious rationalism, and the bludgeoning pragmatics of empiricism. So what if you get egg on your interface! Let's provide that puff of wind to take us out of calm waters. As for research and measurement, banish them forever, and while we're at it destroy all boundaries. The baleful discourses of measurement define themselves against a perceived emptiness or disorder—a disorder that is not preexistent but rather one the discourse of measurement has itself already given birth to within its own capitalist structure. The discourse of measurement belittles other alternative discourses and ways of knowing, thus displacing counterforms of knowledge construction—thereby creating hierarchies of knowledge and ensuring, as we ought to know, cascading processes of marginalization. So, I would recommend that we have the Council on Social Work Education and the Canadian Association of Schools of Social Work make up huge posters that all social work schools would be required to put up as a condition of accreditation with the words, Research Forbidden, Disorder Encouraged. To steal a line from a Wallace Stevens poem, we could be connoisseurs of ambiguity and chaos. If we must theorize, at best a dubious activity, at least let's do it from sites of transgressive, disruptive practice (Stevens, 1972).

The postmodern view is that contradictions are not only inevitable but desirable. To smooth them over in some Enlightenment madness would be bad form, even bad faith. The narrator of Salman Rushdie's novel *Shame* puts it this way: "I myself manage to hold large numbers of wholly irreconcilable views simultaneously, without the least difficulty. I do not think others are less versatile" (Rushdie, 1982, pp. 24–42). Perhaps you crave a definition of postmodernism, an operational definition—how quaint! Nietzsche to the rescue, who once commented, as I recall, only that which does not have a history can be defined. But if you insist, and it seems you do, how about postmodernism as a cultural field of brilliant dreck and jocose rubble?

Provisionality and heterogeneity contaminate neat attempts to tidy it all up, to get some kind of unifying coherence. Narrative continuity and closure are contested, there are no centers, only margins, fractures, dispersals. From our decentered perspectives, the marginal, what Linda Hutcheon (1988) calls the *ex-centric* (be it class, race/ethnicity, gender, gender bending, sexual orientation, etc.), we can surely grasp the possibilities that open when we refuse to participate any longer in the realm of universal objectivity—or middle class, male, heterosexual, white, Western constructions. How limited we've been. Why have we tried to contain everything, instead of embracing the complexity of the world, irreducible to a homogenous vision of single linear codes, single points of view? Let's cross borders, cross thresholds, cross over, cross-talk, cross-dress, split open the present and its single, all-inclusive manner of knowing. Bring on virulent attacks of ambiguity. Please, I implore you, no more certainty. The rational certitudes of modernity now confront ghosts that were banished by the Enlightenment. Gender, as Judith Butler (1990/1999) so eloquently argues, is not fixed in some male/female binary, something essential, but is constructed through our repeat performances of certain ways of being. These can be changed. Not only is there a plenitude of difference in the world, but we can also ourselves be something different—poets of our lives, artists of our self-creations as Nietzsche and Foucault advocated. Let us devote ourselves to repeat performances of noncapitalist acts; forget theory, just perform. Perform repeated acts of social justice, however you want to define it. Find new sites for performance. Let us ghost our present understandings with other stories, with others in endless conversation, dialogue; rewrite the world, redescribe, for as Rushdie says in *Imaginary Homelands,* "it is clear that redescribing a world is the necessary first step towards changing it" (Rushdie, 1991, pp. 13–14). Social justice, where is thy sting?

The way back to the modern is sealed for good. I agree with postmodern novelist Kathy Acker (Acker, Cooper, Scholder, & Winterson, 2002) who says that Enlightenment reason leaves us susceptible to coercive orderliness, tells us to be constantly forcing ourselves to fit within reason's narrow boundaries. We must escape its clutches. Postmodernism adopts an approach of rupture reveling in rich debris and complexity. One imperative might be to engage in acts to destabilize orderly institutions. Advocate unpredictability, unrestricted play, carnivalize our classrooms, promote endless process and indeterminacy. Dispersal to different sites. Let dialogue replace dialectic. Hermeneutic conversation replaces the rigors of Cartesian methods—there's another word that should be banned—methods. Oh, let it slip from sight. Universality always excludes. To hell with that. It's all in our acts of framing at the edge of the world. Push against the frames, then the poetical acquires its potential. No certainties anymore of a politics built on truth and reason—truth, as Jane Flax (1990) has observed, is discourse dependent. Single truths lead to appalling domination. If we are open to, and allow new tenants to inhabit old discourses, then class from a Marxist perspective can be understood in our postmodern multitruthed world as yet one more dimension that constitutes a social formation. Rather than the total, essential determinant.

But we want to think of new sites for social work practice. Disrupt the old codes as do the novels of Kathy Acker and Thomas Pynchon—read biker outlaw magazines, get a tattoo. The sculpture of Thomas Hirschhorn can direct us to the idea of new sites for practice. His sculptures are made from detritus, the materials of waste and impoverishment; they are a bricolage, made from old bits of aluminum and nylon foils, cardboard remnants, paper fragments, all taken from the nonsites of consumer culture, the negative ready-mades of containers and wrappings, materials in which objects have been packed and shipped; he salvages for his work the discarded evidence of our infinite productions of waste. Hirschhorn places his sculptures, which are homages to the tragically failed projects of modernity, in out-of-the-way street corners, stairways of public housing projects, where he invites vandalism by petty theft thereby disrupting codes of private property and controlled museum space (Buchloh, Gingeras, & Basualdo, 2004).

For a postmodern Marxism can we envision class in myriad new sites and a multitude of forms? Class sites occur not only in capitalist industrial enterprises but in households, communities, recreational facilities—class is local, plural, dispersed, decentered, fragmented, multiple. Many class modalities can be used, many social actors like social workers can engage in struggles over class. If we see capitalism not as a systemic, totalizing entity but instead as local, dispersed, and partial, then many sites and spaces open up for creating, performing, and enacting non-capitalist, communal processes. Let us consider working to create public projects of establishing in an artistic way a social ethic of care in our communities, our universities, our classrooms.

There it is, the lecture never given—yet. But I feel the time is coming for a wash and a rinse, and all that is required of me is courage. When Michel Foucault, delivered his inaugural lecture at the Collège de France in 1970, he quoted one of his favorite passages from Beckett's 1965 novel *The Unnamable*: "you must say words as long as there are any, until they find me, until they say me." This is perhaps our work of social work as we imagine establishing dialogic communities of our own making, of our own speaking, of our own social construction.

References

Acker, K. Cooper, D., Scholder, A., & Winterson, G. (2002). *Essential Acker: The selected writings of Kathy Acker.* NY: Grove Press.

Barthelme, Donald (1997). *Not knowing.* New York: Random House.

Beckett, S. (1954). *Waiting for Godot*. New York: Grove Press.

Beckett, S. (1957). *Endgame*. New York: Grove Press.

Beckett, S. (1958). *Krapp's last tape*. New York: Grove Press.

Beckett, S. (1959). *Watt*. New York: Grove Press.

Beckett, S. (1965). *Three novels: Molloy, Malone dies, The unnamable*. New York: Grove Press.

Begam, R. (1996). *Samuel Beckett and the end of modernity*. Palo Alto, CA: Stanford University Press.

Blackburn, S. (2000, October 30). Enquivering. *The New Republic*, 43–48.

Buchloh, B., Gingeras, A. M., & Basualdo, C. (2004). *Thomas Hirschhorn*. New York: Phaidon Press.

Butler, J. (1990/1999). *Gender trouble: Feminism and the subversion of identity*. NY: Routledge.

Colvin, S. (1970). *John Keats: His life and poetry*. New York: Octagon Books.

Fish, S. (1980). *Is there a text in this class?: The authority of interpretive communities*. Cambridge, MA: Harvard University Press.

Flax, J. (1990). *Thinking fragments: Psychoanalysis, feminism, and postmodernism in the contemporary West*. Berkeley, CA: University of California Press.

Foucault, M. (1997a). The masked philosopher. In P. Rabinow, (Ed.), *Ethics, subjectivity and truth: The essential works of Foucault* (pp. 321–328). New York: The New Press.

Foucault, M. (1997b). What is enlightenment? In P. Rabinow, (Ed.), *Ethics, subjectivity and truth: The essential works of Foucault* (pp. 303–319). New York: The New Press.

Higgins, A. (1996). *Samuel Beckett: Photographs*. New York: George Braziller.

Hutcheon, Linda. (1988). *A poetics of postmodernism*. New York: Routledge.

Irving, A., & Young, T. (2002). Paradigm for pluralism: Mikhail Bakhtin and social work practice. *Social Work, 47*(1), 19–29.

Juliet, C. (1989/1990). Meeting Beckett. *TriQuarterly, 77*, 9–30.

McMullan, A. (1994). Samuel Beckett as director: The art of mastering failure. In J. Pilling (Ed.), *The Cambridge companion to*

Beckett (pp. 196–208). Cambridge, MA: Cambridge University Press.

Nehamas, A. (1985). *Nietzsche: Life as literature*. Cambridge, MA: Harvard University Press.

Nietzsche, F. (1968). *The will to power* (W. Kaufman & R. J. Hollingdale, Trans.). New York: Vintage. (Original work published 1883–1888)

Nietzsche, F. (1974). *The gay science* (W. Kaufman, Trans.). New York: Vintage. (Original work published 1882)

Nietzsche, F. (1979). *Philosophy and truth: Selections from Nietzsche's notebooks of the early 1970s* (D. Breazeale, Ed., Trans.). Atlantic Highlands, NJ: Humanities Press International.

Reid, A. (1968). *All I can manage, more than I could: An approach to the plays of Samuel Beckett*. Dublin, Ireland: The Dolmen Press.

Rushdie, S. (1982). *Shame*. London: Cape.

Star, A. (1993). Philip K. Dick (1928–1982). *New Republic,* (December 6), 34–41.

Stevens, W. (1972). *Collected poems*. New York: Knopf.

Weick, A. (1999). Guilty knowledge. *Families in Society, 80*(4), 327–332.

Wittgenstein, L. (1969). *On certainty* (D. Paul & G. E. M. Anscombe, Trans.). New York: Harper.

CHAPTER 11

Makeovers for "Bewhiskered" Research

Diverse Heuristics for Understanding Causality in the Social and Behavioral Sciences*

KATHERINE TYSON McCREA

> Note our temptation to think of nature as divisible into discrete happenings, each of which has one "father" (cause) and one, or several "sons" (effects). This way of looking at the world leads to bewhiskered questions. —Norwood Russell Hanson

Why Is an Up-to-Date Conceptualization of Causality Important?

Norwood Hanson (1958), one of the first and foremost postpositivist philosophers of science, points to the problem that

---

*An earlier version of this chapter was presented as Keynote Lectures for the Summer School at Vytautas Magnus University, Kaunas, Lithuania, entitled "Enhancing Academic Competencies: Practitioner-Relevant Research," Summer, 2002. Lisette Piedra and Deborah Major provided very helpful comments on initial drafts. Many thanks go to Dennis Saleebey and Stan Witkin for their insights and most helpful editing.

research questions can become "bewhiskered" (p. 51) if researchers are constrained by overly narrow linear and unitary beliefs about causality. Like participants in the Transforming Social Work gatherings, he sought to broaden the logical empiricist limits on inquiry that included an overly narrow definition of causal explanations and the methods that can be used to study them scientifically (Saleebey, 1989; Tyson, 1995; Vigilante, 1974; Witkin, 1989). As William Wimsatt (1994) notes, the social and behavioral sciences are pervaded with "causal thicket," (p. 271), because it is so challenging to develop models to organize the complexities of multilayered and interactive causes working between individuals, groups, social systems, and cultures. This chapter suggests some models that can be used to carve paths through the thickets of causal interactions (Wimsatt, 1994). As will be seen, philosophers and scientists past and present offer many alternatives to the linear, unitary model that has "bewhiskered" question asking in the social and behavioral sciences.

This chapter draws from our Vermont meetings and Stanley Witkin's (2001) important editorial, and offers diverse understandings of causality to foster recognizing common conceptualizations of causality and the opportunities provided by the many heuristics for modeling causal processes. Finally, a standard of "causal validity" that can be applied to any research design will be advanced as a way to keep the issue of causal models on the radar screen of the research design process, and to minimize the unfortunate consequences that can result from unrecognized biases in researchers' choices of causal heuristics.

Understanding how we conceptualize causality is important for many reasons. First, clearly it is important for the day-to-day practice of social work. As Stanley Witkin (2001) writes,

> Causes matter. They matter because what we believe about causes and their relationship to "effects" has consequences for the people with whom we work. Consider the history

> of causes believed to underlie conditions such as developmental or physical disability, mental illness, depression, or poverty. As the causes changed so did the effects—that is, who was identified as having these conditions—and the way people so labeled were treated. (p. 201)

Second, causal processes are at the heart of the knowledge base of the social and behavioral sciences, a knowledge base that hopefully influences decisions at the micro-, meso-, and macrolevels of practice. For instance, funding for early intervention programs may be reduced if policy makers accept causal hypotheses that genes override environment in determining academic and career success. Those causal hypotheses have been demonstrated to be false both conceptually and empirically (Lewontin, 1974, 2000).

To start considering the importance of causality for research in the social and behavioral sciences, our scope can be broadened to science in general, recognizing a challenge all scientists face. The noted evolutionary biologist Richard Lewontin underscores in a recent work (2000) that all scientists necessarily use metaphors (alternatively, Wimsatt calls these "heuristics," [1986]). He also emphasizes the ease and danger of confusing the metaphors with the entities themselves:

> While we cannot dispense with metaphors in thinking about nature, there is a great risk of confusing the metaphor with the thing of real interest. We cease to see the world *as if* it were *like* a machine, and take it to *be* a machine [italics in original]. The result is that the properties we ascribe to our object of interest and the questions we ask about it reinforce the original metaphorical image and we miss the aspects of the system that do not fit the metaphorical approximation. As Alexander Rosenblueth and Norbert Weiner have written, "the price of metaphor is eternal vigilance." (2000, pp. 3–4)

By definition, "metaphors" or "heuristics" (per Wimsatt, 1986) can be hard to detect using even the most "vigilant" radar screens researchers have. Research designs contain assumptions that transform the researcher's initial question into another question that can be studied using the researcher's chosen method. The design changes the research problem into a question that can be studied through data collection and analysis processes such as operationalization, standardized measurements, and statistical analyses. The question transformed by the research design may not resemble the original question in important ways. When the research question and the research method contain embedded assumptions about the causal processes at work that are incompatible, the validity of the study is seriously eroded. For instance, Lewontin (1974) indicated that using analysis of variance (ANOVA) requires that the causes studied not be interactive, and yet unfortunately many researchers (incorrectly) used ANOVA to study interactive causes, such as how a genotype combines with environment to produce the phenotype.

Lewontin's central point, part of which was raised in social work in 1979 by Dennis Saleebey and in psychology in 1985 by Kurt Danziger, has been that all research designs and methods contain in them embedded theoretical assumptions, which then (either invisibly or explicitly, depending on the researcher's awareness) determine the questions that can be asked as well as the findings. Researchers may become accustomed to asking only those questions that can be "study-able" using the methods they believe yield the most valid information. They learn (perhaps even without recognizing it) not to ask questions that cannot be answered using the preferred methodologies. As knowledge accumulates, the causal explanations derived from findings using (unjustifiably) privileged methods yield consistent unrecognized biases. For instance, Nash (1999) points out that the human beings whose characteristics are described in statistical analyses are, "simple, one-dimensional, determined *models* about as like to real people as the cardboard police officers one sometimes sees in shopping malls" (p. 453). Because people are actually, "non-determined agents with multiple sources of motivation" (p. 453), privileging of statistical methods can actually inhibit the development of complex models of the causal processes occurring in human choices and interactions.

It is much easier to recognize heuristics when one compares them with alternatives. Consider for a moment the different perspectives one might use to study the origins of effective nonviolent movements for social change. How could nonviolent movements for social change arise in contexts of extreme oppression (Schell, 2003), specifically the civil rights in the southern United States under the Jim Crow laws, the Sajudis liberation movement in Lithuania under the persecution of the Soviet Union, and Mandela's African National Congress (ANC) in South Africa under apartheid? All three of these were contexts of profound, violent societal trauma in which people organized uprisings and protests, risking their lives to bring about more just social orders. Throughout this chapter examples will illustrate how one could formulate and study this research question.

As a first look at answering the question about how effective nonviolent social movements can arise in contexts of extreme oppression, one might look at the past, at historical origins of the ideals guiding the movements (e.g., Schell, 2003), or one could conceptualize the movements as stratified and study the roles of inspirational leadership, or one could assume an egalitarian, horizontal perspective is most relevant and study how members of the movements created and maintained communications with each other. All three of these analyses would yield a different picture of the causal processes at work in engendering the coming together of so many people in such a powerful way despite the constant threats to their lives such actions provoked.

The problem of alternative explanations is among the thorniest facing researchers—the existence of alternative causes that the researcher has not studied, or what are also called "confounders" (Steel, 2004). "An overabundance of plausible mechanisms is a major source of difficulty for causal inference in the social sciences" (p. 65). Yet it is not just the existence of alternative unmeasured causes that can compromise the validity of research findings; validity also can be compromised because those causes may work in ways that the researcher has not taken into account. Thus a solid understanding of the heuristics one is positing for the causal processes in any form of inquiry is of utmost importance. To foster recognizing heuristics that can be used to define causal processes, the following is a summary of the most important contributions that philosophers have made over time in defining causes and the processes by which they work.

Heuristics Used to Model Causal Processes in Historical Perspective

ARISTOTLE'S FOUR TYPES OF CAUSES

Historical understandings of causality in Western thought tend to begin with Aristotle, who in his *Metaphysics* (1910–1952) reviewed the theories of causality of his predecessors and concluded that no one before him had delineated the four causes that he defined: formal, efficient, material, and final. Aristotle approached causality through exploring the process of change (*Physics,* 1910–1952). Distinguishing change from development, he defined change as neither patterned nor goal-oriented. By contrast, he regarded development as a patterned process of change that moves toward a specific goal intrinsic to that entity. Human development, a process of evolving stages in the context of the social environment, is a good example of Aristotle's definition of development. Development is purposive and leads to a goal inherent in the entity itself. The goal is the *final cause*, or, in Aristotle's metaphysics, the sought-for "good" (Coppleston, 1944–1965, 1985, p. 288). Aristotle was both a metaphysicist and an empiricist, and in his view, cause is both what has occurred in the past to lead up to the present event, and also what grows out of it into the future (Jones, 1970, vol. 1, p. 226). In addition to the final cause, Aristotle delineated three other types of causes: material, efficient, and formal (1910–1952).

Lewis (2000) applied Aristotle's three models of causality to his analysis of how human free will interacts with the determinism produced by social structures such as language, culture, and defined social roles that are inherited and impinge upon human choice. Applied to the question about the origins of nonviolent movements for human liberation, individual human agency (e.g., the action of physically confronting Soviet tanks or racist police) Lewis defined as an *efficient cause*. Social structures such as language, cultural roles, and economic stratifications function as *material causes* (Lewis, 2000). They are both the means by which humans act (e.g., language fosters communication of liberation strategies), and they guide and constrain human agency (e.g., communication is constrained when our wished-for conversational partner speaks an unknown foreign language). *Formal causes* articulate how human interactions are regulated—as in the new laws created by the civil rights movement, the ANC, and the Lithuanian Sajudis movement.

MORE THAN ONE CAUSE CAN WORK TOGETHER TO BRING ABOUT A RESULT: THE DUAL CAUSALITY OF ST. THOMAS AQUINAS

Writing almost a millennium after Aristotle, Thomas, canonized as St. Thomas Aquinas, is one of the foremost theologians and philosophers of all time. He studied both the natural sciences and theology, and in his day, theology was regarded as the pinnacle of scientific investigation. St. Thomas Aquinas's central accomplishment was to supplement the insights of Christianity with the empirical naturalism of Aristotle, developing therefrom a theology and philosophy that continue to shape both disciplines to this day. Whereas science conceptualized by positivists has tended to eschew final (or teleological) causality as metaphysical, from St. Thomas's point of view the world is purposively structured, so all scientific knowledge is inherently teleological—all things have a purpose, and all aspects of the natural world can be understood in terms of the ends (final causes) to which they aim, including human behavior (Jones, 1970).

Dissatisfied with the neo-Platonic mysticism of Christianity at the time, St. Thomas did not want to deny or devalue the reality of the sensible world, because that was logically inconsistent with affirming God's creative act and the incarnation. To show that God would work in the world and also that the world grasped through the senses had its own causal processes, St. Thomas had to demonstrate that both God and the sense world could cause results that humans could perceive. In other words, two ontologically different causes could be at work in producing a given, perceptible result (Aquinas, 1920/1981).

How might one apply this concept to social work research? An example is that human behavior need not be reduced to expressions of neurological impulses in order to be scientifically meaningful, but instead can be understood as resulting from many causes working interactively, as will be described further in the discussion of emergent causality later in this chapter. For those interested in transcendent causes, if one incorporates spirituality into social work practice and research, St. Thomas's heuristic of dual causality could be used to posit both spiritual realities and human interventions as generating outcomes (Sermabeikian, 1994).

If one does not include a transcendent ontology, the possibility of dual causality is still of great importance for explaining human events that many might understand as having two ontologically distinct causes. Returning to the example of the three nonviolent movements for human liberation noted above, clearly several causes fostered the organization of the movements. In all three examples, socially organized patterns in the form of a cultural heritage, including powerful values of respect for human autonomy and freedom (in African American spiritual traditions, the native Lithuanian culture, and the heritage of cultural movements such as Ghandi's in South Africa), supplied received values (material causes, per Lewis, 2000) inspiring the movements' participants. Another material cause was the means of communication, the importance of which led Lithuanian revolutionaries to form a human chain protecting their TV tower, even though 14 of them were gunned down by Soviet tanks. Thus, transmitted nonviolent beliefs and communication structures were causes in all three social movements, functioning alongside the courageous choices of individuals to participate.

THE EXISTENCE OF THE RESULT INDICATES THE EXISTENCE OF THE CAUSE: DESCARTES

As was true of St. Thomas, Descartes' discussion of causality was critical to his effort to prove the existence of God. Readers may be familiar with Descartes' invention of his companion "skeptical demon," who questioned him on every effort he made to prove the existence of himself and others, until the only proof that Descartes could offer to refute the demon was the famous "cogito ergo sum" (Descartes, 1637/1993). From this "I think, therefore I am," a number of implications followed. One was that because Descartes had in his mind a thought of God, and he believed that his thought was a result of a cause, then God must exist as the cause of his thought. The important link was an assumption about causality accepted among Descartes' contemporaries, which was, as Descartes said, that there is "at least as much reality in the cause as in the effect" (Jones, 1970, vol. 3, p. 168). In other words, since the thought of God exists in our mind, and given that Descartes saw this thought as a created result, he assumed he had demonstrated the existence of God: "Finally I perceive that the objective being of an idea cannot be produced by a being that exists potentially only, which properly speaking is nothing, but only by a being which is formal or actual" (from *Meditations on First Philosophy*, as cited in Jones, 1970, vol. 3, p. 167).

The basis of Descartes' reasoning was a specific view of nature, causality, and reason: that nature was uniform in patterned ways, and specifically, if results existed, one could assume uniformity between cause and effect and reason from the effect to the cause. We still use this reasoning to a large extent when we infer the existence of gravity every time we drop our pen, or the existence of magnetism when shopping lists adhere to refrigerator doors via a small metallic block. Yet, David Hume's (1896) critique would pull the rug out from under the assumption that one can infer causes from effects, challenging theology and philosophy as they were known and practiced, and the foundations of science.

CAUSES CAN ONLY BE PERCEIVED AS CONSISTENT COINCIDENCES: DAVID HUME

Hume's perspective was grounded in a view of knowledge as made up of ideas and impressions, impressions being those ideas that were stronger and therefore connected with more powerful experiences. Hume offered what he called the *empirical criterion of meaning* (1894): in order for an idea to be meaningful, it must be connected to a memory of an experience. Having reduced knowledge to ideas and impressions only, it followed then that he could tear apart the assumption that impressions are connected:

> All events seem entirely loose and separate. One event follows another; but we never can observe any tie between them. They seem conjoined, but never connected. And as we can have no idea of any thing which never appeared to

> our outward sense or inward sentiment, the necessary conclusion seems to be that we have no idea of connection or power at all, and that these words are absolutely without any meaning, when employed either in philosophical reasonings or common life. (Hume, 1894, section VII, parts 1 & 2)

Notice that in Hume's view, causality as connection did not exist; causality consisted only of observable events contiguous in time. Accordingly, his view of causality was limited to "priority, contiguity, and constant conjunction" (Salmon, 1989, p. 107). In other words, Hume assumed that causality could be reduced to a linear process, determined by a sequence in time (Edwards, 1967, p. 58). In concert with this viewpoint, Hume challenged the validity of inductive generalizations, which he saw as unfounded, since he believed that the knower always begins every moment with a fresh set of unrelated sense perceptions. Furthermore, because evidence of the connection itself could not be perceived, the most a causal explanation could refer to were classes of contiguous events, and not the cause of any particular event such as the origin of the universe (Jones, 1970, vol. III, p. 327).

Although scientists have in fact reasoned about causes, including about the origin of the universe, Hume's view of science has been deeply influential, perhaps most of all in contemporary variants of logical empiricism in the social and behavioral sciences. For instance, it is not uncommon for some contemporary researchers to state that all they can know about causation are coincidences or correlations, they cannot make inferences about causation.

CAUSALITY IS A CATEGORY THAT IS A PRECONDITION FOR EXPERIENCE: KANT

Immanuel Kant lived in the same era (the 18th century) as David Hume, yet his view of causality diverged profoundly from Hume's. Kant's thought is highly complex and this summary can only start to give the reader an experience of his very different way of modeling causality. He began from a starting point in which he asked: what are the conditions that make experience possible? In other words, rather than starting, as the empiricists sought, by trying to derive laws from the given of experience, Kant examined the process of experience itself. He essentially overturned Hume's empirical criterion of meaning by demonstrating that in order for there to be experience, the human mind must bring order to that experience via patterns he called categories (1929/1965). The categories in turn allow the mind to organize and synthesize representations. Kant demonstrated that Hume's empiricist criterion of meaning was a concept that was itself devoid of any matching percept, or experience, and that it failed because it did not meet its own criterion for meaningfulness.

Demonstrating that the mind experiences patterns in enduring ways, even though the specific contents vary, Kant described the fundamental patterns, or categories, that humans use to organize their experience. *A priori* categories are givens before experience itself, and according to which all experience is organized. *A posteriori* categories are those that are acquired in the course of experience. Examples of *a priori* categories, that all humans bring to their experience, are time, space, and causality (1929/1965).

Kant described causality as a process of change in substance, noting that it occurs always in accordance with a given period of time and always means that while something of the substance remains, also something of it alters. (1929/1965, p. 216, section A187). Kant's demonstration that experiences are necessarily ordered by anterior cognitive categories is the conceptual foundation on which all modern notions of heuristics and social constructivist thought rest.

Elements of a Causal Explanation

CAUSES, EFFECTS, AND MECHANISMS

Great scientific discoveries have invariably included the discovery of (1) an entity, (2) a causal process (or "mechanism"), and (3) a result. Traditionally, scientific explanation has focused on all three factors (Salmon, 1989). Taking these in turn, following Bhaskar (1989), we know that what something can cause is contained in or assumed by its definition. Defining an entity (ontology) simultaneously implies an epistemology—how that posited reality can be known. One has only to consider that the discovery of microbes, gravity, atoms, genes, and quantum particles all include theories of a new reality, what that reality can cause, how it can cause it, and a new way of knowing that reality. Customarily, causal explanations include a definition of the result of the causal process. The result can differ substantially from the mechanism bringing about the result, and even from the agent acted upon (although, per Kant, something of the original substance remains). A caterpillar evolves into a beautiful winged creature. Social work treatment can be the mechanism by which a traumatized human who only haltingly loves others or participates in society can become a fully loving human being who contributes meaningfully to her or his community.

The mechanism of action through which a cause brings about a result also is of great importance to a causal explanation, and can be defined "as sets of entities and activities organized so as to produce a regular series of changes from a beginning state to an ending one" (Steel, 2004, following Salmon; Machamer, Darden, & Craver). In social life, mechanisms can be identified through many means, among them identifying stable patterns in social roles and interactions that bring about characteristic results. Steel emphasizes that qualitative data can yield reliable causal inferences through "process tracing" (2004, p. 74). Process tracing relies on detailed descriptions of social practices and social roles to identify stable patterns of relating that yield specific cause and effect relationships over time. One has only to consider Mary Richmond's (1922) detailed case analyses in *What Is Social Casework?* to understand how social workers have traditionally identified causal mechanisms through process tracing. With her famous insight that social casework brings about change through "the impact of mind upon mind" (p. 131), Mary Richmond was emphasizing the power of a specific type of human relationship (social treatment) as a mechanism through which one mind can bring about constructive change in the mind of the person seeking that change.

Time: Distal and proximal causes. Chaos theory and recent research about human development raise different questions about time and causality, such as how long do social and behavioral causes take to have their effects? Some causes are coincident in time—for instance, when the appearance of a caregiver's face causes an infant to smile ecstatically. Other causes operate over great periods of time. Virginia Seitz's fascinating research (Seitz, Rosenbaum, & Apfel, 1985) demonstrated that combined medical and social interventions for poverty-level, single, first-time mothers and their children seemed to result in no appreciable differences by comparison with families who had not received the intervention after a few years. However, when she again measured the differences between the families receiving the intervention and a control group of families 10 years later, she found the mothers who received the interventions were more likely to be employed and to have had fewer children, and the children had better school attendance and fewer behavioral problems. The program more than paid for itself by comparison with the services required by the control group. Such findings are now the norm in early intervention research, leading many to conclude that small efforts provided early in a human family's life continue to have exponential effects over time. This example also illustrates the possibility that one can measure *distal* as well as *proximal causes*, in this case, for a family's improved social and behavioral functioning, and that distinguishing distal and proximal causes can be helpful for studying social interventions and also for understanding psychopathology.

Necessary and sufficient causes. Traditionally, philosophers have understood causality as a process of change, beginning with specific conditions and yielding a specific result. They have conceptualized both *necessary and sufficient conditions* to bring about a result. Some conditions are necessary for a result to occur: "*conditiones sine quibus non*—that is to say, those conditions which were such that, had any of them not occurred, the change in question would not have occurred either" (Edwards, 1967, vol. 2, p. 62, following A. J. Ayer). Other conditions are sufficient, for example, the totality of causes that "all of them having occurred, the effect in question could not fail to occur" (p. 63). Clearly, conditions can be necessary without being sufficient in order to bring about a result. An example is that it is virtually a truism given considerable amassed research evidence that humans will not abuse their young unless they have experienced abuse (e.g., abuse is a necessary cause of child abuse). However, it is also well known that many people abused as children do not abuse their young, so clearly having been abused as a child is not in itself sufficient to cause a parent to abuse a child. A recent study suggests that in order for a person abused as a child to become criminally aggressive, a sufficient cause must coexist—the deprivation of any better form of a caregiving relationship throughout the preceding period of time (Beathea, 2003).

Contemporary Perspectives on Causal Explanations

LEVELS OF ORGANIZATION AND MULTILEVEL REDUCTIONISTIC ANALYSIS: WIMSATT

One of the most seminal contributions to conceptualizing the complexities of biological and social realities remains William Wimsatt's (1976, 1994) elucidation of levels of organization. Wimsatt offers scientists ways of identifying the ontological assumptions they use to carve up natural (including social) systems for study and comparing these assumptions to recognize the biases inherent in any one definition of a system. To delineate the borders between systems under study and the environment that is not being studied, he used the term *the environment-system boundary* (1976). One can analyze the bias that is created as one defines the system for study by changing the environment-system boundary and moving up and down levels of organization—a procedure that Wimsatt called multilevel reductionistic analysis. Wimsatt defines levels of organization using size, mass, and internal interactive patterns (regular, irregular, periodic, etc.). While social scientists are familiar with the division of macro-, meso-, and microlevel systems (Bronfenbrenner, 1977), Wimsatt's originating formulation goes smaller (to the cellular and atomic), and larger (global). Consider that levels of organization are defined by many factors in addition to size, as, for instance, a black hole the size of a pinprick is immensely massive.

To apply these ideas using the example of the three nonviolent social movements, consider that a researcher could study the level of individual agency (the choices of individuals to participate in the movements). Alternatively, a researcher could choose a different level of organization and examine interactions between groups, for instance, how church-led organizations interacted with each other in forming the social movements. Still another level of organization would be to examine interactions between the participants and national-level systems, such as the March on Washington and civil rights legislation in the civil rights movement, the surrounding of the Lithuanian Parliament building by nonviolent protestors (Vardys & Sedaitis, 1996), and the imprisoned Nelson Mandela's meetings with apartheid government officials reacting to international pressures. Clearly, interactions at all of these three levels of organization are critical to understanding the mobilization and change processes of these three social movements, and choosing to study any one level of organization will yield very different information from making another choice.

Peruzzi (2004) describes horizontal causes as working within the same level of organization, and vertical causes as working across levels of organization. He also pointed out that causal models include constraints, also called the boundedness of causal influence. For instance, Nelson Mandela's impact on the ANC clearly was bounded horizontally and vertically by his imprisonment; KGB infiltration was an ever-present constraint on organizing the resistance movement against the Soviets; the work of the Ku Klux Klan and other homicidally racist activities imposed clear constraints on the causal efficacy of civil rights workers.

THE CAUSAL IMPACT OF SOCIAL STRUCTURES: ROY BHASKAR'S CRITICAL REALISM

To study the question of how nonviolent social movements can arise in contexts of profoundly traumatic social oppression assumes that societies can be traumatizing and that social movements are entities that can be studied. For some social scientists and philosophers, these are debatable assumptions. (Lewis, 2000; Nash, 1999). By comparison, critical realists following Roy Bhaskar's (1989, 1991) tradition claim that

> the social bonds that constitute social systems are just as real, if not in the same way, as the molecular bonds of things like sticks and stones. Moreover, the emergent social systems themselves have properties that are not those of their individual elements, just as material entities have properties distinct to their organization. (Nash, 1999, p. 447)

This realist position is very much in tune with the natural sciences (Salmon, 1989). The foundation for critical realism's contention that social structures are causal was outlined by Roy Bhaskar (1989, 1991), who emphasized that any definition of an entity will invariably include a definition of what that entity can cause. Moreover, he noted that there are two ways in which science ascribes reality to entities: some through perception (e.g., your chair), and some because of changes the entities bring about in material things (e.g., gravity, or magnetism). The latter are termed *causal ontologies*. Bhaskar described society (and social organizations) as a causal ontology (Manicas & Secord, 1983), in that social structures bring about changes in material things just as perceptibly as gravity and magnetism.

Applying the critical realist position to the example, discriminatory and oppressive social structures can be studied as real causes that produce real effects (such as impoverishment and learned helplessness), and likewise social structures can be studied as having powerfully remedial effects (e.g., civil rights legislation in the United States, parliamentary democracy in Lithuania, the new liberation from apartheid in South Africa). Social organizations possess values that are acted upon by humans, and in this way human values also are causes that can be studied scientifically (Bhaskar, 1991).

Although one defines an entity and what it causes simultaneously, this is not the same as asserting a causal law that the entity will invariably be able to bring about that cause. An apple will only fall toward the earth if the conditions and other associated contextual factors are favorable. An astronaut in outer space might well find the apple floating in quite other directions. Similarly, many oppressive societies persist without publicly manifest opposition, and, tragically, participants in many nonviolent social movements have been slaughtered without bringing about desired social changes. Accordingly, contemporary philosophers of science recognize that developing causal explanations is best understood *not* as a process of invariant laws, but rather as probabilistic, highly dependent on initial conditions and context (Manicas & Secord, 1983). The aim of contemporary science, then, is *not* to discover laws that apply as uniform predictions (as in the symmetry thesis of the logical empiricists), but rather to develop context-sensitive explanations that are inherently probabilistic. Consider that we can look for the cause of the movements of resistance in oppressive societies as some stable feature in human motivation, and yet the conditions that make those movements possible may vary considerably, including, for example, contextual conditions such as *glasnost* in the Soviet Union, international pressure against the apartheid regime in South Africa, and Presidents Kennedy's and Johnson's stand in support of the integration of schools, all of which formed more supportive climates for the nonviolent social movements.

CAUSES, AGENCIES, AND INTERACTIVITY: LEWONTIN

In addition to contextual factors influencing the probability that causes will bring about effects, Lewontin (2000) points out that causes can work through multiple pathways: "Agencies are alternative paths of mediation of some basic cause, a cause that always operates, although through different pathways. If the cause does not operate through one agency it must operate through another" (p. 103). Lewontin's example is that death occurs because humans are composed of biochemical parts that wear out. Yet the mechanisms, or "agencies" by which death occurs vary considerably and may not be limited to the individual's biochemical body parts. Infectious diseases were chief causes of mortality in Europe in the 19th century, yet 90% of the decrease in mortality from infectious diseases had occurred by the time of the First World War. Ruling out other explanations, Lewontin says the most plausible is that there were socioeconomic changes, specifically an increase in the real wage, which resulted in improved nutrition and a decrease in the number of hours worked. With their bodies better nourished, clothed, and rested, people were more able to recover from infections (p. 105). Lewontin's distinction between agencies and causes is particularly helpful when analyzing forces operating from different levels of organization (here, biochemical and socioeconomic) that may work together to bring about a result.

EMERGENCE

Yet another form of causal relationship was identified in the last part of the 20th century. The debates about the relationship between consciousness and the brain that were so important in the last part of the 20th century combined with other insights about the organization of systems to yield a definition of a specific type of causal process termed *emergence*. Whereas a condition of aggregativity obtains when the whole can be understood as the sum of its parts, an emergent property is dependent on the mode of organization of a system's parts (Wimsatt, 1997, p. S373). "Classical cases of emergence are those motivating the claim that 'the whole is more than the sum of the parts'—like Huygen's [1673/1986] discovery that pendulum clocks hung together on a beam became synchronized and kept better time than either did alone" (p. S374). Part of what is mysterious about emergence is how the parts are organized to produce a unique whole: "Emergence involves some kind of organizational interdependence of diverse parts, but there are many possible forms of such interaction, and no clear way to classify them" (p. S375).

Emergence is actually the most common type of causal process operating in nature. Emergent systems can unfold in patterned ways, within specific constraints, and predicting their behavior can be uncertain and probabilistic, because of emergent causes' dependence on both context and internal organization. In a fascinating book exploring emergent causal processes in nature, human systems, and software, Steven Johnson (2001) describes the slime mold as an example of emergence. The slime mold, comprised of single cells, can, without any identifiable form of leadership, merge into one mass, organize itself, and transport itself across large spaces of forest. Characterized by spontaneous, horizontal, self-regulating organization rather than by vertical patterns of discernible leadership, emergent systems are flexible and responsive both to internal state changes and changes in their contextual conditions.

Emergence is a way to define the relationship between consciousness and the brain, specifically, that consciousness is dependent for its existence on brain function. At the same time, consciousness can also regulate important aspects of brain functioning (Sperry, 1993). This way of understanding consciousness has revolutionary implications, in that subjective mental states have a causal impact on brain function. In addition, a bidirectional causality can be posited, in that while brain function causes subjective mental states, it also can be influenced by those states.

> The cognitive-consciousness revolution thus also represents a revolt against the long-time worship of the atomistic in science. Reductive microdeterministic views of personhood and the physical world are replaced in favor of a more wholistic, top-down view in which the higher, more evolved entities throughout nature, including the mental, vital, social, and other high-order forces gain their due recognition along with physics and chemistry. (Sperry, 1993, p. 879)

Returning to our example, one can illustrate multiple causal models and generate a hypothesis about the complex processes at work in the nonviolent movements for human liberation (the U.S. civil rights movement, the Lithuanian Sajudis, and Nelson Mandela's movement to free South Africans from apartheid). Again, the question posed initially is: Given that we know that traumatizing and oppressive environments tend to have disabling psychological effects on humans, what psychological mechanisms can explain the rising, organization, and ultimate victory of these movements for justice and freedom? Looking first at the microlevel system, one can postulate an innate motive for compassionate self-determination in all humans desiring love, truth, and justice, resembling in some ways the assertions of W. R. D. Fairbairn and Heinz Kohut (Mitchell & Block, 1995) that humans have an innate capacity to love that, in a caregiving relationship, can be strengthened so that it is a source of creativity, gratitude, generosity, and stable love of others. This inborn capacity is not an instinctual drive, but rather a meaning-creating intention to develop self-determining autonomy that includes the capacity to perceive and know truth and fairness (justice). Humans are not born with destructive motives (although they are naturally assertive), rather destructiveness is acquired when children are both deprived of good caregiving and subjected to traumatic experiences they identify with and struggle to cope with. It is possible that this motive for compassionate, just self-determination exists in a human from birth, and throughout development continues to exert an ongoing influence on the individual's other motives, an influence in the direction of seeking genuinely caring relationships, fairness, truth, and self-determining autonomy (Tyson, 2005).

The expressions of this motive for compassionate self-regulation, truth, and justice in everyday life cause clients to seek out social workers for care, and social workers' care for clients. This innate motive may be expressed in the social movements named above—because it is innate it can persist despite external oppression and continues to exert a force for justice, truth, caregiving love, and respect for others' autonomy even in life-threateningly oppressive circumstances. At the microlevel, other motives may be present in the person, and yet the person may choose to express justice and compassion rather than fear and hatred. In addition, any individual's choice and action may be the expression of several types of motives (motives to use music for inspiration and solidarity, for instance, which characterized all three movements).

Clearly, communities can operate in exclusionary, discriminatory, and even genocidal ways, apparently overwhelming individuals' capacity for justice and love, so causes stemming from other aspects of reality must be operative in an effective nonviolent community, including cultural values and received beliefs, as noted previously. In the example of these three movements, Gandhi's satyagraha was an important set of principles that was actively studied by Lithuanian and U.S. civil rights leaders and pervaded the work of the ANC.

One can also postulate an interactive causal pattern, in which participating in a community dedicated to the aims of justice and love will strengthen each person's individual motive and affirm synergistic cultural values. A committed experience of authentic relating enables the individuals to develop, to know the truth, and to respect each others' freedom and autonomy. Thus we can understand the uprising and organizing of these important movements for social justice as originating in each individual's motive for compassionate self-determination, which then was strengthened through interactive processes of inspiration, education, planning, and solidarity that occurred as the communities took shape.

These movements express an emergent causal pattern—their organization in coming together, cohering, and bringing about change in individuals and their societies is more powerful than simply the sum of individual parts. Finally, the causal impact of these movements was not just horizontal (the change in each participant, for example), but vertical as well. Although they were community movements, they grew and effectively changed important aspects of the regulatory governing bodies at the national level and continue to inspire global movements for peace and liberation.

Causal Validity

To allow research to adequately venture into the "causal thickets" of social and behavioral realities, researchers need a diversity of causal heuristics from which to choose. With a diversity of heuristics, researchers may be more able to (a) recognize the biases in the heuristics they choose for a specific research design and (b) compare heuristics in deciding how to understand what the posited realities cause. Returning to our core problem: *It is not just the existence of alternative unmeasured causes that can compromise the validity of research findings, but also that those causes may work in radically different ways from ones the researcher has taken into account.* Causes can interact with each other, work in tandem, be circular, emergent, necessary or sufficient, distal or proximal, and so on. *Evaluating the causal validity of research designs responds to the central question: Is this design as a whole a sound heuristic for studying the causal process(es) that are the focal points for this study?* To address this question the researcher can break the design into component parts, asking

- Are the ontology and epistemology to be used in this study sound approximations of the entities, and what they can cause?
- Are the causal processes assumed by the methods of data collection and analysis (a) logically consistent with the ontological and epistemological assumptions and (b) sound ways of knowing about the entities and what they cause?

Conclusion

From a historical overview it becomes clear that causes, including their definitions, mechanisms, agencies, and results, have been conceptualized in radically different ways over the history of Western thought. Scientists both past and present have used diverse methods to study causes and causal processes. Because every method is a heuristic that conceptualizes causality in a particular way, the requirements of received (positivistic) approaches to research (e.g., that variants of experimental design methodology are needed in order to study causality) have unjustifiably oversimplified causal realities. Roger Sperry (1993) eloquently captures the implications of limiting the ontologies, epistemologies, and causal mechanisms that can be used to understand humans in an article that described the implications for understanding consciousness of the revolution in brain science over the past several decades. The fact that consciousness has its own status as emergent from the brain, and can exert regulatory control over brain function, signifies that the human capacity to create meaning and choice can be freer than heretofore imagined:

> Volition remains causally determined but no longer entirely subject to the inexorable physiochemical laws of neurocellular activation. These lower level laws become supervened by higher level controls of the subjective conscious self in which they are embedded (just as, introspectively, it seems to be). The implications become critical for scientific treatment of personal agency and social interaction. Overall we still inhabit a deterministic universe, but it is ruled by a large array of different types, qualities, and levels of determinism. (p. 879)

The very diversity of causes that exist, in the mind, societies, and nature can signify not more determinism, but more freedom as we become more reflective about them.

References

Aquinas, St. Thomas. (1920/1981). *The Summa Theologica of St. Thomas Aquinas*. Part 1. Fathers of the English Dominican Province (transl). Westminster, MD: Christian Classics.

Aristotle. (1910–1952). *The works of Aristotle translated into English.* J. A. Smith (Ed.) & W. D. Ross (Trans.). Oxford: Clarendon Press.

Beathea, C. J. (2003). *"Now think about that!" Understanding the aggressive acts of African-American Women on probation and parole*. Unpublished doctoral dissertation, Loyola University of Chicago.

Bhaskar, R. (1989). *Reclaiming reality: A critical introduction to contemporary philosophy*. London: Verso.

Bhaskar, R. (1991). *Philosophy and the idea of freedom*. Oxford, UK: Basil Blackwell.

Bronfenbrenner, U. (1977). Toward an experimental ecology of human development. *American Psychologist, 32*, 513–531.

Coppleston, F. (1944–1965/1985). *A history of philosophy* (vols. 1– 9). New York: Doubleday.

Danziger, K. (1985). The methodological imperative in psychology. *Philosophy of the Social Sciences, 15*, 1-13.

Descartes, R. (1993). *Discourse on method and meditations on first philosophy* (D. C. Cress, Trans., 3rd ed.). Indianapolis, IN: Hackett. (Original work published 1637)

Edwards, P. (Ed.). (1967). *The encyclopedia of philosophy*. New York: Macmillan.

Hanson, N. R. (1958). *Patterns of discovery: An inquiry into the conceptual foundations of science.* Cambridge, UK: Cambridge University Press.

Hume, D. (1894). *An enquiry concerning the human understanding* (L. A. Selby-Bigge, Ed.). Oxford: Clarendon Press.

Hume, D. (1896). *A treatise on human nature* (L. A. Selby-Bigge, Ed.). Oxford: Clarendon Press.

Johnson, S. (2001). *Emergence: The connected lives of ants, brains, and software.* New York: Scribner.

Jones, W. T. (1970). *A history of Western philosophy.* New York: Harcourt, Brace Jovanovich.

Kant, I. (1929/1965). *Critique of pure reason* (Norman Kemp Smith, Trans.). New York: St. Martin's Press.

Lewis, P. (2000). Realism, causality, and the problem of social structure. *Journal of the Theory of Social Behavior, 30,* 249– 268.

Lewontin, R. C. (1974). The analysis of variance and the analysis of causes. *American Journal of Human Genetics, 26,* 400–411.

Lewontin, R. C. (2000). *The triple helix.* Cambridge: Harvard University Press.

Manicas, P. T., & Secord, P. F. (1983). Implications for psychology of the new philosophy of science. *American Psychologist, 38,* 399–413.

Mitchell, S., & Black, M. (1995). *Freud and beyond: A history of modern psychoanalytic thought.* New York: Basic Books.

Nash, R. (1999). What is real and what is realism in sociology? *Journal of the Theory of Social Behaviour, 29*(4), 445–466.

Peruzzi, A. (2004). Causality in the texture of mind. In A. Peruzzi (Ed.), *Mind and causality.* pp. 199–228. Amsterdam: John Benjamins.

Richmond, M. E. (1922). *What is social case work? An introductory description.* New York: Russell Sage Foundation.

Saleebey, D. (1979). The tension between research and practice: Assumptions of the experimental paradigm, *Clinical Social Work Journal, 7,* 267–284.

Saleebey, D. (1989). The estrangement of knowing and doing: Professions in crisis. *Social Casework, 70,* 556–563.

Salmon, W. (1989). *Four decades of scientific explanation.* Minneapolis: University of Minnesota Press.

Schell, J. (2003). *The unconquerable world: Power, nonviolence and the will of the people.* New York: Henry Holt.

Seitz, V., Rosenbaum, L., & Apfel, N. (1985). Effects of family support intervention: A ten-year follow-up. *Child Development, 56*, 376–391.

Sermabeikian, P. (1994). Our clients, ourselves: The spiritual perspective and social work practice. *Social Work, 39*, 178–183.

Sperry, R. W. (1993). The impact and promise of the cognitive revolution. *American Psychologist, 48*, 878–885.

Steel, D. (2004). Social mechanisms and causal inference. *Philosophy of the Social Sciences, 34*(1), 55–78.

Tyson, K. (1995). *New foundations for scientific social and behavioral research: The heuristic paradigm*. Needham Heights, MA: Allyn & Bacon.

Tyson, K. (2005, June). Developing self-determination from the child's perspective: Effective social services for traumatized children. Invitational lecture for International Social Work Conference, University of Lapland Department of Social Sciences, Rovaniemi, Finland.

Vardys, S., & J. Sedaitis (1996). *Lithuania: The rebel nation*. Greenwich, CT: Westview Press.

Vigilante, J. (1974). Between values and science: Education for the profession during a moral crisis or is proof truth? *Journal of Social Work Education, 10*, 107–115.

Wimsatt, W. (1976). Reductionism, levels of organization, and the mind-body problem. In G. G. Globus, G. Maxwell, & I. Savodnik (Eds.), *Consciousness and the brain: A scientific and philosophical inquiry* (pp. 205–267). New York: Plenum.

Wimsatt, W. C. (1986). Heuristics and the study of human behavior. In D. W. Fiske & R. A. Shweder (Eds.), *Metatheory in social science: Pluralisms and subjectivities*. Chicago: University of Chicago Press.

Wimsatt, W. C. (1994). The ontology of complex systems: Levels of organization, perspectives, and causal thickets. *Canadian Journal of Philosophy*, Supplementary Volume 20, 207–274.

Wimsatt, W. C. (1997). Aggregativity: Reductive heuristics for finding emergence. *Philosophy of Science, 64,* S372–S384.

Witkin, S. L. (1989). Towards a scientific social work. *Journal of Social Service Research*, *12,* 83–98.

Witkin, S. L. (2001). Complicating causes: Editorial. *Social Work, 46*(3), 197–202.

CHAPTER 12

Notes on Teaching Social Work Ethics

MARGARET RHODES

At the 2001 Transforming Social Work gathering, I participated in a small-group discussion focused on "doing theory" differently. In particular, interest centered on new ways to think about theory from social constructionist and feminist viewpoints. Many in the group expressed the view that too often the teaching of theory within social work (including our own teaching) seemed to narrow and oversimplify, rather than expand and enrich, our students' understanding of clients and their worlds. Particular interest was expressed in the ways that many theories, while claiming universality, did not encompass the interests and voices of marginalized groups, thereby in effect ignoring power differences that need to be addressed to achieve social justice. Our discussion ranged from theories that undergird our psychological and sociological understanding of clients and their worlds to the ethical theories that form the basis of the National Association of Social Workers (NASW) *Code of Ethics* (1979, 1996).

Well after the conference ended, I found that I kept coming back to the questions we had posed. How do we use theory to open up possibilities, rather than narrowing them, particularly in a social work world requiring specific outcomes? How do we incorporate the dialogues of everyday life more fully into theorizing? How do we convey the ways in which theory privileges some voices while excluding others, and how do we challenge these ways? What discourses enable us to question and revise our assumptions about what has value and what is true? As a teacher of social work ethics, I was already engaged in rethinking my approach, and the discussion served as a spur to explore ways to think about and teach ethics to address some of the questions we had raised.

I shall begin with my experience understanding and teaching social work ethics and its connection to the Vermont conversation. I shall then use a case to probe the strengths and limitations of a traditional approach to social work ethics, one that is widely used and that I myself have often used, followed by an exploration of alternative ways we might think about and teach ethics, and my reasons for preferring this account.

Social Work Ethics

When I first began teaching social work and human service ethics more than 20 years ago, the fields of bioethics and social work ethics were just emerging as legitimate areas of serious study. While social workers had always seen the importance of values, there was a relatively small literature at that time on the relevance of ethical theory to practice (Reamer, 1998). The NASW *Code of Ethics*, developed in 1960 and revised in 1979, delineated social workers' basic responsibilities to the client, agency, colleagues, profession, and society, but there were few courses or trainings devoted to ethical issues per se. When I worked in child protection from 1967 to 1970, for example, I received training about legal but not ethical issues. Discussion of ethics was subsumed into discussion of practice but often not specifically addressed. In the 1970s and 1980s, as the interest in bioethics and social work ethics increased, there was a real excitement and sense of experimentation to discover what principles, what textbooks, what trainings would best serve social workers and other professionals.

Today, social workers have a greatly expanded *Code of Ethics* (NASW, 1996). Besides providing general principles, this code lists 155 specific guidelines, or rules, for conduct (Reamer, 1998) and serves to adjudicate unethical conduct, as well as to describe overarching values of the profession (NASW, 1996). Social work can also boast of a significant literature on ethics, and within social work schools, ethics forms a specific part of many practice courses, as well as sometimes meriting a course in its own right. Textbooks often provide detailed steps of ethical decision making, based on a set of articulated ethical principles (see, e.g., Dolgoff & Loewenberg, 1988; Reamer, 1982; Rhodes, 1986). While this increased interest in ethics has resulted in many important contributions, I worry that ethical decision making is increasingly presented as a set of rules to be plugged in, a complex set of legalistic directives, a kind of *Diagnostic and Statistical Manual of Mental Disorders* (*DSM*)*-4* of ethics that does not do justice to the complexities of ethics in practice (B. Fenby, personal communication, October 2000). The *Code of Ethics* in particular seems more focused on the special mandates of managed care than on the needs of the unempowered (Freud & Krug, 2002).

In addition, I, and many of us at the gathering, had begun to question the theoretical structures that most frequently inform discussion and teaching of social work ethics—that is, human rights perspectives, consequentialism, and Kantian ethics. These perspectives derive from Enlightenment-era notions of what an ethical theory is and what a theory can do. In the 18th century, theorists labored under the optimistic idea that it was possible to provide laws or principles under which one could subsume all ethical knowledge. And even though today philosophers and social workers are much more cautious in their claims for reason, the theories still figure prominently in our teaching of social work ethics. This is not surprising, since the theories form the underpinnings of many of our institutions, and they can and do helpfully inform ethical decision making about particular cases. In various combinations they form the basis of several texts on social work ethics (referenced above), as well as providing the underpinnings of the *Code of Ethics*.

And it was precisely these theoretical underpinnings that we, in our transforming social work conversation, were questioning. Participants, borrowing from social constructionist theorizing, suggested that Enlightenment theories, rather than in fact subsuming all truth within their principles, gave a partial understanding of our world, one that distorted by assuming it could give the Truth with a capital *T*, and one that was inevitably shaped by existing power relations and conditions within the society that developed it. In our conversation, we were interested in what had been left out.

I had found, as my colleagues had, that using these enlightenment theories to understand ethical problems could be as problematic as it was helpful. While I believe that students need to understand these perspectives, reliance on them as frameworks for understanding ethics can result in thinking that is formulaic and rigid; the complexities and power dynamics of the situations can too easily be overlooked. Students too often plug in the theories in ways that both distort the complexity of the original theory and are insensitive to the theory's limitations.

In addition, in applying these theories/principles, our mandate to promote social justice for clients often gets buried under our concern to promote the well-being and self-determination of individual clients, with well-being and self-determination being conceived in the most immediate and sometimes superficial way. Borrowing in part from these social constructivist ideas, I was interested in finding new ways to teach that could broaden our understanding of clients' worlds and better encompass our mandate to work for social justice.

While social justice encompasses many different aspects, including issues of punishment and protection, I am focusing here on "social justice" as an ideal of economic and social access and participation in the basic services and institutions of our society: jobs, housing, education, child care, health care. I would argue that this sort of justice or equality is essential to our much-touted concept of personal liberty or client self-determination. That is, liberty in the sense of self-determination becomes an empty ideal if not enacted in a context of equality, that is, a context in which the disempowered have access to services that enable them to make meaningful choices. (Roberts, 1997). This idea is captured in our *Code of Ethics* by the stipulation that we act to "help meet the basic needs of all people, with *particular attention* to the needs and *empowerment* of people who are *vulnerable, oppressed and living in poverty* [italics added]" (NASW, 1996, p. 1). Social justice in this sense has been a central theme of social work ethics since its inception (Abramowitz, 1998; Reisch, 2002; Swenson, 1998; Witkin, 1998).

In our Vermont conversation, we were searching for ways to apply our concern for social justice and our interest in a more context-driven understanding of theory to social work practice. I shared that interest, particularly in relation to ethics. I began to examine my approach further (using cases plus theory) to teaching ethics and its limitations, and I turn to that now.

Teaching Theory Through Cases

There are many excellent reasons for adopting a case-plus-theory approach to teaching social work ethics: (a) engaging a student through real-life examples, (b) integrating theory with practice, (c) positing difficult dilemmas that a student will encounter in future practice, and (d) probing a student's actual beliefs through the student's choice of what to do in the case. Consider, for example, a typical kind of dilemma, in an abbreviated case example.

A social worker at a family service agency is assigned to work with a 28-year-old white woman, call her Ellen, who has two children, a boy aged 2 and a girl aged 6. Ellen has come to the agency struggling with severe depression and with her inability to handle the responsibilities of her children. She is living in a one-bedroom apartment in the inner city and working at a fast-food restaurant from 8 a.m. until 4 p.m. While she is at work, she is able to leave her son with a friend who lives near the restaurant. She is afraid, however, that a complaint of child abuse will be filed by the school, since her daughter misses school often and is home alone sometimes after school. Ellen has been prescribed medication for her depression and you, the social worker, have three follow-up appointments to deal with Ellen's other issues. In the course of the second session, she tells you that her boyfriend, who lives in her apartment, sometimes sells drugs from her home and while she doesn't like it, he then helps with her rent, which she could not otherwise pay in full. She also tells you that her daughter is often there with him and that her boyfriend does not like her daughter and she sometimes worries about her daughter's safety. How can you, as the social worker, help her? What are the ethical issues?

In a case such as this one, in an ethics class, in addition to probing the psychological and relational issues, students are usually encouraged to articulate any ethical problems and to describe different options, framing them in terms of ethical principles or theories that help us understand what is at stake and the rationales for acting one way or another. In this case, given the way it is presented, students might well see a conflict between the social worker's duty (ethical and legal) to report information if a child is at serious risk (child abuse) and her duty to respect the confidence of the client (her client's privacy and right to make her own decision). The case may even have been set up to probe this conflict, to probe the limits of a social worker's legal and ethical responsibilities around confidentiality.

In discussing the case, students would examine different options and the rationales behind each, looking for ways to respect the wishes of the client and to promote her and her children's welfare. The social worker will try to honor the mother's need for help with her depression, her job, and her children, and in doing so, she is acting on a principle of promoting welfare, which can be connected to the perspective of utilitarianism (increase happiness, minimize pain). She will also consider her obligation to honor confidences, which is connected to a principle of individual liberty—control over personal information. She may come to believe that the welfare and liberty of the mother (in keeping the situation as it is) conflicts with the welfare of the children (making the boyfriend move out or reporting him). In this case, the legal mandate to report child endangerment (to prevent harm) will trump the welfare and privacy of the mother.

In addition, if the mother refuses to take any action, then the social worker may have another dilemma, for she must add to the analysis the ethics of paternalism—that is, how does she evaluate her expertise to decide what is good for the client versus the client's right to make her own good or bad decision for herself (again the principle of self-determination and privacy)? And she must reconsider any laws with respect to violating confidential information and reporting child abuse. This is a very typical sort of dilemma, and the *Code of Ethics* gives guidelines to help in the decision making by providing principles that must be honored.

In discussing a case such as this in class, I have found that students often become very engaged in the different options and tease out many of the relevant factors to making a decision. It enables students to see some of the complexities involved, as well as the relevance of different theoretical principles at stake in the situation. What then is the problem? What is left out or distorted? Why should we change our teaching or our understanding of the theories involved?

I have become increasingly uneasy in my use of analyses such as these because they seem to me sometimes to be contrived and at times to encourage a too-facile kind of decision making, one that students may embrace precisely because it enables them to feel they know what they are doing. I'm also made uneasy because such ethical analyses seem too often to leave out considerations of social justice. We figure out what to do so that we are respecting confidentiality or so that we are not liable if we break it, but Ellen is left with no apartment, homeless, or with her children removed from her care. Social justice is left to the policy makers. Let me explain more fully.

In this case, because of the way it is described, the focus becomes that of the client's welfare, her children's welfare, and her autonomy about this decision (her privacy and right to make her own decision). Other important ethical dimensions of the case (and of her welfare) are downplayed: for example, her having to work at a grueling, low-paying job without benefits; the absence of decent, low-cost housing; the absence of low-cost, safe after-school care; or the harm to her children from living in a neighborhood where gang violence is common. Might one not argue that these factors should form the focus of any ethical discussion, rather than the issue of confidentiality? At the least, there needs to be a way to make these dimensions more salient, because otherwise the discussion itself may leave the impression that these factors, which reveal unethical levels of poverty within our society, are not as important as the factors focused on or that they are not factors we can do anything about. Either way the result is unfortunate.

Cases are often discussed to emphasize one or another principle within the code so that students can see the importance of one aspect of ethics without having to focus on all the other, complex dimensions of it. For example, in this case, through the discussion, ideally students will understand better the importance and limits of keeping client information confidential, in both legal and ethical terms, and the importance and limits of reporting abuse. Issues of social justice, such as the absence of adequate child care or housing, even though they could be viewed as part of Ellen's welfare, are taken up in policy classes. Because the focus in ethics discussions is usually on the individual liberty and well-being of the client, the social, economic, and political dimensions and contexts for individual behavior and decision making are too often ignored or de-emphasized.

The NASW *Code of Ethics* itself separates issues of social justice from those of client well-being, putting them in separate sections of the code—social justice in part 6 and with an emphasis on action separate from one's work with a particular client. While it makes sense to delineate and separate different dimensions of ethics, I worry that the separation is too great and can result in the sense that political and economic issues of social justice do not belong in our decision making about individual clients—they do not fit with practice per se. This sort of separation is sometimes reiterated through the way social work schools set up classes, separating classes about practice from those on social justice and policy issues.

I'm sure many would argue that to do otherwise would be to expect too much of classroom teaching of students, many of whom are 22 years old and without much experience of social work. How much can one absorb, without the complexity leading to confusion and paralysis? My point, however, is that the result seems often to be an emphasis on satisfying our legal and other professional obligations, with little focus within practice on the broader social justice mandates of the profession.

The danger is that ethical decision making can easily degenerate into a narrow focus on what to do next, based on a cursory, or at least less than full, analysis of the meaning and reach of the principles. The principles become reduced to a kind of checklist that students must run through. And it is the broader social justice issues, these intractable issues of the profession such as poverty and disempowerment, that may too easily be set aside to consider at some later, undefined time. This is particularly true if, within practice, as is often the case, one is rushed for time and a decision needs to be made immediately. We need some way to encompass more fully in our consideration of particular cases the range of economic and political forces often arrayed against our clients, those historical and economic particularities that often silence our clients and that may prevent us from seeing the larger picture within a particular case.

Let me make the point another way. Students in an ethics class will be encouraged to use as a framework a set of ethical principles or ethical theories. The principles most often invoked are some version of those in the code: promoting client welfare and self-determination; honoring confidentiality; avoiding conflicts of interest; honoring obligations to the agency, colleagues, and the profession. We notice and act on situations that manifest one of these principles or values. While promoting social justice is also included in the *Code of Ethics* and is accepted as one of our most important mandates, we seldom focus on it in practice—we are not clear how we are to define it or integrate it in our work with individual clients. Consideration of it may get short shrift in the analysis of particular case studies involving ethics.

Case and Principles Reformulated

I want to suggest ways to teach and think about social work ethics that further problematize our analyses of cases and that make room for social justice. Let me return to our hypothetical example.

Often, discussion in this sort of case will begin with asking students to identify the most important ethical issues at stake, followed by a discussion of the issue or issues. Sometimes a student will bring in a case because of a specific conflict the student wants help in resolving. When I presented the case earlier, I described it as if this process had occurred, with the issue of confidentiality versus child safety emerging as the primary issue to be discussed.

In asking students to articulate the ethical dimensions/problems posed by this case, for example, one might begin by asking them to think about different ways it might be described. From whose viewpoint is the case currently described? How might other participants in the case describe it? Are we leaving out participants whose viewpoint needs to be included—a grandmother or teacher or the children's father? And what does each of the children think about it? Do the ethical issues change as we shift viewpoint? Students might even be asked to rewrite the case from the viewpoint of different participants. What we see and how we describe it will determine much about what ethical principles we view as having relevance. Social work students (and all of us) can benefit from reformulating and revisioning case descriptions. Such reformulations are, I would claim, first and foremost an ethics' process—what we include, exclude, and emphasize. In this way, we may broaden our understanding of what is involved and begin to make room for the voices of those who are not heard.

In addition, once a case has been examined in terms of one ethical issue, which will highlight some ethical principles rather than others, students can be asked to reexamine the case, putting a different ethical principle or value at the center of the discussion. For example, in the case as it was described earlier, the focus centered on how to honor confidentiality while making sure that the children were safe. Suppose that students were then asked to reexamine this case, but to do so putting the principle of equality of opportunity at the center, rather than that of privacy. How do the ethical dilemmas and the possible resolutions then shift? If social equality and the sort of economic equality necessary to achieve social equality are set forth as the primary concerns, then the case dilemma may look different. We may conclude that the most urgent ethical dimensions are other than those first formulated—perhaps finding different housing or job or education for Ellen.

What would this mean in actual practice, given how hard it is to change economic circumstances or find resources? I suspect that we avoid focus on powerlessness and inequality because of the difficulty of being able to effect any change in these areas. However, if we are asked to redirect our attention to a principle such as equality of opportunity, then new space may open up, not only in our own understanding of priorities, but in the mind of the client. Discussing our concerns with the client may be a relief to the client who is apt to have these matters on her mind and who is experienced in understanding this aspect of her life.

In a class discussion, this shifting of what principle or value to put at the center could also result in discussion of which social work principles are most valued in practice in different social work settings. And students could probe how their agency is or could be structured to meet the challenge of honoring different principles.

I would suggest more generally that as students move through formulating and examining cases in terms of their ethical dimensions, they consider multiple viewpoints at each step, as a way to complicate and enrich their theorizing while still leaving them with a structure to guide their decision making. Through considering multiple viewpoints, we can combine our concern for the well-being and autonomy of the individual client with our concern to include viewpoints that have gone unvoiced, viewpoints that are crucial if we intend to honor our commitment to diversity, the unempowered, and social justice.

One might argue that social workers already consider multiple viewpoints. Considering such viewpoints and the economic and political realities that affect the client is tantamount to incorporating an ecological viewpoint, one that is much discussed already in social work schools. However, while as social workers we are strongly committed to viewing clients through multiple lenses, these lenses are not always incorporated into practice decisions about ethics. We pay lip service to this perspective more than we find ways to interrogate our own ethical positions and to challenge the oppressive social-economic-political contexts of our clients. And this is not surprising, as it is very hard work and we often do not know where to start.

In fact, an opposite criticism of this approach might be that there is little an individual social worker can do to affect these deep inequalities, as they affect a particular client. However, if we do not find ways to put these concerns at the center, then in effect we are narrowing our ethics to fit what is achievable in existing circumstances, a kind of acceptance of the status quo at odds with what we say we stand for.

By highlighting equality (a central part of social justice—see earlier comment regarding social justice), we in effect put an emphasis on changing the conditions that contribute to the unequal and often oppressive circumstances of our clients' lives. And through multiple viewpoints, we attempt to include what may have been overlooked. This sort of equality at the center moves us to begin to incorporate economic/political change in order to achieve it and forces us to look for what has been left out of our own accounts of the role of ethics in our clients' and in our professional lives.

The Enlightenment ethical theories of the 17th and 18th centuries were themselves once dynamic, radical critiques of both earlier theories and existing conditions in the society promoted by the old religious outlooks. A new faith in the power of reason to uncover the Truth replaced an earlier faith in divine revelation and divine right in the works of John Locke, John Stuart Mill, and other leading Enlightenment thinkers who provided the basis from which our social work *Code of Ethics* eventually emerged. I am not suggesting that we discard the concepts and principles provided by these theories—our commitment to individual liberty, to individual welfare, and the common good. I am suggesting, though, that if we separate these values from our concern for the sort of economic and social equality that is essential to social justice, then our social work ethics will run the risk of becoming part of the status quo, rather than leading the way to uncover and change the unethical practices and conditions of clients' lives today.

I also am not suggesting that equality of opportunity should be the only principle put at the center, though I think it is particularly important in addressing power differences. Rather, I am suggesting that we experiment with putting different principles at the center, even in cases when they do not seem relevant, to examine how they change the way we look at the situation. Thus, we might examine what our case looks like if respect for diversity becomes the central concern. Varying the ethical principle we put at the center becomes another way to create multiple viewpoints.

Ethical Steps Reformulated

Before concluding, I want to elaborate on four basic steps of ethical decision making and how we might use them to include multiple viewpoints in our ethical analyses.

PERCEPTION

When we examine a dilemma or problem in social work ethics, we in effect have noticed some features of the situation that we identify as ethical and as requiring further inquiry. In any situation, we focus on some aspects of it to the exclusion of others: If you are looking for a place to eat when you are hungry, all you notice are restaurants, while if you are not hungry these eateries may barely register as you pass. So, within social work ethics, we may focus on some aspects of situations as demanding ethical attention, while ignoring others. We may do so for a variety of reasons. We may do so because we are in fact acting ethically and so do not question what we are doing. Ethical norms may be built into the skills we have learned (Rhodes, 1992). Alternatively, if we are committed to a belief system that itself is unethical in some respect, we may fail to question that aspect, as, for example, with racism within the segregated structures of our society in the past. Also, if a particular way of doing things has become routine within an agency, then we too may fail to question it—for example, the past practice of not making case records available to clients. What we notice as ethical will depend on a complex of factors derived from our background and training, as well as from the context and accepted practices of a setting. Some settings, for example, may promote strict confidentiality guidelines (as in private practice), whereas in others (such as probation) confidentiality would be inappropriate because of the kind of service offered (Fleck-Henderson, 1991). The history of ethics has consisted in part of problematizing aspects of the culture that have been taken for granted—slavery, women's inequality, racism, and so on.

In social work practice, we need to hone our skills of looking for what we are not seeing. This is of course very hard to do—how does one see what one is blind to ethically? Putting ourselves in the position of different actors in a situation can be a way to expand our understanding of what is at stake ethically. In addition, as teachers we need to expose students and ourselves to points of view that will expand or challenge their and our understanding of ethics and its boundaries. Sometimes we can do this by making a group as diverse as possible to include different viewpoints. A diverse class will have a better chance of opening us up to "see differently" than will a homogeneous one. In agency settings as well, case conferences and other meetings should include representatives from client groups, the community, and other populations whose ideas can broaden our own.

In addition, we should make efforts to include children's views whenever possible. Children's views are regularly discounted, even in situations where children have a large stake, yet they often have creative solutions to problems (Konrad, 2004). We should also pay more attention to our own childhood experiences and the knowledge these experiences give us that can deepen our understanding of clients (Weick, 1999).

FORMULATION

Perception and formulation are closely linked. What we notice is determined in part by the language and categories we have for expressing thought. The language we use and the questions we pose will determine the answers we get. Expanding our categories and ways of thinking is also challenging. Here, feminist and constructionist writings have been valuable in teaching us to look more closely at how we construct our world and how that affects the decisions we make. An exciting literature has emerged that challenges some of our categories and shows how our concepts have limited our understanding of clients and thus our ethical vision as well.

Let me give a few examples to suggest the richness of this approach to ethics. Stanley Witkin (2000) has pointed out how our categories of disability work to keep the disabled invisible and how they also keep us "from noticing the complexities and differences among people identified with these labels" (p. 101). Another challenge is presented in the insightful historical/philosophical exploration by Nancy Fraser and Linda Gordon (1997) in "Genealogy of Dependence." They challenge the view of welfare recipients as unhealthily dependent, by tracing the way in which "dependence" has shifted from meaning anyone whose work depends on others (laborers are thus dependent) to being a term reserved for welfare "dependents." They show through their analysis how racial and gender prejudice inform our understanding and the policies directed toward those we choose to call "dependent," and thus how unacceptable inequalities in the society are reinforced. This sort of analysis, while it does not offer any solutions to the "problem" of "welfare," invites us to think about women who are caring for their children in a different way. It also invites us to analyze our concepts differently through locating them in their political and historical contexts.

Another example of expanding/questioning our categories can be found in Ruth Malone's (1999) analysis of our concept of *marketing* and how it affects our view of health care that is increasingly discussed in terms of *products, consumers, delivery,* terms that downplay the moral agency of the participants and the public nature of the goods at stake, thereby impoverishing the policies we come up with.

Dennis Saleebey (1994) and Joan Laird (1998), among others, have written about how clients' stories and myths can serve as instruments of empowerment, with clients serving as experts on their own lives. This approach has expanded the ways in which we think about clients and thereby has expanded our ethical vision. Saleebey's now widely accepted strengths perspective can itself be viewed as a way of looking at clients' worlds differently, of shifting the focus on clients' lives from deficits to strengths, and thereby changing the evaluative lens, the ethical focus (Saleebey, 1994, 1997).

In our teaching, students should be encouraged to probe the concepts within which a case is couched and to look for alternative ways to think about them. To return to the case of Ellen, students might probe the concept of *confidentiality* and examine its historical development. Why is it so important in our culture, given that it is not a recognized value in many cultures or even subcultures in our country? Does it serve to prevent communication in families or encourage it? In what context did it develop, and whose interests does it serve?

DISCUSSION

If one includes multiple viewpoints in describing and formulating a case, then discussion can more easily encompass many points of view, though even here we need to examine how we set up discussion and whether we do so in ways that privilege some viewpoints over others. In urging multiple viewpoints, I do not mean to suggest that all viewpoints are equally valid. Any meaningful ethical discussion must privilege reasoning and evidence over simply having an opinion. However, all thoughtful viewpoints deserve a hearing, so that we are not too quick to dismiss a point of view we do not understand. And the criteria of what is thoughtful or reasonable and what counts as evidence should remain open to discussion.

RESOLUTION

One might argue that if we are successful in eliciting many viewpoints and expanding our awareness to include new dimensions, then any sort of timely resolution or agreement will become all the more difficult, if not impossible. And how is one to agree on criteria for deciding among competing viewpoints? Such deliberations may be all very well in a classroom, but in the "real" world of case decisions, one must act and usually quickly.

My hope is that even when students must act quickly, this sort of process will spur them to look for and consider more broadly and to have greater humility about the "rightness" of any decision they make, to hold their ethical truths lightly. Ethical principles and ethical theory are not set in stone but open to changing interpretations and emphases, and we need to find ways to build such uncertainty into our understanding of ethics. It is my hope that this chapter, this way of thinking about teaching social work ethics, can contribute to this process.

Conclusion

Nafisi (2004), in her book *Reading Lolita in Tehran*, states that "The highest form of morality is not to feel at home in one's own home" (p. 94). I think what she means is that the heart of ethical thinking is questioning, trying out new viewpoints, being uncomfortable, a kind of discomfort that forces us to expand our understanding of the ethical and to "question what we took for granted" (Nafisi, p. 94). I am suggesting a way of teaching social work ethics that attempts to problematize, through both considering multiple viewpoints and shifting what principles we put at the center, in particular giving equality, a principle often left on the periphery, a central place. In this way, we might begin not only to expand our understanding of ethics, through our consideration of multiple viewpoints, but also to integrate our concern for social justice more fully into our practice, by both giving attention to new voices and privileging equality, a central part of social justice in social work.

Notes

My rethinking of theory has been inspired by and based on the reading of many theorists, and in particular the following works have been important in shaping my thinking:

Benhabib, S., Butler, J., Cornell, F., & Fraser, N. (1995). *Feminist contentions*. New York: Routledge.

Farmer, P. (2003). *Pathologies of power: Health, human rights and the new war on the poor*. Berkeley, CA: University of California Press.

Harding, S. (Ed.). (2004). *The Feminist standpoint reader: Intellectual and political controversies*. New York: Routledge.

Nicholson, L. (Ed.). (1990). *Feminism/postmodernism*. New York: Routledge.

Okin, S. (1989). *Justice, gender and the family*. New York: Basic Books.

References

Abramowitz, M. (1998). Social work and social reform: An arena of struggle. *Social Work*, 43(6), 512–526.

Dolgoff, R.., & Loewenberg, F. (1988). *Ethical decisions for social work practice*. Itasca, IL: Peacock Press.

Fleck-Henderson, A. (1991). Moral reasoning in social work practice. *Social Service Review*, *65*(2), 185–202.

Fraser, N., & Gordon, L. (1997). The genealogy of dependence. In N. Fraser (Ed.), *Justice interruptus: Critical reflections on the "postsocialist" condition* (pp. 121–150). New York: Routledge.

Freud, S., & Krug, S. (2002). Beyond the code of ethics, part 1: Complexities of ethical decision making in social work practice. *Families in Society*. *83*, 483–492.

Konrad, S. (2004, November). Notes from workshop on social work with children in contested divorces. University of Maine, Portland.

Laird, J. (1998). Theorizing culture. In M. McGoldrick (Ed.), *Revisioning family therapy: Race, culture and gender in clinical practice* (pp. 20–36). New York: Guilford Press.

Malone, R. (1999, May/June). Policy as product: Morality and metaphor in health policy discourse. *Hastings Center Reports*, 16–21.

Nafisi, A. (2004). *Reading Lolita in Tehran: A memoir in books*. New York: Random House.

National Association of Social Workers. (1979). *Code of ethics of the National Association of Social Workers*. Silver Spring, MD: NASW Press.

National Association of Social Workers. (1996). *Code of ethics of the National Association of Social Workers*. Washington, DC: NASW Press.

Reamer, F. G. (1982). *Ethical dilemmas in social service*. New York: Columbia University Press.

Reamer, F. G. (1998). The evolution of social work ethics. *Social Work, 43*(6), 488–501.

Reisch, M. (2002). Defining social justice in a socially unjust world. *Families in Society, 83*(4), 343–354,

Rhodes, M. (1986). *Ethical dilemmas in social work practice*. Milwaukee, WI: Family Service, America/Families International.

Rhodes, M. (1992). Social work challenges. The boundaries of ethics. *Families in Society, 73*, 40–47.

Roberts, D. (1997). *Killing the black body: Race, reproduction and the meaning of liberty*. New York: Vintage.

Saleebey, D. (1994). Culture, theory and narrative: The intersection of meanings in practice. *Social Work, 39*(4), 351–359.

Saleebey, D. (1997). *The strengths perspective in social work practice*. New York: Longman.

Swenson, C. (1998). Clinical social workers' contribution to a social justice perspective. *Social Work, 43*(6), 527–539.

Weick, A. (1999). Guilty knowledge. *Families in Society. 80*(4), 327–332.

Witkin, S. L. (1998). Is social work an adjective? *Social Work, 43*(6), 483–486.

Witkin, S. L. (2000). Noticing. *Social Work, 45*(2), 101–104.

CHAPTER 13

Postmodern Call and Response
Social Work Education in the Modernist University

SUSAN E. ROCHE

For the past 15 years, my department of social work has committed our curriculum and our scholarship to a maturing postmodern philosophy that emphasizes critical social construction, particularly as it informs human rights, social justice, and a strengths perspective in social work. By postmodernism, I am referring to a critique of all universal theories and of discourses that marginalize and disqualify some people's realities by privileging the beliefs of others (Chambon, Irving, & Epstein, 1999; Faubion, 2000; Foucault, 1995; Parton, 1994). Postmodernism changes the tradition of expert, repositioning teachers as facilitators, social workers as consulting partners, and everyone as colearners and coconstructors (Pease & Fook, 1999; Roche et al., 1999).

Social constructionism (Berger & Luckman, 1967; Gergen, 1994, 1999; Witkin, 1991, 1999) has been called a source and a strand of postmodernism. As we define it in our department,

> critical social constructionism provides a conceptual framework for understanding, analyzing, and critiquing knowledge

> claims and for generating new perspectives. From a constructionist standpoint, knowledge is created through historically, culturally and politically situated processes of social interchange rather than being the product of individual minds or a reflection of the external world. . . . Since no one perspective is considered to have privileged access to truth, social construction supports intellectual diversity and tends to oppose the elimination or suppression of forms or models of understanding. As a sociohistorical product, knowledge is intimately connected to power. This connection encourages social workers to engage in "oppositional discourses of criticism and resistance" (Lather, 1991, p. xvii). These qualities of critical social construction connect it with the program's third emphasis on human rights and social justice. (Department of Social Work, 2006)

When I first joined the department, the philosophy was largely made up of traces of ideas whose substance and implications had yet to be developed and owned by the faculty. Today, the philosophy infuses every major curricular and policy decision we make as a faculty.

This description is not to say that ours is a postmodern department, or that we have consensus on the meaning and implications of constructionist social work. If anything, we have raised more questions about this than we have answered. My particular versions of such questions pertain to my teaching of practice and combine to form one of the impetuses for my return each year to the Transforming Social Work gathering. Participating in the relaxed, creative dialogues and informal activities there provides opportunities to pursue these questions in a uniquely conducive setting.

In the beginning of this chapter, I discuss some of my own questions related to teaching postmodern social work in modernist educational settings. In the remainder of the chapter, I summarize conversations in a discussion group at the Transforming Social Work gathering in 2002 that expand on my questions, and then present an array of examples related to these conversations that are drawn from foundation practice classes. The inquiries in both represent a postmodern call and response we pursue despite the difficulties.

Teaching Questions

Because I teach "foundation" and "advanced" practice courses, my abiding questions in regard to our philosophy are how to translate it into social work practice, and how to support students and alumni in this practice. These questions are born of intellectual, institutional, and interpersonal struggles I have witnessed students experience.

Two of the master's of social work (MSW) courses I teach span the entire year of foundation practice, from social work with individuals, groups, and families, to social work with communities and organizations. Early in the foundation year, I often hear a mix of reactions from students who are grappling with their introduction to postmodern thinking. For some, it is an exciting learning project, but for others the intellectual challenges produce self-doubt or anger at the faculty. The language of postmodernism (e.g., *discourse, deconstruct, binary, essentialize*) is particularly vexing for these students, as it was for at least some of us on the faculty when we began studying it formally. As Thomas (2002) points out,

> Some of the ideas have come from philosophers and it can be a bit of a stretch to engage with their ways of writing and to understand all the implications of what they are trying to convey. Some of these writers originally wrote in languages other than English (mainly French) and so their writings have had to be translated and this hasn't necessarily helped

> with the ease of reading. But another reason why [these] ideas are sometimes hard to understand is because we're not used to them. (p. 88)

Later in the semester, as students become more familiar with the language of social construction and its rationale as an antioppressive orientation, they describe their beginning attempts to act from it in their field practica. This is a time when their need for encouragement is high, and yet the reactions they receive from some professionals in their practica can be discouraging. These negative reactions may be subtle ("You don't have to take psychopathology?"), while other reactions are not ("You can leave all that ivory tower stuff in your classes; in this agency, you'll learn real social work.").

I feel a special responsibility to assist students in navigating these intellectual challenges and the repercussions they experience as they encounter institutional demands and interpersonal pressures on them to stick to the status quo. This sense of responsibility expands my original questions to include others that are reflective of my location in a largely modernist university, such as, *How can I, as a social work educator, wisely and humanely work within academia to transform oppressive relationships embedded in and embedding the professions' practices? How can I counter the demoralizing impact of unquenchable institutional and professional demands in order to be the encouraging, creative educator to which I aspire? How can I resist the culture of evaluation that surrounds and divides us in academia?* The following report of the social work educators' discussion provides some ideas about this from the perspective of shared concern.

The Social Work Educators' Discussions

One of the regular features of the Transforming Social Work meetings is spending several hours talking with other participants in small groups organized by topics we rank in order of preference before we arrive at the meetings. In 2002, I participated in a group composed of social work educators and doctoral students on the topic, Practicing Postmodernism in a Modernist University.

Day One: Challenges and Possibilities. Eight professors and doctoral students, whom I refer to as the social work educators, met in the informal conference center to discuss our ideas on this subject. We sat together in the morning, after lunch, and again the next morning. The piano room provided us a comfortable, intimate setting to get to know each other and share our ideas. In the afternoon, the incandescent light was enhanced by a colorful fall day shining brightly through a large window. The informality of the setting was reflective of the type of postmodern dialogue across differences (e.g., of gender, experience, and notoriety) that we were there to have.

Our first day's discussion focused on institutional, intellectual, and interpersonal issues, and we began to consider promising possibilities for reconstructing them. Unsurprisingly for social work educators, the primary institutions of interest in these discussions were the university and human service organizations. The intellectual focal point was the boundary between modern and postmodern thinking in agencies' policies and practices and in what and how we teach, research, and consult in social work. Interpersonal topics included formal teaching-learning relationships, the connections and disconnections between universities and communities (e.g., field education), and social workers' relationships with difference.

One broad challenge shared by all was the corporatization of the university and the impact of the concomitant ideological demands it places on faculties' postmodern scholarship and teaching. These demands include funders' privileging of classical outcome research and university administrators' equating of productivity with obtaining external funding. The group perceived these demands as subjugating of postmodern scholarship and the priorities of social work faculties while enforcing the assumptions and methodologies of classical empiricism and rational objectivity.

A related process, the corporatization of human service agencies through managed care, was discussed in terms of its parallel emphasis on fiscally driven outcome measures in agency practices, such as evidence-based practice. From the perspective of the social justice mission of social work, the languages, purposes, and compliance practices of behavioral health (known in social work as the "mental health field") were notably pervasive and seemed particularly ripe for deconstruction and transformation. I had come to the Transforming Social Work meetings because of the possibilities for countering and reconstructing subjugating practices that I perceive in postmodern thinking such as social constructionism, post-structuralism, and strengths perspectives. Troubling to me, therefore, was the fairly widespread lack of understanding and criticism of postmodern practices we found ourselves and our students surrounded by. We all had seen the privileging in field agencies of funder- and procedure-driven practices that contradicted our teaching aims of supporting students to think differently, not just act differently, and of educating for uncertainty.

Other closely related challenges we noted were the skewed reactions to postmodern approaches to authority vis-à-vis students' and field agencies' preferred practices. One example someone used was that of working to establish a collaborative classroom despite students' resistance to this. Another was the demand from students and field practica for social work courses that teach recipes for techniques and decontextualize the historical and cultural influences and their current implications for harmfully assuming the universal applicability of such methods.

Encouragingly, the participants' accounts of struggle were followed by stories of promising practices influenced by postmodern understandings. One person told how her school of social work got reappointment, tenure, and promotion decision making moved from the university to the school level. Her faculty deconstructed the definitions of teaching, scholarship, and service, and the related criteria and processes that varied across schools and the university level. Then they successfully argued for turning the decisions over to the school. In turn, this enabled the school of social work to expand its own reappointment, tenure, and promotion approach to include multiple forms of scholarship, each with its own criteria.

Many of the promising examples indicated the significance of adopting dialogical practices that pool the knowledge and skill of all involved, rather than privileging that of the "experts." For example, another social work education story was told about a new MSW program. As part of the intention to build a learning community made up of academia and community organizations, the program established dialogical "circles" of six students, two agency-based social workers, and one client mentor. These circles promoted mentoring as both a support for students and a feedback loop between the program and the agencies.

This postmodern approach to knowledge-power also was located in social work practice settings outside of the university. Someone else explained and illustrated the notion of "open dialogue" methods that move social work practices beyond the "systems of care" approach. One of these is a children's capacity circle in the Midwest that involves 40 foster children in a circle of support. These children meet with whomever they want to talk about topics they choose related to what is and is not going well. The agency that organizes this circle also has a council of teens who have previously been clients of the agency. The young people on the council provide mentoring and advising to foster children currently in the agency's care.

By the end of this first day's discussion, I had taken copious notes as I followed the development of our dialogue and attended to our negotiation of meaning. Although and perhaps because the focus of this conversation about academia was broader than teaching, these exchanges gave me new language and new ways of thinking about my questions. As the group disbanded for the evening's activities, I anticipated returning to the conversation in the morning.

Day Two: Promising Approaches. We again met in the piano room. This time the member of our group who was serving as the facilitator distributed a set of questions that she thought we might want to use to guide our last discussion. These questions are presented below in bold italics. After each question, I summarize the responses.

What would we tell an individual who has just completed a Ph.D. about how to maintain postmodernism in the new faculty position she or he has just accepted? Most of the responses to this question reflected the significance of relationships with others in academia. Early in the discussion, someone suggested that individuals seeking an academic position for the first time probably could benefit from assistance in considering which schools might be a good match for his or her postmodernism.

The issue of preventing the new faculty member from becoming isolated elicited a number of comments. Someone suggested that it is helpful to have a sense of oneself as someone who appreciates scholarship and other scholars. Someone else pointed out that, although postmodernism challenges long-held values in academia, new faculty should not assume that their postmodern thinking is so completely unique that they will not find colleagues in their university for whom a postmodern orientation is resonant. Along this same line, someone commented that new faculty members should develop ways to extend their own views while remaining open to others' ideas. Some of the means that were mentioned for doing this include a writing support group, a teaching support group, a reduced load for new faculty, incentives for senior faculty who publish with students, and a collaborative culture. As one person summed up, "It's about being in a relationship, and how we want to be. It's also about how our language affects this. Encourage him or her to notice the language. Being 'multi-partial' (as H. Goolishian calls it), for example, from 'my' to 'our.' "

How can we create a culture of postmodern transformation? Someone noted that our discussion about the first question seemed to contain this implicit question. The responses to this question focused less on what the newly hired faculty member can do than on what the unit (department, program, or school) to whom she or he is responsible can do. The discussion focused primarily on the evaluative processes through which faculty members are hired and promoted. One person suggested that those who are more senior should construct supports for new faculty to maintain their postmodernism *and* meet the reappointment, tenure, and promotion standards. Someone else pointed out that we had said little up to this point about the tension of standards that clearly conflict with postmodern appreciations, for example, valuing particular forms of scholarship or research paradigms over others, or evaluating productivity by quantifying publications and students without consideration of an author's or professor's treatment of difference.

How do we construct conditions that sustain collaboration? Someone pointed out that it would be worthwhile to investigate how conducive a school's environment is for collaboration before accepting a faculty position. Someone else suggested that bringing people together around common interests, for example, "teaching excellence," is a way to sustain collaboration. Another person suggested finding ways to discover the hidden gifts that people have to offer and then incorporating these explicitly in their faculty responsibilities, in effect shaping institutional expectations according to their gifts.

How can constructing conditions that sustain collaboration advance social justice and our other transformative agendas? The day before, the group had noted that as an antioppressive commitment and one that is concerned with multiplicity and difference, postmodern practice is collaborative and dialogic. In considering the relationship between conditions that sustain collaboration and social justice and other transformative agendas, one person commented that collaborative relations carried out between scholars and practitioners can challenge the tension between research and practice. She pointed to a variety of other constructions of separation that collaboration disrupts and the way it lessens the oppressive impact of some forms of separation between groups, such as marginalization, isolation, and loneliness. The group returned to the university itself in considering this question further, recognizing that although universities differ by size, political and economic interests, and productivity guidelines, the modernist university expects entrepreneurial, individualistic modes of work and productivity. However, in the postmodern world this metanarrative of the "higher order" structuring of work is destabilized. The postmodern narrative undermines modernist separations between professor and student, researcher and research subject, social worker and client. In place of the expert who knows and imparts this knowledge to students, the professor is the consultant and facilitator whose authority is open to question and challenge. Professor and students become colearners in shared inquiries. Knowledge and knower proceed on the basis of knowing *and* not knowing, both of which are equally valued for their contributions. Like knowledge, the notion of self is no longer fixed, but is multiple and transitory. Someone pointed out that orienting new faculty members to this perspective includes assisting them to assess where they are situated institutionally from the perspective of their multiple selves.

What is the developmental process of postmodernism? After a brief foray into the postmodern assumptions of nonfoundational, nonlinear developmental processes, this discussion led to someone expanding the question by asking, *"What about the postmodern transformative process enables us to become so strong and so clear that we act in congruence with its transformative agenda despite the hardships?"* As the last question this also seemed to be the ultimate point toward which the rest of our discussions had led us in terms of the social work values it simultaneously took for granted and made central. The responses weaved back and forth across issues of difference and the exercise of institutional privilege and power as follows: translating across worldviews, undermining the institutional weight, creating semipermeability, maintaining connection with communities, and attending to the borders, the margins.

Although this conversation was directed more specifically at scholarly agendas than at teaching, it had addressed my questions in a manner that reminded me of a conception of discursive therapy I had read. The dialogue had provided me "words and discourses [to] be resourcefully and improvisationally drawn from, where certain limiting meanings and ways of talk [e.g., modernism and postmodernism in opposition] had previously dominated" (School of Psychology, n.d., para. 20). Little did I know as we ended the group just how soon I would be drawing "improvisationally" on this resource, as I will illustrate in the first of the following examples derived from my practice classes.

Social Work Practice Students' Examples

The Practice Class. The location of the Transforming Social Work gathering in the county where I live and work and the schedule of activities enabled me to teach my MSW foundation practice class on the evening of the second day. Sated from the day's discussions, I drove from the conference center to the campus. During my drive I wondered how the students in my class would respond to the subject of postmodernism in a modernist university. I began to imagine their voices in the conversations I had just left. By the time I arrived on campus, I had decided to revise several parts of my class plan by adapting the discussion group's questions and applying these to an experiential learning activity.

Along with my teaching colleagues, Marty Dewees and Gail Rafferty, I had been revising this course for several years to keep pace with the department's developing postmodern thinking and the changing conditions of contemporary social work. By the time of this example, the course purpose was defined as "developing knowledges, ethics, and skills to translate the department's social work philosophy into sustainable, accountable practice with individuals, groups, and families in diverse situations." The course content, class plans, and assignments were organized around two general themes in sequence: (a) Discerning Context and Meaning: Philosophical Framings and (b) Translating Context & Meaning into Practice. Social work practice was defined in the course syllabus as the professional discourses, relationships, and activities of social workers. The course examined both modernist (e.g., Mattaini, 2001; Middleman & Wood, 1992; Turner, 1996) and postmodernist (e.g., Kemp, 2001; Lane, 1999; Swan, 1998; Tangenberg & Kemp, 2002) practice content. The methods infuse postmodern emphases on meaning, context, language, power, and relationship throughout the course. For example, students share leadership with me for aspects of each class session (e.g., facilitating openings and closing classes); assignments include collaborative learning, a practice perspectives paper, and a structured (integrated) essay. My class plans are fluid, allowing for responsiveness to the group and providing opportunities for shared improvisation.

By this seventh week in the semester, the full-time students in the class had been studying social construction with other local participants in the Transforming Social Work gatherings. They were introduced to it most broadly in Human Behavior and the Social Environment (HBSE) with Stanley Witkin. Many also had developed their understanding of this postmodern thinking further in an elective in Child Abuse and Neglect taught by Brenda Solomon. The part-time students in the class had been developing their postmodern understanding and its implications for social work for a year, after having completed most of the foundation curriculum except practice and field, both of which they and the full-time students were taking concurrently. They also had the benefit of having applied postmodern thinking to groups, communities, and organizations in their second HBSE course, taught by Suzy Comerford.

In this course, the students had become practiced at noticing what they do and do not notice and interrogating practice metaphors. They had considered historically influential direct practice approaches in social work (e.g., behavioral, structural, cognitive-behavioral) through reading and examining the dominant approaches in their field practica. In keeping with the course design, the theme for this midpoint in the course, Engaging the Metaphors of "Story," launched our most explicit inquiry into social work perspectives and approaches that were developed in response to postmodern conceptions of multiplicity, difference, and power. Post-structural feminist, strengths, deconstruction, narrative, and solution-focused practices were scheduled to shape our conception of social work practice for the remainder of the semester.

Two course objectives provided focus for this three-hour class plan: (a) "to be able to listen radically to and work collaboratively with the personal and cultural stories of problems and unique outcomes that people tell about their lives and relationships" and (b) "to be able to demonstrate in writing and class discussions, a beginning familiarity with strengths-based, narrative social work, as informed by social construction and the intended impact." The class was assigned to read the first part of Morgan's (2000) *What Is Narrative Therapy?* prior to this class session. The reading introduced story as a social and practice metaphor;

the methods of externalizing, historicizing, exploring the effects of, and situating/deconstructing the problem; discovering and tracing the history and meaning of unique outcomes; and naming an alternative story.

While accompanying classes through this section of the course in the past, I had noticed that the deconstructive purposes (i.e., the postmodern emphases) of the method often eluded students. As Vodde and Gallant (2002), point out, "externalization does not stop with challenging the assumptions that locate the problem within persons but extends to revealing those social forces whose interests lie in maintaining such personification" (p. 443). I thought that discussing the postmodern influences on narrative practices might increase this understanding, as would adapting some of the questions from the Transforming Social Work discussion group for a collaborative learning activity and debriefing discussion.

In my introductory explanation of the class plan, I told the students about the Transforming Social Work meetings. They were fascinated to know that a number of the authors they had read in their courses were gathering nearby and that we would consider questions similar to those the authors were considering at the meetings. This provided a "storied" opening that engaged the class in the evening's agenda in keeping with the narrative metaphor.

After discussing what the students found compelling and discomfiting in the reading, I facilitated a discussion in which we highlighted its postmodern underpinnings. Following this discussion, we prepared for the experiential learning that would occur after the break. Together, we reviewed the method and rationale of externalizing, as well as that of what we call "real playing" (an alternative language for "role playing" that emphasizes drawing on their own responses rather than trying to fabricate those of an imagined other).

The basic instructions for this collaborative learning activity were performance specific; first, I asked the students to work together as "social worker" and "client" in the dyads to which they had been randomly assigned at the beginning of the course. Then, I asked the students in the social worker position to adopt a stance of genuine interest in asking and listening to their partners' responses to some variation of the question: *What is it about the postmodern aspects of our MSW program that feels difficult to you at this time?* (Although I felt a bit uncomfortable that this question was one-sided in the direction of struggle, it did take up where we had left off the week before when some students voiced being troubled by this content.) I also asked them to externalize problems their partner discussed in ways that allowed for three processes: (a) situating these separately from their partners' identities (Morgan, 2000, p. 17), (b) naming the problem in language that comes from and is amenable to their partners (p. 22), and (c) "making visible the relations of power and injustice that constitute the personification of the problem" (i.e., defining oneself as the problem) in the partners' narratives (pp. 22–23; Vodde & Gallant, 2002, pp. 442–443). I asked the students in the client position to do two things: (a) participate in the conversation to provide their partners with actual experience in facilitating an externalizing conversation (Carey & Russell, 2002; White & Epston, 1990), and (b) give themselves a first-hand experience of this method and its impact on the meaning they make of their identities vis-à-vis the issue.

The students' consultation sessions lasted 30 minutes. Most pairs of students were animatedly engaged in their conversations as I walked among them, and the allotted time ended before their conversations did.

The debriefing and analysis discussion lasted 40 minutes. I opened it by asking the students what happened in the dyads, why (theoretically speaking), and what they wanted to remember about these experiences in their practices as social workers. As the discussion turned toward the content of the dyad's consultation, I used the chalkboard to list the various features of postmodern thinking that felt difficult to them.

Most items on the list pertained to ambiguity, language, or "how-to" application. Some individuals talked about the ambiguity they experienced in trying to navigate multiple realities (or truths) in their field practica and competing conceptions of good practice between the MSW program and their field agencies. Others identified the sense of confusion, and in some cases alienation, they felt in reaction to the vocabulary in postmodern and narrative texts. These students shared the concern they had harbored that intellectually they were not up to graduate work.

Another issue entailed the lack of distinct social work techniques that some individuals perceived, despite the narrative approach processes they had read and just practiced. This perception was accompanied by feelings of insecurity and frustration. As one student commented, *"When I came to graduate school, I thought I would learn what to do in specific situations. I guess I thought it would be more practical, like tell me what techniques to learn for particular situations."*

After we discussed the challenges of learning postmodernism for social work, a student provided the ideal segue for considering the social justice aspects of the externalizing process. She commented that she would not want the list of challenges that had been generated to obscure what she found compelling about postmodernism, particularly its antioppression emphases. This comment is intriguing because it contradicts one of the common criticisms of postmodern thinking—that it does not take a position on right and wrong, but simply elucidates how these are socially constructed. However, the comment also points to the stream of postmodern thinking in which she was immersed in the child abuse and neglect course—a Foucauldian (poststructural) social work critique of power and social control by professions (Chambon, Irving, & Epstein, 1999). On cue, I asked the question considered by the social work educators, "*What is it about the postmodern transformative process that might enable us to become so strong and clear that we act in congruence with the social justice agenda of social work despite the hardships?*"

The responses to this question referred to postmodern emphasis on the heterogeneity of reality and to its interrogation of taken for granted discourses and practices. The former was credited with assisting them to respond to different and opposing perspectives so that they can speak persuasively to alternate issues and realities. The latter was attributed with enabling them to recognize and helpfully question norms that were taken for granted in society and social work. As one student commented, "*Postmodernism asks what meaning a practice has for the multiple perspectives of those who are affected by it. This helps us to be clear about clients' meaning so that we are less likely to impose our own.*"

Examples from Subsequent Practice Classes. In reaction to the intellectual challenges of postmodernism, students in these fall practice classes have questioned whether it really matters which theoretical perspective social workers use. On one hand, I recognize this as a typical question of social work students in their first semester in an MSW program. On the other hand, I recognize it as a particular reaction to the countercultural effort students must invest in understanding postmodernism and its significance to social life and social work. This question usually gets raised at a time when more than one student is poised to begin to get what he or she is learning, but is not quite there yet. Therefore, the question and ensuing discussion are endowed with an intensity that can be contagious.

Not used to, and provoked by, the discursive methods and social constructionist content in which they have been engaged throughout the program by this time, students often extend their remarks to theory in general. They question whether theory and thinking about their thinking is useful at all, as long as they are responsive to their clients. These questions are often attached to the explanation that because this is a practice class, they expect to learn concrete approaches, particularly those that they are compelled to employ in their agencies (e.g., those based on a medical model, like diagnosis). In the course, we do consider a variety of practice approaches, use some type of experiential learning every week, and look closely at one approach (narrative practice). Therefore, while I listen mindfully I have found offering a postmodern method—deconstruction—to be a useful response.

In this case, I start by generating questions to deconstruct the theories and methods constituting the approaches used in students' field practica or their own preferred methods. Students contribute to these questions once they recognize this process from their other courses. We ask questions, such as *what and whom do we find when we uncover the normative assumptions of any practice theory? Whose realities are privileged and whose are marginalized or made invisible yet implicit by taken-for-granted practice assumptions?* White (2003) refers to this idea as "absent but implicit" (p. 30). These discussions lead to examining the assumed split between theory and action. In turn, students gain greater appreciation for the way that theory and the cultural beliefs tied up in it are embedded in and created by all that they *do* as social workers, providing a segue for considering the way that various practices privilege and subjugate some people's interests.

The ability to interrogate one's own theory and its language as well as those of institutions and other practitioners has remained a critical issue for students from the perspective of difference and diversity. In order to situate and be attentive to students' learning, I usually start with students' immediate experiences in the classroom and their experiences in the field practicum and beyond, rather than theory. The theory is generated or consulted spontaneously through their reflections and dialogue about the experiences and what it suggests to them about social work practice.

Jillian. For the sake of credibility and responsiveness, it has been important to ensure room for interrogating the discourses of postmodernism as well as those of modernist theories, instead of making such a binary opposition between the two. One memorable example of this occurred when "Jillian" carefully probed the appearance of postmodernism's Eurocentrism from her cultural vantage point as a white South African. Although she had lived in the United States for many years, she came to graduate school with the hope that she somehow could make a difference as a social worker in the lives of people living in abject poverty in South Africa and Namibia. Without rejecting her new learning, she painstakingly questioned its origins and relevance to that commitment, noting it is not the language of the people she wants to assist.

Her care in questioning the language of postmodernism was coupled with a similar care for how she spoke to and referred to me throughout this critique. Therefore, when she seemed to have satisfied her own issues, I asked her if we had enough of a relationship established for me to encourage her to look at the language of care she had used in response to me. She answered affirmatively, and with the participation of the class, she uncovered her South African assumptions about the authority of the professor. By the end of that discussion, we had all learned something about deconstruction as a method, applying it to our professional relationships, and the culture of expert-power and its alienating effects.

Manisha and Tiffany. A similar example of these issues occurred more subtly for "Manisha," a student whose field practicum was at a statewide domestic and sexual violence coalition. She asked her field instructor, Tiffany, if the coalition used postmodern ideas. Tiffany, herself newly familiar with this paradigm, first made a joke about talking more like people speak in the grocery store than a philosopher. Then she told Manisha that she leaves postmodernism to academics, because as a practitioner, her job is to speak the languages of the women and children with whom she works and for whom she advocates.

In thinking aloud about Tiffany's comment, Manisha noted to her practice class that although her field instructor's disclaimer was funny and profound in its unfussiness, Manisha also perceived it as postmodern in its resistance to mystifying expert-power. This recognition was significant to the class discussion of what could be helpful to people about social workers' postmodern perspectives, even when its academic language and the barriers it may produce are not.

Rachel and Crystal. The type and quality of relationships between students and their "clients" is a favorite topic in the practice classes. Another promising aspect of this inquiry into the translation of postmodernism into practice is how it can enable students to form partnerships of resistance and care. This is especially gratifying when the partnership is forged with those whose lives do not conform to the attitudes, beliefs, and expectations of those with more social privilege and power (by virtue of relations of gender, race, class, age).

In her field practicum, "Rachel" was assigned to work with "Crystal," a young pregnant woman who was viewed as "noncompliant" by practitioners where she went for prenatal care. In private conversations with Crystal, Rachel discovered that the expert-authority asserted by the professionals intimidated her, and in reaction, she seethed with anger during her appointments with them. Nevertheless, because Crystal was a minor in the custody of the state, her desire to keep her baby after the birth obligated her to go to the many appointments scheduled for her. This helplessness in the face of professionals' power over Crystal fed her self-contempt, and along with their attitudes toward her, prevented her from trusting them. When for unavoidable reasons, Crystal could not keep her appointments, she did not explain, and the practitioners saw her absences as indicative of her inability to be a good mother.

Rachel, like Crystal, was initially intimidated by the professionals because of her inexperience, their esoteric language, and seeming insensitivity to Crystal. Feeling caught in the middle, she finally confided in "Blake," her field instructor. She described to him the developing quagmire that she perceived between the health practitioners and the young woman. Blake, an alumnus of our program, assisted her to engage the woman in a deconstructive conversation. In that discussion, Rachel and Crystal were able to identify oppressive social beliefs in the professionals' reactions to Crystal and in the diagnosis they had assigned her.

Rachel narrated this situation in a class about the reading we had done on feminist social work approaches (e.g., Tangenberg & Kemp, 2003). In particular, she was struck by the similarity of her own and Crystal's reactions, even though their roles were so different. For the members of the class this became a stock illustration of how the body is not only a biological site but also a social site in which culture is inscripted (Gatens, 1992, 1996; Grosz, 1990, 1994). This idea was pivotal in moving to considerations of how Rachel could counter such inscriptions by asking Crystal questions that could enable her to identify and strengthen her own knowledges and skills, which were obscured by professionals' reactions to and about her.

Beth and Jackson. Over the year, some students seem to become more adept at deconstructing institutional claims about people, despite the demands placed on them to conform to these claims. "Beth," an MSW student whose foundation field practicum was in child protection, was assigned to work with a 15-year-old African American male named "Jackson." Jackson had been adopted as a baby by white parents and was one of the only people of color living in his rural community. In his first meeting with the student, Jackson remained studiously silent until near the end of their scheduled time together when he finally expressed his outrage about the constancy with which white adults singled him out for surveillance. (His angry outbursts were the primary basis for his referral to juvenile services.)

Beth acknowledged to Jackson that as a white woman whose life experiences had been very different from his, she had no idea what it meant to be him, but that she did have other bases for understanding what it is to feel angry about receiving prejudicial treatment. Moreover, after silently deconstructing the diagnosis he had been assigned, she said that she would like to understand his reality as *he* experienced it. Jackson, who had been labeled a hostile and defiant adolescent, seemed to melt as his eyes filled with tears in response to her words. Then he abruptly left the room where they had been talking. When he had regained his composure, he returned and told her that he had not until that moment really been able to trust his own perceptions about what was happening to him. He described how clerks in local stores followed him, but not his white friends, as if he were going to steal something. However, adults he cared about and who purported to care about him had trivialized or disputed these experiences when he had explained his anger to them. In turn, their reactions had led him to mistrust his own perceptions and to distrust and react hostilely against adults more generally.

Beth discovered herself pulled between her agency's "more experienced" conclusions about Jackson and her education and compassion when she chose to convey to him the limits of her expertise out of respect for his own knowledge. She translated her concern about Jackson's growing alienation from himself and his community into a request to learn from him, recentering him in the position of his own knowledges and skills. In response, Jackson told her how much her words relieved the pressures on him to disbelieve himself. This was a turning point in his willingness to actively participate in social work meetings with her. It ultimately led her to link him with an adult African

American man in a nearby community who could assist him to consider new options for navigating multiple identity claims about who and how he was.

When I asked Beth what enabled her to communicate with Jackson as she had, her reply reflected the promise of postmodern thinking. She said she had remembered the reading and discussions about starting with strengths, using radical listening, and excavating frames of mind in order to dialogue and collaborate meaningfully with those who are different from us—all postmodern-inspired processes (McKee, 2003; Saleebey, 2002; Weick & Chamberlain, 2002; Wood & Roche, 2001).

Temma and Carl. In the first section of a practice perspectives paper, "Temma" narrated a conversation with "Carl" who was a member of a social clubhouse program for individuals diagnosed with mental illnesses. As Carl jumped from one focus to the next, Temma attempted to stay present with each focus and to externalize each problem he agonized over. She also attempted to situate each problem culturally and locally to the point of exhaustion and discouragement. Her compassionate openness and perseverance in response to Carl's shifting realities revealed her conscientious approach to applying what she had learned while doing no harm. Her reflections on the assumptions she made and her struggle to notice these were moving in their demonstration of her willingness to not know and to "story" her colearning as his accompanist. Gradually, she discovered just how strong a hold the belief in doing things the "right way" has on practitioners, even when they are encouraged not to for learning purposes.

Abbey. In another practice perspectives paper, "Abbey" described a heated discussion that occurred in a meeting at her field agency. By the time she completed her narrative, she was surprised to realize that the conversation she remembered participating in was a conversation she had had with herself as she sat silently in the meeting.

Reflecting on the assumptions underlying her actions and subsequent perspective "shift within a shift" demonstrated to Abbey just how far away from our "embodied practices " (Kemp, 2001) our assumptions can take us. Connecting theory to experience, she referred to the postmodern concept of the evaluative gaze (Foucault, 1973) of institutional and cultural power, noting as she did how the gaze recruits people into policing themselves into silence and into not noticing that we are doing so.

Closing Reflections

What have I learned from this? That the following five principles (among others) guide my approach to translating the postmodern philosophy into social work practice: (a) *anticipate students' struggles and my own without predetermining them*; (b) *engage in colearning without abdicating my responsibility to teach*; (c) *start where the students are*; (d) *create opportunities* with *students to learn through experience, dialogue, and reflection*; and (e) *blur the separations between theory and action*.

I also have been reminded that social work educators and students translate postmodern philosophy into social work practice in modernist contexts through relationships, shared experience, and conversations. We create safe havens in small groups and communities. And we honor our social work commitments to social and economic justice by sometimes blurring distinctions between ourselves and others, and at other times, narrating them.

References

Berger, P. L., & Luckmann, T. (1967). *The social construction of reality*. London: Penguin.

Carey, M., & Russell, S. (2002). Externalizing: Commonly asked questions. *The International Journal of Narrative Therapy and Community Work, 2*, 76–84.

Chambon, A., Irving, A., & Epstein, L. (Eds.). (1999). *Reading Foucault for social work*. New York: Columbia University Press.

Department of Social Work. Mission statatement. Department of Social Work program philosophy. Retrieved August 2, 2006, from http://www.uvm.edu/~socwork/directorswlecome/missionstatement.htm

Faubion, J. D. (Ed.). (2000). *Michelle Foucault: Power*. New York: The New Press.

Foucault, M. (1973). *The order of things: An archaeology of the human sciences*. New York: Vintage Books.

Foucault, M. (1995). *Discipline & punish: The birth of the prison* (A. Sheridan, Trans.). New York: Vintage Books. (Original work published 1975)

Gatens, M. (1992). Power, bodies and difference. In M. Barret & A. Phillips (Eds.), *Destablizing theory: Contemporary feminist debates* (pp. 120–137). Stanford, CA: Stanford University Press.

Gatens, M. (1996). *Imaginary bodies: Ethics, power and corporeality*. London: Routledge.

Gergen, K. J. (1994). *Realities and relationships: Soundings in social constructio*n. Cambridge, MA: Harvard University Press.

Gergen, K. J. (1999). *An invitation to social construction*. London: Sage.

Grosz, E. (1990). Philosophy. In S. Gunew (Ed.), *Feminist knowledge, critique, and construct*. London: Routledge.

Grosz, E. (1994). *Volatile bodies: Toward a corporeal feminism*. St. Leonards, NSW, Australia: Allen & Unwin.

Kemp, S. P. (2001). Environment through a gendered lens: From person-in-environment to woman-in-environment. *Affilia, 16*, 7–30.

Lane, M. (1999). Community development and a postmodernism of resistance. In E. Pease & J. Fook (Eds.), *Transforming social work practice: Postmodern critical perspectives* (pp. 135–149). New York: Routledge.

Lather, P. (1991). *Getting smart: Feminist research and pedagogy with/in the postmodern*. New York: Routledge.

Mattaini, M. (2001). The foundation of social work practice. In H. E. Briggs & K. Corcoran, *Social work practice: Treating common client problems* (pp. 15–35). Chicago: Lyceum.

McKee, M. (2003). Excavating our frames of minds: The key to dialogue and collaboration. *Social Work, 48*, 3, 401–408.

Middleman, R. R., & Wood, G. G. (1992). *Skills for direct practice in social work.* New York: Columbia University Press.

Morgan, A. (2000). *What is narrative therapy?* Adelaide, South Australia: Dulwich Centre Publications.

Parton, N. (1994). Problematics of government, (post)modernity and social work. *British Journal of Social Work, 24*, 9–32.

Pease, B., & Fook, J. (1999). *Transforming social work practice: Postmodern critical perspectives*. New York: Routledge.

Roche, S. E., Dewees, M., Trailweaver, R., Alexander, S., Cuddy, C., & Handy, M. (1999). *Contesting boundaries in social work education: A liberatory approach to cooperative learning and teaching.* Alexandria, VA: Council on Social Work Education.

Saleebey, D., (2002). The strengths approach to practice. In D. Saleebey (Ed.), *The strengths perspective in social work practice* (3rd ed., pp. 80–94). Boston: Allyn & Bacon.

School of Psychology. (n.d.). *What is discursive therapy?* Retrieved November 20, 2004, from http://therapy.massey.ac.nz/diplo maintro.html

Smith, D. E. (1999). *Writing the social: Critique, theory, and investigations*. Toronto, Ontario, Canada: University of Toronto Press.

Swan, V. (1998). Narrative & Foucault: Implications for feminist practice. In S. Madigan & I. Law (Eds.), *Praxis: Situating discourse, feminism & politics in narrative therapies* (pp. 65–80). Vancouver, BC, Canada: Yaletown Family Therapy.

Tangenberg, K. M., & Kemp, S. (2002). Embodied practice: Claiming the body's experience, agency, and knowledge for social work. *Social Work, 47,* 9–18.

Thomas, L. (2002). Poststructuralism and therapy: What's it all about? *The International Journal of Narrative Therapy and Community Work, 2,* 85–89.

Turner, F. J. (1996). Theory and social work treatment. In F. J. Turner (Ed.), *Social work treatment: Interlocking theoretical approaches* (4th ed., pp. 1–17). New York: Free Press.

Vodde, R., & Gallant, J. P. (2002). Bridging the gap between micro and macro practice: Large scale change and a unified model of narrative-deconstructive practice. *Journal of Social Work Education, 38,* 430–458.

White, M. (2003). Narrative practice and community assignments. *The International Journal of Narrative Therapy and Community Work, 2,* 17–55.

White, M., & Epston, D. (1990). *Narrative means to therapeutic ends.* Adelaide, South Australia: Dulwich Centre.

Witkin, S. (1991). The implications of social constructionism for social work education. *Journal of Teaching in Social Work, 4,* 37–48.

Witkin, S. (1999). Constructing our future. *Social Work, 44,* 5–8.

Weick, A., & Chamberlain, R. (2002). Putting problems in their place. In D. Saleebey (Ed.), *The strengths perspective in social work practice* (3rd ed., pp. 95–105). Boston: Allyn & Bacon.

Wood, G. G., & Roche, S. E. (2001). Situations and representations: Feminist practice with survivors of male violence. *Families in Society, 82,* 583–590.

CHAPTER 14

Epilogue

DENNIS SALEEBEY

The chapters in this volume, as you know, come from the invitation to reflect on encounters, conversations, dialogues, experiences, and relationships occurring as a part of an annual gathering at a retreat on Lake Champlain, Vermont. Since the retreat is devoted to discussions around the general call to think about the transformation and renovation of some of the root assumptions, practices, and conceptual schemes that run through social work education, inquiry, and practice, Stan and I wanted to encourage the participants to write freely and engagingly about ideas spurred by their experience. We think the authors, in very different ways, have done that.

My task here will be to extract what I think are some of the themes found in these chapters. Inevitably, I will be adding my own interpretations of these based on my experiences within certain discussion groups at these gatherings.

Transformation

Transformation implies change, transfiguration; the modification of structure, appearance, and shape. In the case of a person, it might suggest the alteration of perspective, behavior, relationships, philosophy, and/or values. It seems clear that for many of the contributors to this volume, transformation occurred in different ways and for different reasons, certainly not just because of their experience at these gatherings, but also because they were already undergoing, to one degree or another, some critical examination of their careers, commitments, and contributions to the profession, of their intellectual lives, of the communities of their interests, as well as the relationship of these to movements and tempos in the larger culture and in social, political, economic, and spiritual institutions. Others may be in the midst of transformative movement because of stress, adversity, and serious challenges in their lives.

Personal Transformation

The transformation of the individual may be a slow, inexorable but subtle process. Or it may unfold so rapidly and dramatically it startles. Transformation may come as the individual confronts adversity and challenge. Or it may come because the person has the luxury and time to consider and configure it. It may be an epiphany, welcome because of the spiritual, intellectual, interpersonal opportunities it brings. Or it may be imposed from the outside, the enduring effects of institutional, interpersonal, or ideological demands.

In a sense, being transformed has to do with seeing or, rather, with a different way of seeing. The familiar becomes transfigured, or the heretofore invisible suddenly looms on our horizon.

Annie Dillard (1994) describes two kinds of seeing. The first is seeing as a kind of running account, reflecting a verbalization that brings the objects or process into view. "But there is another kind of seeing that involves a letting go. When I see this way I sway transfixed and emptied" (p. 704). I believe, as you have read the accounts, you have encountered narratives involving both kinds of seeing.

In my experience in groups at these gatherings, it seems that some of us were seeking an understanding, an accounting or affirmation of the transforming going on within us. That is, propelled by events, experiences, crises, or developmental urges, something clearly was changing, at least in part, in the way that we saw ourselves. Perhaps we were seeking something beyond the institutional roles we played. Perhaps we were in revolt against the modernist project. For some of us the insurrection was against the hegemony of science with a big *S*; for others it was against the rules, regulations, and roles that emanated from that most modernist of institutions—the university. For most us, the gatherings were an opportunity to dust off some ideas, skills, projects that had been muted or derailed. But for all of us, I believe it was an opportunity to engage in real talk ("good talk" as Ruth Dean says), genuine conversation, and authentic dialogue. No posturing, preening, prepackaged propositions, and practiced papers. And most of us, even those of us who were regular habitués of the gatherings, relished the rare opportunity for such contact. And frankly, sometimes it was difficult to slide into the discourse and dialogic modes.

Personal transformation as rebellion. The universities and agencies wherein we practice are often conservatories of the usual, the conventional, and the officious. We sometimes grant them ease and expressions of gratitude because they have, after all, given us a degree of freedom that might be hard to find in manual labor, the corporate world, or the sociopolitical establishment. For example, the university, as Max Weber knew, can be a behemoth that suppresses the truly innovative and may exculpate the bureaucratic and mundane. Isn't it odd to think the spatial, temporal, and interpersonal opportunities for transformation might be at a premium in such supposedly intellectually stimulating contexts? But it may be that when we meet in Vermont, we are more than ready to let the conceptual and philosophical dogs run loose.

Personal transformation as development. As some writers (Baltes & Baltes, 1993; Vaillant, 2002) on the virtues and prospects of aging well often remind us, the self (or ego) is in a constant process of maturation, and part of that maturation, all things being equal, is an expanding ability to master change and confront challenge as the years pass. We are never fully the same person that we were a biographical moment ago. The plasticity of our brain, that is, its continuing capacity to change in the face of challenges and opportunities, ensures that. Richard Restak (2003), the neuroscientist, says this: "[W]e now know that the brain never loses the power to transform itself on the basis of experience, and this transformation can occur over very short intervals. . . . think of the brain as a lifetime work in progress" (p. 8). Your brain (your self) is never the same, different today in some ways from what it was yesterday. In a sense, we are creatures of transformation, even though we may seem to ourselves as staid and durable over long periods of time. Intriguing, isn't it, to think that at the Vermont gatherings our brains, ourselves, have changed as a result of relaxed conversation, play, and exploration.

Institutional Transformation

I think it would be fair to suggest that most of us at these meetings would wish that our universities, colleges, schools, agencies, and institutions would (a) more energetically foster the process of individual transformation and (b) engage more pointedly in transforming themselves as organizations. It does seem to be the case that today many organizations, in the public and private sector alike, are faced with changes—fragmentation of functions, uncertain market forces and financial support, a dramatic increase in the volume of information that flows through the organization, and decreased loyalty to the organization. (As one example of the last, apparently some universities and schools are offering "signing bonuses"—think baseball here—in order to lure faculty and staff away from their current organization.) And as many have pointed out over the years, there are just some nagging dysfunctions that characterize many organizations: one-way flow of information from the top down; fixed communication channels; specialization so that no one, except at the top, has an idea of the organization's internal decision making and choice processes; and rigid boundaries between what is inside the organization and what is outside its parameters. The university itself reflects the principles of the dominant culture. bell hooks (2003) writes: In our nation most colleges and universities are organized around the principles of dominant culture. This organizational model reinforces hierarchies of power and control. It encourages students to be fear-based, that is, to fear teachers and to seek to please them (p. 130).

We teach and learn in such institutions, and we take it upon ourselves to do what little we can to transform such institutions, perhaps by altering the atmosphere of the classroom, by engaging in collaborative relations with students, by seeing and acting toward them as agents and adults who know things and desire things, and by engaging our colleagues in genuine collegial relationships.

In explorations of new ways to think about and act in organizations, Anderson et al. (2001) pose the idea of the "appreciative organization." Such organizations are founded on the idea that we live our lives through meaning making; this is how we fund the world of our experience. The meanings that we make are forged in relationships, and these "constructions" always inform decisions and actions. The appreciative organization is a network, ever in flux, of approval, enjoyment, and assent of others' meanings. Such fluidity is the groundwork of continuing transformation as internal and external environments continually change. Ricketts and Willis (2001) write:

> Appreciative Inquiry (AI) is a transformational organization change process. People experiencing an AI inspire each other to leverage their most powerful collective stories in order to dream and design a new affirmative future. In the process of truly hearing each other's hopes and dreams, people create community—they discover affinity, build relationships, and develop common language with those who were previously only colleagues in the most formal sense. (p. 5)

I think it is fair to say that, even though we meet once a year for only three days, we have created a kind of appreciative organization in Vermont. We do engage in dialogue (see below), we do affirm each other's experiences, we do provide a range of opportunities for interacting, from hikes and power walks to visits to places with local color to meals together and having fun and play. Thus, our knowing of each other changes as we interact in different contexts with different purposes.

The Interaction of Dialogue and Naming in Transformation

Since it is only in league with others that meaning is made, that values are affirmed or created, transformation—personal and institutional—is very much a phenomenon born of dialogue, discourse, and relationships. These are the dynamic of our gatherings. The chapters in this volume are, in a modest way, examples of reflection and action (or praxis). That is, what we say and name here may well turn into action in our home bases. Seeing and saying, for example, the oppressive uses of conventional science may lead to a different way of teaching research conceptually and pedagogically, sharpening the edge of critique in the teaching/learning environment.

Dialogue is given its fullest accounting in Paulo Freire's (2000) *Pedagogy of the Oppressed*. In his view to exist authentically is to be able to name the world, using true, indigenous words. It is together that we speak and act on our worlds in order to transform them, to liberate them from oppressive institutions and individuals. While he certainly was speaking of the serious domination of native groups, rendered powerless by oppressors, and while our situations clearly do not have the same urgency as those he describes, the idea is the same: that only in dialogue can the world of our interest be named, acted upon, and, thus, transformed.

> If it is in speaking their word that people, by naming the world, transform it, dialogue imposes itself as the way by which they achieve significance as human beings. Dialogue is thus an existential necessity.... Dialogue cannot exist, however, in the absence of a profound love for the world and for people. (pp. 88–89)

So, for us dialogue means conversation, "good talk," flowing in an environment of respect, interest, concern, and, not unimportantly, fun. In the end, we know that the dialogical relationships we have may, in fact, not just transform us in some way, but allow us to act differently, however modestly so, in the environments we return to. Dialogue is in its best sense the antithesis of a one-sided, dominative interaction. It is, in some way, a supreme human accomplishment.

Ann Lamott (1995), in her wondrous and funny treatise on writing and going mad, *Bird by Bird,* says this about good dialogue in the novel: "Good dialogue is such a pleasure to come across while reading, a complete change of pace from description and exposition and all that *writing*" (p. 64).

I think that for us at these gatherings the opportunity to engage in good dialogue is a precious thing—not always achieved by any means—but so priceless because in our daily contexts, we may be dominated much of the time by exposition, by lecturing past one another, as Jacques Barzun once famously observed.

Self, Narrative, and Transformation

Jerome Bruner (1986) argues that there are two modes of cognitive processing, two ways to frame the world. One he calls *argument*, and it is meant to stand as the scientific, logical ideal, at its best, the fulfillment of a rational, formal, even mathematical accounting of the world available to our senses. The ultimate goal of this mode of thought is explanation and description, the development of a paradigmatic way of understanding the world, the creation of propositions or "possible worlds" that can be generated and tested against observable phenomena. The language and narratives of this way of perceiving and thinking revolve around categorization and conceptualization and the manufacture of explanations that are context independent—ultimately, though rarely, universal.

The application and appreciation of "the narrative" leads "to good stories, gripping drama, believable (though not necessarily 'true') historical accounts. It deals in human or human-like intention and action and the vicissitudes and consequences that mark their course. It strives to put its timeless miracles into the particulars of experience, and to locate the experience in time and place" (Bruner, 1986, p. 13). Narratives typically are about human nature, the human condition, and contrast action and consciousness in plots and scenarios that are context dependent. Verisimilitude, "lifelikeness," is the stuff of stories.

At the Vermont gatherings, it is narrative and stories, the subjunctive and the imagined that suffuse our conversations. We regale each other, inform each other, draw upon each other, and hope together about our individual and collective futures. We seek not the truth but as Kenneth Gergen (2001) suggests, "intelligibility." And such intelligibility cannot be achieved without mutual assent and engagement in dialogue and egalitarian discourse.

Let it not be assumed that all of our interactions together are "love-ins" or "teach-ins." Certainly civility requires some degree of consensus about what we are doing, what events, people, and experiences mean, but we also occasionally undergo conflict, fractiousness, and disagreement. But what is interesting is how often these phenomena are forgiven, forgotten, or just gotten past. While our culture tends to dote on conflict, argument, and disagreeableness, the certainty is that most people, most times, rise above it and carry on—together. Bruner (1990) observes, "In human beings with their astonishing narrative gift, one of the principal forms of peacekeeping is the human gift for presenting, dramatizing, and explicating mitigating circumstances" (p. 95). So, too, we explicate as much as we reconcile. And from this we learn about ourselves and others.

Transformation in Context

There are, of course, immediate and distal contexts that affect the course of our dialogues and conversations, our interactions and relationships together. The most profound immediate context is the lovely natural setting in which we meet. Lake Champlain and the woods surrounding the retreat center are at once inspiring, calming, and restoring. And we make sure that we take advantage of this bounteous gift of nature. Hikes through the woods, music and drumming sessions at a lakeside beach, boat trips across the lake, rides through the countryside all place us in the midst of this astonishing natural world.

Distal contexts (only distal in terms of geographic distance; emotionally they are often intimate) also play a hand in how we interact, discuss, and act. For example, one of our meetings occurred only three weeks after the malign horrors of 9/11. We began our gathering assuming that we would launch into some of the topics that had been proposed earlier. It soon became clear that the emotional, spiritual, and factual weight of that September day and all that was to come after had to be dealt with, whatever that would mean. I can only speak for myself, but the emotional, reflective, even brooding and urgent thoughts and words of that day had a genuine impact on how I was to come to understand this agony. The eloquence of some of the people is something that I will remember for a very long time; every time there is a discussion of 9/11, terrorism, cultural antagonisms, and misunderstandings, many of their thoughts spring to mind.

Being social work practitioners, social work educators, and social work students means that we cannot ignore during these meetings the continuing hints and murmurs of, and even fanfare for, the dismantling of the welfare society, the beggaring of the public over the private, the rise of the marketplace as the replacement for the ideals of social and economic justice. These drumbeats of conservatism are always within earshot.

Risible Transformation

Laughter, fun, play, humor, and creativity also mark our Vermont gatherings. These are not, for the most part, planned or staged. Rather, they seem to be an outcome of being relaxed, enjoying one another's company, and being outside the "box" of the customary. Humor is transformative. It allows you to see things differently or to see things as they are without cringing, crying, or capitulating. George Vaillant (1993), in constructing a hierarchy of ego defenses, from psychotic through immature, to neurotic, and, ultimately, to healthy, regards humor as one of the healthiest of defenses. He recounts that a friend once wrote him:

"Humor can be marvelously therapeutic. It can deflate without destroying; it can instruct while it entertains; it saves us from our pretensions; and it provides an outlet for feeling that expressed another way would be corrosive" (p. 73).

Humor allows you to call a spade a spade, to confront a stark and grave situation with perspective, even equanimity. But humor does not cut like sarcasm or sting like wit. Rather it displays and celebrates our ordinary humanity and fallibility. It also allows us to see things differently, to change our perspective, to re-form our ideas. Creativity is humor's handmaiden. As a wag once pointed out, hahas often turn into ahas. Diane Ackerman (2004), the gifted essayist, in her book about the brain, *An Alchemy of Mind*, writing about humor, play, and laughing says we laugh when we're embarrassed, when surprised, when we flirt, when we ridicule, to forge alliances; we laugh for any number of reasons. "Humor, on the other hand, as distinct from laughter, may be something uniquely human." Play is, on the other hand, "enthusiastic and widespread among mammals. It sharpens the senses, builds muscle strength and coordination, and helps animals rehearse for adult life" (p. 197). So humor is humble and utterly human, perhaps in its atavistic forms, utterly mammalian.

At the end of our group meetings we ask each group to present to the whole group the substance (or remnants) of what they discussed, considered, concluded, or commemorated. And we encourage them to be free to do it in any way they want. More often than not we get "performances." These are moments when we do what is beyond us, outside the "commodifed self," wherein we creatively imitate (not mimic) our roles, others' roles, institutional foibles, and we perform other possibilities (Newman & Holzman, 1997). These are pure fun and play. We know each other, in a small way, differently after these.

Keeping an Eye on Practice, Inquiry, and Pedagogy: Critique and Integration

In the end, we are dedicated to the practice of critique. Critique, like critical pedagogy, seeks to delve beneath oppressive ideologies, radically altering our own teaching routines and professional customs by launching a sociopolitical, spiritual, and/or axiological analysis of subjects. Rather than accepting the value of concepts, or even examining evidence for their claims to truth, we seek to examine ideas as social and political constructs with effects in the real world. We interrogate the manner in which ideas are constructed and the social positions and intent of those who produce them. We might very well ask: What, if any, forms of inequality (especially in the realms of race, class, and gender) does accepting concepts like person/environment or clinical intervention support? What effects do our ideas and practices have on reifying the authority of dominant groups or the inferiority of subordinated ones? We return, almost always, to viewing ideas and knowledge as social constructs that serve the interests of some groups and not others.

However, authors such as Giroux (1994) and hooks (1993) posit that while critique is essential, it is important also to construct a "pedagogy of hope" (the title of Paulo Freire's last book as well) that encourages us and our students or clients to believe that alternative ways of constructing educational and personal experiences are possible. While ideologies can become hegemonic and gain unquestioned acceptance, the pedagogy of hope argues that contrary ideas can be "counterhegemonic" and offer hope for resistance and change in the social order (Saleebey & Scanlon, 2005). We have commented at times on the fact that schools and universities can reproduce inequality and a docile professional class (social workers) that inadvertently does the bidding of governmental and marketplace entities. But it seems to many of us, and our conversations strengthen this notion, that a critically informed educational institution can challenge social inequality through fostering dialogue, critique, and student and client voices.

A serious question for all of us is how can these ideas, these possibilities, be introduced into the sometimes insistent beat and obstinate parameters of academic and agency bureaucratic life? We think a little local insurgence might be a good place to start. That is, (a) you find colleagues who have similar interests and dissatisfactions and begin informal conversations about changes, small at first, that might bring your organization closer to the ideals that we have so ardently upheld in these gatherings; (b) you take some degree of responsibility for making informal presentations about these ideas in staffings, in-service trainings, coffee lounge and lunch encounters, and faculty and staff retreats; (c) you employ the tools available to you—newsletters, bulletin boards, informal exchanges, and the like—to forward some of the basic ideas of our endeavor; (d) you plan to have a mini gathering for your faculty that mirrors some of what happens in Vermont; (e) you keep in touch with some of the participants of the gathering during the year; and (f) when you do these things, you are—and this is the nature of these ideas, really—engaging people in conversation, dialogue about possibilities and loyalty to our professional past and values. The upshot is that we are simply encouraging ourselves to understand that transformation moves backward (to social work's past) and forward (to a more vigorous future).

We seek then, as best we can, through these annual gatherings, and the conversation and dialogue they inspire, ways to integrate and incorporate the ideas, propositions, and assertions that emanate from them into our practice, teaching/learning, and scholarship. In spite of the suggestions above, this is not always a matter of ease, and once away from the sylvan setting, the sometimes tricky realities of institutional life often trump the dedication to a more postmodern, less practiced way of performing our lives. But, thanks to these get-togethers, we all know that we have allies and compatriots in our attempts to forge a more dialogical, open-ended relationship with those we teach and serve. Integration mightily depends on our collective ability to live the life, sing the song of transformation and possibility.

References

Ackerman, D. (2004). *An alchemy of mind: The marvel and mystery of the brain.* New York: Scribner.

Anderson, H., Gergen, K. J., McNamee, S., Cooperrider, Gergen, M., & Whitney, D. (2001). *The appreciative organization.* Taos, NM: Taos Institute.

Baltes, P. B., & Baltes, M. M. (1993). Psychological perspectives on successful aging: The model of selective optimization with compensation. In P. B. Baltes & M. M. Baltes (Eds.), *Successful aging: perspectives from the behavioral sciences* (pp. 1–34). Cambridge, UK: Cambridge University Press.

Bruner, J. (1986). *Actual minds, possible worlds.* Cambridge, MA: Harvard University Press.

Bruner, J. (1990). *Acts of meaning.* Cambridge, MA: Harvard University Press.

Dillard, A. (1994). Seeing. In P. Lopate (Ed.),*The art of the personal essay: An anthology from the classical era to the present* (pp. 692–706). New York: Anchor.

Freire, P. (2000). *Pedagogy of the oppressed.* New York: Continuum.

Gergen, K. J. (2001). *Social construction in context.* London: Sage.

Giroux, H. A. (1994). *Disturbing pleasures: Learning popular culture.* New York: Routledge.

hooks, b. (2003) *Teaching community: A pedagogy of hope.* New York: Routledge.

Lamott, A. (1995). *Bird by bird: Some instructions on writing and life*. New York: Anchor.

Newman, F., & Holzman, L. (1997). *The end of knowing: A new developmental way of learning*. New York: Routledge.

Restak, R. (2003). *The new brain: How the modern age is rewiring your mind*. New York: Rodale.

Ricketts, M. W., & Willis, J. E. (2001). *Experience AI: A practitioner's guide to integrating appreciative inquiry with experiential learning*. Taos, NM: Taos Institute.

Saleebey, D., & Scanlon, E. (2005). Is a critical pedagogy in the profession of social work possible? *Journal of Teaching in Social Work, 25*(3&4), 1–18.

Vaillant, G. E. (2002). *Aging well.* Boston: Little, Brown.

Vaillant, G. E. (1993). *The wisdom of the ego.* Cambridge, MA: Harvard University Press.

About the Authors

Stanley L Witkin is a professor in the Department of Social Work at the University of Vermont. He holds a BA in social welfare from the University of Minnesota and MSSW and PhD degrees (social welfare) from the University of Wisconsin, Madison. In 2004 he was awarded an honorary doctorate in social science from the University of Lapland, Finland. From 1998 through 2001, Stanley served as editor in chief of *Social Work*, the membership journal of the National Association of Social Workers. In this position he wrote 20 editorial essays, many of which have been widely cited and used in social work education. In addition to these essays, Stanley has been a frequent contributor to the social work literature and a presenter at national and international conferences. Currently, his primary interests are the applications of social constructionist thought to social work and creating spaces of dialogue and connection to further the cause of developing a more just and humane world. In 1999, he codeveloped a unique summer program, called Social Work from a Global Perspective (www.ulapland/summerschool), that brings together social work students and instructors from around the world. In 2004, he cofounded (with Dennis Saleebey) the Global Partnership for Transformative Social Work (www.gptsw.net), a worldwide collective of social workers interested in exploring the transformative possibilities of social constructionist and related frameworks.

Dennis Saleebey is professor emeritus of social welfare at the School of Social Welfare, University of Kansas. He was the Lucy and Henry Moses Distinguished Visiting Professor of Social

Work at Hunter College in New York for the 2002–2003 school year. One of his primary interests has been the development of a more strengths-based approach to social work practice. For the past 20 years he has been involved in a number of strengths-based community building and community outreach projects in Fort Worth, Texas; Kansas City, Missouri; and Kansas City, Kansas. Dennis has written widely and made many presentations nationally and internationally to a variety of social work and human service groups. Saleebey is author and editor of the fourth edition of *The Strengths Perspective in Social Work Practice* (Boston, MA: Pearson/Allyn & Bacon, 2006). His *Human Behavior and Social Environments: A Biopyschosocial Approach* was published by Columbia University Press in 2001. His latest publications include "The Power of Place: The Social Environment Revisited," published in *Families in Society*, 2004, *85*(1), 1–16; "Balancing Act: Assessing Strengths in Mental Health Practice, in S. A. Kirk (Ed.), *Mental Disorders and the Social Environment* (New York: Columbia University Press, 2005); and (with Edward Scanlon), "Is a Critical Pedagogy in Social Work Possible? in the *Journal of Teaching in Social Work*, 2006, *25*(3&4), 11–18.

About the Contributors

Fred H. Besthorn is associate professor of social work at the University of Northern Iowa in Cedar Falls. He is the author of numerous published works on the interface between the natural environment and social work practice and has been a featured presenter and keynote speaker at many national and international conferences focusing on the impact of global environmental decline, economic globalization, and consumer culture on a range of human developmental issues. He is the creator of the Global Alliance for a Deep-Ecological Social Work (http://www.ecosocialwork.org/) and is the founder of the online journal *Earth Consciousness: The Journal of Environmental Social Work and Human Services* (http://ecosocialworkjournal.org/).

Adrienne Chambon is a professor on the faculty of social work at the University of Toronto. She writes on narrative and discourse, refugees, and immigration. She is coeditor (with Allan Irving) of *Essays on Postmodernism and Social Work* (Toronto, Ontario, Canada: Canadian Scholars' Press, 1994) and *Reading Foucault for Social Work* (New York: Columbia University Press, 1999) with Allan Irving and Laura Epstein. A main focus of her work is on public space and the space of relations, by examining art practices in contemporary times (installations), and in the premodern period in northern Italy (primarily frescoes). She is currently pursuing a project on "The Heuristics of Art Practices for Social Work" with funding from the Social Sciences and Humanities Research Council of Canada.

Ruth Grossman Dean is professor and head of the Practice Sequence at Simmons College School of Social Work in Boston, where she teaches courses in clinical practice, narrative therapies, and orientation to knowledge. In addition to running her small private practice, she volunteers at the Children and Families Unit of the South End Health Center, where she engages in community-based practice and consults at a primary school in a dense and diverse Boston neighborhood. In 1999 Ruth Dean received an award for the Greatest Contribution to Social Work Education from the Massachusetts Chapter of the National Association of Social Workers.

Mel Gray is professor of social work at the University of Newcastle in New South Wales, Australia, and co-editor of *Australian Social Work*. Her interests range from creativity, morality, spirituality, and theory and philosophy in social work to experiential social work education. She is currently working on several books on social work as art, culturally relevant social work, theorizing social work, and values, ethics, and morality in social work. She is a strong believer in local, culturally relevant social work practice. Permeating Mel's intense interest in philosophy, morality, values, ethics, aesthetics, spirituality, epistemology, and so forth, in social work—perhaps even its practical mysticism—is its history and how it is interpreted, for an understanding of history is so important to an appreciation of where we are today. Mel has always appreciated Jane Addams's style of social work, which is why her debate with Richard Pozzuto—recounted in this book—hooked her in with such intensity. She hopes you enjoy their conversation across miles and cultures as much as they did.

Allan Irving is a professor in the School of Social Work, King's University College at the University of Western Ontario. His current scholarly interests are in the intersections of art, postmodernism, and social work practice. He is virulently anti-

Enlightenment in his outlook and believes in Nietzsche's comment that "we have art lest we perish of the truth."

Katherine Tyson McCrea is a professor at the Loyola University of Chicago School of Social Work. She also is a psychotherapist who treats children and adults, and she consults with social workers in public and private mental health and school settings. She obtained her undergraduate and Masters of Divinity degrees from Yale University, and her Masters and PhD from the University of Chicago, School of Social Service Administration. She has been a consulting editor for *Social Work* and other human services journals and has presented extensively in this country and abroad on clinical social work treatment of adults and children and social work's philosophy of research. She has published several articles about the treatment of children and residential care for severely mentally ill, homeless adults, and also published a book and several papers about a practitioner-relevant approach to research for the social and behavioral sciences. She is the founding editor-in-chief of *Illinois Child Welfare*, a multidisciplinary, international journal dedicated to improving child welfare services. Her current interests focus on effective psychotherapy for children and disadvantaged clients and on social work models for international and culturally diverse, socially traumatized communities, especially collaborative community development and parent support programs.

Nigel Parton is the NSPCC (National Society for the Prevention of Cruelty to Children) Professor in the Centre of Applied Childhood Studies in the School of Human and Health Sciences at the University of Huddersfield, England. Over the last 25 years he has written several books and articles on the general themes of social work, social theory, and child welfare. He has a particular interest in child protection policy and practice. His recent books are *Constructive Social Work: Towards a New Practice*, with Patrick O'Byrne (New York: St. Martin's, 2000); *Constructing Clienthood in Social Work and Human Services: Interaction, Identities and Practices*, edited with Chris Hall, Kirsi Juhila, and Tarja Poso (Philadelphia, PA: Jessica Kingsley, 2003); *Constructive Work With Offenders*, edited with Kevin Gorman, Marilyn Gregory, and Michelle Hayles (Philadelphia, PA: Jessica Kingsley, 2006); and *Safeguarding Childhood: Early Intervention and Surveillance in a Late Modern Society* (New York: Palgrave Macmillan, 2005). From 1995 to 2005 he was coeditor of *Children and Society,* published by John Wiley & Sons in association with the National Children's Bureau, England.

Richard Pozzuto is associate professor, School of Social Work at East Carolina University, Greenville, North Carolina. He is a founding editor of the online journal, *Critical Social Work*. Currently he is active in the Knowledge for Practice Research Cluster at East Carolina University whose focus is the forms and uses of knowledge in professional practice. Richard has a long-standing interest in critical theory and the use of "knowledge" for social integration and/or social control.

Margaret Rhodes is associate professor of philosophy at the College of Public and Community Service, University of Massachusetts/Boston, where she teaches undergraduate courses in the humanities and the master's course in human service ethics. She also teaches ethics in the PhD program at Simmons School of Social Work. She is author of *Ethical Dilemmas in Social Work Practice* (Milwaukee, WI: Family Service America, 1991) as well as several articles, among them "Constructionism and Ethics," coauthored with Ruth Dean, published in *Families in Society*, 1998, *79*(3), 254–261. She has served on the Massachusetts National Association of Social Workers Ethics Commission, including its hotline, and on the Donaldson

Adoption Institute's Ethics Advisory Committee, which developed information papers on adoption and the new reproductive technologies. She regularly gives workshops and talks on social work ethics, particularly in the Boston area. She did her undergraduate work at Stanford University in philosophy, graduating Phi Beta Kappa, and received her PhD from Brandeis University.

Susan E. Roche is associate professor in the Department of Social Work at the University of Vermont. She teaches, writes, and consults about feminist practices, gender violence, human rights, and social work education from a constructionist, global-local perspective. She is the lead author of *Contesting Boundaries in Social Work Education: A Liberatory Approach to Cooperative Learning and Teaching* (Alexandria, VA: Council on Social Work Education, 1999), serves on the editorial board of *Affilia: Journal of Women and Social Work*, and is the university cochair of the Anti-Violence Partnership: A Community Collaboration at the University of Vermont. She has presented at social work, human rights, and domestic violence conferences in the United States, Canada, China, and Australia. Her most recent project involved coordinating the Vermont Sexual Violence Prevention Project and writing *The Vermont Approach: A Strategic Plan for Comprehensive, Collaborative Sexual Violence Prevention in Vermont, 2006–2010*. This project resulted in bipartisan support and state legislation to support implementation of that plan. The plan itself is informed by postmodern conceptions of research, sexual violence, and transformative practices.

Brenda Solomon is associate professor of social work at the University of Vermont. She is interested in using institutional ethnography to explore discourses in use. Her studies concern the construction of work and family, the production of women workers, intersections of oppression, and the everyday practices of frontline workers in welfare-to-work, child welfare, and schools. Further, she is beginning a new research project in meaning making and sibling death.

Sally St. George is an associate professor and co-director of the Family Therapy Program at the University of Louisville. She is dedicated to creating and using social constructionist principles in her teaching and clinical practice. Sally serves on the Boards of Directors for the Taos Institute and Global Partnership for Transformative Social Work. She is also a co-editor of *The Qualitative Report*, an open-access online interdisciplinary journal committed to creating a learning community of writers and reviewers to present solid, interesting, and novel works of qualitative inquiry.

Dan Wulff is an associate professor and co-director of the Family Therapy Program at the University of Louisville. His research and practice efforts center on an integrative practice of social work and family therapy. Dan also serves on the Boards of Directors for the Taos Institute and Global Partnership for Transformative Social Work and a co-editor of *The Qualitative Report.*

INDEX

C